Babycham Night

PIER APPROACH, RYDE, ISLE OF WIGHT

ALSO BY PHILIP NORMAN

FICTION

Slip on a Fat Lady
Plumridge
Wild Thing
The Skaters' Waltz
Words of Love
Everyone's Gone to the Moon

BIOGRAPHY AND JOURNALISM

Shout: The True Story of the Beatles
The Stones
The Road Goes On For Ever
Tilt the Hourglass and Begin Again
The Age of Parody
Your Walrus Hurt the One You Love
Awful Moments
Pieces of Hate
The Life and Good Times of the Rolling Stones
Days in the Life: John Lennon Remembered
Buddy: The Biography
Sir Elton

PLAYS

The Man That Got Away
Words of Love

PHILIP NORMAN

Babycham Night

MACMILLAN

First published 2003 by Macmillan
an imprint of Pan Macmillan Ltd
Pan Macmillan, 20 New Wharf Road, London N1 9RR
Basingstoke and Oxford
Associated companies throughout the world
www.panmacmillan.com

ISBN 0 333 90097 9

1 3 5 7 9 8 6 4 2

A CIP catalogue record for this book is available from
the British Library.

Typeset by Intype London Ltd
Printed and bound in Great Britain by
Mackays of Chatham plc, Chatham, Kent

FOR SUE

Who made none of it matter any more

A chield's amang you, taking notes

– Robert Burns

Contents

Prologue xi

Part One

LEARNING THE MOHAWK

I

Part Two

'HAPPY CELEBRATION, DING-DONG-DING'

107

Part Three

THE REST ROOM

233

Prologue

THE FIRST TASTE OF glamour in my life was Babycham.

I was ten when it appeared in 1953, the year we crowned Queen Elizabeth II. No one in the pub trade – my family's trade – had ever seen such a bizarre concoction. It came in an undersized dark brown bottle with a sky-blue label and a cap smothered with matching foil. Inside was a pale gold fizzy drink that looked just like champagne, tasted vaguely like it, and was described with the wonderful freedom of advertising in those days as 'Genuine Champagne Perry'.

Its trademark (no one yet said 'logo') was a baby deer all too obviously inspired by Walt Disney's Bambi, with spindly legs, protruding eyes, two underdeveloped horns, and an outsize pale blue bow around its neck. In its first cinema and television advertisements, this winsomely smiling little creature pranced through the air on a cloud of stardust to land on the open palm of an elegant fifties mannequin. 'I'd love a Babycham!' she exclaimed in tones both demure and suggestive. The unmistakable inference was that, as well as sipping the bubbly nectar, she would lavish kisses and hugs and who knew what else besides on her horny little visitor.

Babycham brought a revolution – one might almost say an early splash of feminism – into the gloomy, male-dominated pubs of post-Second World War Britain. Those were still days when respectable women were not supposed to frequent bars or even drink, and the choice of tipples available to them was consequently meagre and unalluring. Women of the world like my father's girlfriend, Miss Salsbury, drank gin and orange, gin and 'French' (an ice-less version of the dry Martini) or gin and 'It' (sweet Italian vermouth). Inexperienced girls drank port mixed with lemonade ('Port and lemon, please') or Carlsberg lager, about the only brand available, prettified by a dash of lime juice. Elderly ladies drank stout, but only for medicinal purposes, which they underlined by calling it 'milk stout' and taking it in tiny sips, with the patiently closed eyes of early Christian martyrs. Wine barely existed outside the realm of expensive restaurants and gentlemen's clubs.

Babycham was the first drink a woman could order in a bar without feeling like a tart or a crone. Indeed, it was the first mass-produced alcoholic beverage in the UK with a direct appeal to feminine susceptibilities. From its dinky sky-blue and brown bottle it was poured into a shallow champagne glass rimmed with gold, crested with an effigy of the little prancing fawn and garnished with a maraschino cherry on a stick. For dowdy, downtrodden fifties womanhood, it was a heady sip of the high life which most knew only from films and magazines – the world of the cocktail rather than saloon-bar – where people wore evening dress, soft music played and white-coated barmen shook up exotic iced concoctions in silver flasks. All for just one old shilling and sixpence (7½p), then only half the price of a single tot of whisky or gin.

The life-changing elixir was created by a cider-making family firm called Showering's, of Shepton Mallet in Somerset. My wicked, irresistible Grandma Norman also originally came from Somerset and, through her cousin Aunt May Chapman, was distantly related to the Showering family. When I was nine, she took me on a motor-coach trip through the West Country and in Shepton Mallet we stopped off to visit our cider-making kinfolk. The Showerings company was run by three brothers, who had built themselves substantial red-brick houses all in a row, with one at the end for their elderly mother. We were invited to tea with this matriarch and, later, shown round the cider factory, where I collected dozens of scarlet bottle-tops from its wet stone floor.

That very day, according to Grandma Norman, the Showering brothers were discussing a problem which had long exercised them: how to make a drink from fermented pear juice that would sell in quantities equalling their apple-based product. Not long afterwards, they conceived the idea of 'Genuine Champagne Perry', a brilliant illusion that told no actual lie. 'Perry' was an old word for pear cider, no longer recognized except in the deepest West Country regions. The 'cham' in Babycham did not mean champagne, as everyone presumed, but signified the baby deer, or chamois, that was its mascot. Champagne in those days was sufficiently unprotected as a brand for the gloriously self-contradictory tag-line 'Genuine Champagne Perry' to bring no protest from the houses of Moët et Chandon or Veuve Clicquot.

Our tenuous family link with Showerings was one of my father's few natural assets as a seaside showman. When he ran Ryde Pier Pavilion later in the fifties, he faced constant difficulties over supplies of such essentials as beer, ice-cream wafers and mashed potato powder (usually a consequence of his reluctance to settle bills). But with Babycham there was never any problem. One phone-call would bring an express delivery of those scaled-down varnished wood crates, each containing two dozen interlocked rows of sky-blue labels and foil tops. I can see myself now, on my knees in my dirty white barman's jacket, stacking them next to the Schweppes tonic waters, tomato juices and bitter lemons.

We never heard directly from the Showerings, either the brothers or their old mother. As the summers went on and my father's business at the Pier Pavilion plunged deeper into trouble, I nurtured unspoken hopes that as our cousins, however distant, they might rally to our aid. But, far off in Somerset, they could not have realized how bad things really were. And, I supposed, the obstinate family pride that clung to us – especially to Grandma Norman – prevented us from telling them.

Nonetheless, they were a benign presence in my teenage life, and the ever-increasing success of their golden elixir became one of my few sources of triumph. I thrilled each time I saw their TV ad in black and white, and their cinema ad in splendiferous Technicolor. Their promotional material was the most extensive of all the breweries and drinks companies we dealt with, and some of the bounty their sales reps showered on my father he would pass on to me. I had Babycham pencils, a Babycham pen and jotter and key-ring, all bearing effigies of the little chamois. Once he presented me with a yellow plastic statuette of the chamois, about two feet high, that was meant to have been displayed among the liqueur bottles behind the bar. He intimated that the statuettes were much sought after and that I should feel greatly honoured. I did.

As one of the company's most favoured customers, possibly even as the son of a distant cousin, he was also given a Babycham neon sign with which to beautify the Pier Pavilion's otherwise bare wooden exterior. It consisted of a chamois the size of Godzilla, prancing beside a tilted champagne glass. Like much British neon in the 1950s, it was never a hundred per cent reliable. Sometimes a wing of its blue bow-tie would flicker and dim; sometimes one of its legs, or the champagne glass-stem, or the best part of its winsome, inviting smile.

Ryde Esplanade, of course, had neon signs in garish abundance – 'Arcadia', Dinelli's Café, Abell's Gift Shop, the King Lud. But our Babycham neon was the only one here far out at sea, winking its summons to glamour and sophistication across the flickering waves of the Solent. They could see it from the visible mainland, in Portsmouth and Southsea, and from the ocean liners that passed us *en route* to and from Southampton.

During the era when my father put on dances at the Pier Pavilion, Babycham's largesse was a major factor in making them go with a swing. Each Thursday throughout the summer season he staged a gala evening, with dancing to the music of an electric organ and games and competitions of the raucous kind traditionally beloved by the British holidaymaker. At perhaps one in three galas, the prizes would be donated by Babycham and consist of Babycham. So powerful was the presence of the prancing little chamois that each gala became known as Babycham Night.

An enduring memory of my early adolescence is the moment when our Babycham neon sign would be switched on, presaging the long night of revelry ahead. In my mind's eye, it is an evening towards the season's end, when the nights have begun to cool and dusk no longer falls after ten but before eight. At one moment, the sign is dead, a tracery of colourless tubes, as inanimate as stranded jellyfish. At the next, bright energy like St Elmo's Fire is zigzagging and quivering all around its little-horned head, bulbous eyes, bow-tie and champagne glass: not all sectors working at full efficiency perhaps, but the figure unmistakable, irresistible – and created by distant cousins of ours. When the tubes are working at full strength, they emit a loud, continuous buzz, as if a thousand Mediterranean cicadas are singing in the wires.

To this, add the pumping bass of an electronic organ, playing 'Mack the Knife' at quickstep time; the creak of a Portsmouth ferry riding at its berth; the rasp of a diesel tram travelling along its track from shore; scraps of laughter, a clink of bottles and the never-tiring bluster of sea wind.

I'd love a Babycham? I *loved* a Babycham. Welcome to Babycham Night.

Part One

LEARNING THE MOHAWK

One

IF EVER YOU cross the water from Portsmouth to the Isle of Wight, you cannot help seeing my childhood home. It slants out from Ryde like a marching column of rusty iron legs – Britain's second-longest seaside pier.* Forget the purely ornamental Victorian piers of Brighton or Blackpool: this is a serious industrial artefact, which in times past was an indispensable component of the Island's holiday trade. Ryde pierhead was where the vast majority of summer visitors landed, pouring off the Portsmouth ferries to be dispersed to other Island resorts by train or bus. A pier of such unnatural length was needed because the tide here goes out half a mile, marooning the town within a wilderness of dark, wet sand for many hours each day. The iron legs had to stretch to far-off deep water, where large passenger-boats could tie up at will.

Today the visitor has a wide choice of quicker and more convenient ways into the Island. There are alternative passenger services from Lymington to Yarmouth and Portsmouth to Cowes, and the huge-capacity and efficient car-ferries to Yarmouth and Fishbourne. Hovercraft, the Island's own invention, roar over from Southsea to fetch up like skimmed

_____
* The longest, if you care, is Southend pier.

stones on the pier's easterly side. For almost four decades now, Ryde has been bypassed and in economic decline, its main thoroughfare, Union Street, a mere shadow of its former classy self, the broad beaches, even at mid-season, as empty as the Sahara.

The only passenger service from Portsmouth to the pier is by 'Sea Cat' catamaran – insubstantial, rocky craft, delivering visitors by the dozen where they used to come by the hundred thousand. For those who have not landed here before, the impression must be of some vast, seagull-haunted scrapyard. The structure in fact consists of three separate, interlinked piers, one built to carry pedestrians and cars, the second to carry a double-track tramway, the third to carry steam trains from the Island's formerly plentiful routes, both coastal and inland, to their terminus at the pier-head. The tramway has been allowed to rot into rusted ruin. On what used to be the railway now run two superannuated London Underground trains, tricked out in the garish colours of a Disneyland ride.

The parts of the pier that still function present an equally sad and ghostly aspect. The plank promenade is defaced by yellow 'No Parking' lines and speed bumps; the lyre-patterned iron railings, once sea-green, are now a dull, flaking black. The flights of steps to side jetties from which people fished or swam or took pleasure-boat trips have all long since been amputated. Between ferries, it's rare to see a single ped-estrian along the pier's entire length. Rarer still is any human silhouette in the two surviving windbreak shelters with their seats back to back like Irish jaunting carts and their roofs like Chinese pagodas.

Looking at the desolate pier-head today, you would not easily guess that it once offered holiday amusements as various as any on the distant shore. Its dominating feature used to be a wooden pleasure dome, the Pier Pavilion, built as a theatre for minstrel and variety shows but with an ancillary warren of bars, restaurants, function-rooms, sun-decks and kitchens. The Pier Pavilion was pulled down in the mid-1960s, unluckily just before the era that might have preserved it as a unique Victorian architectural extravagance. Its site is marked by a yawning gap, next to the rotted wooden platform of the tram station that once adjoined it. The demolishers took away its labyrinths of wood and marble and glass and Formica but were defeated by its iron legs, which remained rooted as immovably as wisdom teeth in the chalk seabed.

I return to the pier-head sometimes and gaze at that pattern of disembodied stilts, standing in water as dark and turbulent as if the Pavilion's shadow still loomed above. I remember all that was once contained in that circle of empty air – the effort, the hope, the uproar, the disappointment, the anguish, the cruelty, the farce. However far I may travel from this wind-swept, sea-swept place, Ryde Pier Pavilion will always haunt my dreams.

*

YOU MUST PICTURE a gigantic octagonal-shaped structure with walls of yellow slatted wood, serried windows picked out in green and a dome that seems to be made of overlapping grey fish-scales. Attached to its right flank are two identical smaller domes, set side by side like a salt and pepper cruet. Flowing out from between these is a sun-deck, fenced with fancy green iron railings, that forms the roof of the pier-head tram station.

Picture a July morning in 1951, two years B.B. (Before Babycham), with the sky around the fish-scaly dome a deep, cloudless blue and the sun shining as it only ever does in remembered childhood. The tide is at its highest, a weed-skeined grape-greenness, heaving and sploshing only a foot or two below the pier-head's concrete platform. Ryde is a far-off mirage of perpendicular hills, pale ice-cream colours and beaches on which hardly a single square foot of sand remains unoccupied. Out in the cooler Solent, some great transatlantic liner, the *Queen Elizabeth*, the *Mauretania* or the *United States*, is making her silent way westward to Southampton, passing between the circular sea-borne forts built a century ago as safeguards against attack from France. The misty sea passage throngs with freighters, tankers, battleships and air-craft-carriers from the Portsmouth naval base, and hundreds of white-sailed yachts all tilted at the same acute angle, like tiny, jostling crescent moons.

This is the last great age of the railway 'cheap day' excursion ticket and of the seaside day-tripper. Every few minutes, the trains pull into Portsmouth Harbour station, crammed with city dwellers agog for however fleeting a taste of the Island's Riviera atmosphere. From 'Pompey', as sailors have known Portsmouth since Nelson's time, there is a further half-hour's journey across the six choppy miles of water between the nearest of the two seaborne forts to Ryde Pier-head. The black and white, yellow-funnelled ferries – some modern steamships, some still antiquated 'paddlers' – ply virtually non-stop on their diagonal course. More often than not they approach the pier-head with their eager passengers all crowded on the disembarkation side, making the deck heel over almost to the waterline.

As the crowds struggle down the narrow gangways, three voices booming over loudspeakers from widely separate quarters greet them with a bewildering diversity of information, exhortation and advice.

Voice number one comes from the pier-head railway station, from which steam trains pulling scarlet carriages with running-boards connect with the Island's west coast resorts (all prettier and more famous than Ryde but without facilities for ships to dock there). The voice belongs to a British Railways official known as Taffy, a portly Welshman who wears his black serge uniform with the swagger of a Napoleonic hussar and rolls his r's like a bard declaiming poetry. 'Good morning, ladies and gentlemen, good morning. This is Rrryde Pier – Rrryde Pier Head. Upon disembarking, Rrryde passengers go to the rright after you pass the gate and straight down the pier on the trram. Trrain passengers to left for services to Rrryde Esplanade, Rrryde St Johns, Brrading, Sandown, Shanklin, Wrroxall and Ventnor . . .'

Voice number two comes from a small wooden hut with a striped awning situated next to the ticket-barrier for Ryde-bound holidaymakers. This is the pier-head rock shop, operated by my father's arch-enemy, Alfie Vernon. Mr Vernon himself has the microphone and is speaking in his usual damnably light, fluent and persuasive tone: 'Hello there, ladies and gentlemen, just across here at the shop, you've got plenty of time, we'll serve you straight away. We've got bars of chocolate, boxes of chocolates, boiled sweets and toffees as well as rock in three flavours, peppermint, greengage or pineapple . . .'

Voice number three issues from two pairs of square-mouthed loudspeakers, mounted on the Pavilion's seaward-facing perimeter, and belongs to my father: 'Morning coffee and biscuits, tea, minerals and light refreshments are now being served on the sun-roof or in the restaurant upstairs. The entrance is on the tramway station. There is no queuing and no waiting. Make certain of your meal in comfort before you leave the pier . . .'

I can see him in his office, which he calls 'the Amplifier Room' and has a window overlooking the ticket-barrier where the arriving crowds collect in a huge pool, like debris in a blocked sink, then filter through in twos and threes. He is standing next to a wood-encased Trix amplifier, holding a bulb-headed microphone with a heavy base, the kind used by old-fashioned radio announcers. In the summer we're speaking of, he would have been not quite thirty-eight. He's wearing his usual pier-showman's garb of blue-grey shirt, RAF squadron tie and lovat-green trousers hanging low on the waist and billowing over brown suède shoes. He is an extraordinarily handsome man in the clean-cut, no-nonsense style of male movie idols fifty-odd years ago. I think of him whenever I see black-and-white films starring Trevor Howard, John Mills, Jack Hawkins and, especially, Humphrey Bogart. Like Bogart, he has dark, wavy hair, close cropped round his ears and neck and forming a deep V on a high forehead. He has somewhat the same eyes, soulful yet combustible; the same razor-roughened cheeks and cleft chin. His mouth, a perfect cupid's bow, almost touches the microphone as it shapes the words:

'Tea, coffee and biscuits, buttered buns or doughnuts at reasonable prices can be obtained in the restaurant or on the sun-roof upstairs. The entrance is on the tramway station. Make certain of your meal in comfort before you leave the pier.'

It is the voice that makes, and will soon unmake, my world. A low, level voice with only the faintest trace of its original south London origins – one that today we would call 'classless', but back then, after the huge social dislocations of World War Two, pointed to upper-class rather than lower. Indeed, child though I was, I already sensed something in it at odds with this hectic seaside scene and the task of wooing customers to our entertainments. Even when speaking about buttered buns and doughnuts, it had an air of sadness and pessimism, of forcing itself to a task inherently distasteful. In childhood he had had a marked speech impediment that his mother, Grandma Norman, did not seek to correct but actively encouraged, collecting his toddler mispronunciations into a treasury from which she still often quoted with bright-eyed adoration. Though its more obvious features had disappeared when he grew up, there were still certain words that gave him difficulty, as if they were somehow too tiring for the cupid's bow lips to shape. Like chronic stammerers, he tended to over-compensate, articulating these troublesome words with a vehemence that made them sound like their phonetic representations in the dictionary. 'Costume', for instance, would come out as 'kos-choom', and 'minerals' (that era's word for soft drinks of the non-cola variety) as 'minroows'.

I found it strange, too, that my father's broadcasts made no mention of the Pavilion's chief attraction, the penny-in-the-slot machines with which he had filled its former theatre auditorium. I'm talking about Victorian slot-machines, made of iron and varnished wood and brass; the kind which nowadays are bought and sold for thousands of pounds apiece. He had crane-grab machines and weighing-machines and punch balls, and glass-fronted cabinets in which articulated iron figures enacted jerky tableaux amid a whirr of ancient gears and a pinging of little bells. He also had dozens of 1930s pinball games, and a rifle range whose 'genuine Remington .22 rifles' shot darts with festive coloured plumes. 'Come in and try your luck on the Allwyn de Luxe or the Copper Mine,' his loudspeaker broadcast might have added, or: 'Roll up for the rifle-range . . .' But his overmastering sense of dignity, even in the most undignified circumstances, simply would not let him. Consequently, even when summer's crowds were at their height, you seldom saw more than a dozen people at once in our penny arcade.

His war with Alfie Vernon had been inevitable from the moment they first found themselves working adjacent pitches on the pier-head. Indeed, Mr Vernon's very appearance guaranteed that my father would loathe him. In total contrast with that light, agile microphone voice, he was a classic fat man, shaped like a beachball, with the sleekly flattened hair and cherubic face of a traditional wooden doll. He usually wore a cream-coloured linen jacket and a flowing silk tie of garish hue, decorated with little dogs, vintage cars, pirates' treasure-maps or high-kicking dancing-girls. In short, he looked exactly like what he was, and what my father all too obviously was not – a born seaside huckster.

Although their premises were separated by only a few yards of concrete car-park, the two were essentially not in competition. The Pavilion sold morning coffee, lunches, afternoon teas and light refreshments; Alfie Vernon sold rock, sweets, chocolate, ice-cream, cigarettes, postcards, children's buckets and spades and plastic windmills. My father resented the rock shop simply for being there, catching the ferry-crowds first as they disembarked and skimming off the first cream of their holiday cash. Most of all, he resented Mr Vernon's loudspeaker announcements, which he regarded as plagiarism of the most blatant kind. By his account, he had been first to approach their common landlord, British Railways, for permission to have a pier-head loudspeaker over and above the official one. 'Then, of course, Alfie goes to them behind my back and says *he's* got to have one, too . . .'

My father always referred to his enemy as Alfie with the condescending sneer of an immeasurable social superior, even though their London origins probably were not that much different. Such was the legacy of the Royal Air Force, which had raised a lower-middle-class Clapham boy to the rank of Wing-Commander, with a batman and mess-bills and uniforms made to measure by Gieves. He had belonged to the most élite and stylish fighting force Britain had known since her nineteenth-century Foot Guards and Lancers, wearing the magic blue-grey uniform in brotherhood with national heroes such as Guy Gibson, Douglas Bader and Leonard Cheshire. He had flown with Bomber Command's 57 Squadron, commanding his own Blenheim bomber until (as I understood it) a crash landing in Alsace-Lorraine had got him invalided out of the service, two years before the war's end. The broken jaw he suffered in the crash had been rebuilt by pioneer plastic surgeon Sir Archibald McIndoe, entitling him to membership of McIndoe's famous Guinea Pig Club. Though he had not actually received any medals, he was still a war hero as authentic as any to be encountered in films or books. Mr Vernon's wartime career, by contrast, seemed unlikely to have involved anything more glorious than catering or, possibly, forces entertainment.

Even when I was as young as seven or eight, the sound of their two voices battling over the summer airwaves placed me in an uncomfortable ethical dilemma. I could never repress that guilty feeling that our announcements were too sombre and inexplicit to catch the crowds' attention, and that Mr Vernon's easy, conversational 'Hello there, ladies and gentlemen', and the expressive gusto with which he enumerated his rock flavours ('peppermint, greengage OR pineapple . . .'), were far more enticing to the ear. But I knew, in the very marrow of my bones, that the way my father did anything was the only right and proper way to do it. I knew that Mr Vernon's persuasive fluency marked him as a 'spiv', a 'line-shooter' and other terms of RAF anathema, whereas my father's mournful boom somehow shared some of the same lofty ideals of 'the Few' or the Dambusters. I knew that, though to the casual eye 'Alfie' might appear the better pier-head businessman, morality always remained firmly on our side.

The two foes' only common frontier was a short strip of railing that ran between the rock shop and the Pavilion's wide front steps. This rail did not overlook open sea, but an enclosed square of water known, perversely, as the Triangle. On top of the fancy iron railing work was a roofed wooden shelf on which stood four slot-machines belonging to my father and four belonging to Mr Vernon. My father's were the standard Victorian type, with names like 'the Caley' and 'the Allwyn de Luxe', where you shot a silver ball around a coloured spiral into a row of cups. If the ball landed on either of the end cups you lost but if it landed on any in between, you won. Mr Vernon's four machines were typically racier American-style one-arm bandits with silver-and-crimson streamlined cases, though offering prizes of only single copper tokens with holes in them rather than the jackpots of their distant Las Vegas cousins.

Holidaymakers who paused to amuse themselves at this row of machines naturally assumed they all belonged to the larger collection inside the Pavilion. Whenever a Vernon one-arm bandit went wrong, the aggrieved player would as likely as not seek out my father to lodge a complaint. This provided one of his few moments of triumph in the war, for Mr Vernon's Achilles' heel was knowing nothing whatever about the workings of slot-machines, whereas my father knew everything. He would direct the complainant to the rock shop, then retire to his Amplifier Room and watch with grim satisfaction as Mr Vernon emerged with a key to the faulty machine, opened it up and cluelessly poked around inside.

As my father's son, I knew it was treason to enter the rock shop or even to approach too near it. Yet I couldn't help finding its garish confectionery displays more alluring than anything offered by the Pavilion. Remember, this was still the era of government sweet-rationing, when purchase of even a small bar of chocolate required a coupon from a buff-coloured ration-book as well as money. Despite myself, I would be drawn into the hut's tiny interior where Mr Vernon's painted-doll head, huge bulk and jazzy tie almost filled the space behind a high counter. He seemed to bear me no grudge for my parentage, calling me 'Son' in his lightweight cockney voice and invariably giving me a few extra free sweets along with what I had bought. Sometimes his wife would be in charge; an opulent-looking woman with a head of rich curly auburn hair, who was just as amiable and welcoming.

Indeed, I gathered that Mr Vernon prosecuted the war with far less ferocity than did my father, and, on one occasion at least, had tried to bring it to an end. Meeting my father unexpectedly in some pub or club on shore, he said, 'Come on, Norman – why don't we bury the hatchet?' 'Yes, in your head,' my father replied. Even that brusque rebuff did not turn him against me or my mother, whom he always treated with the greatest politeness. 'I've got nothing against you, Mrs Norman,' I once overheard him say to her. 'You're to be pitied.'

The psychological skirmishing between my father and Mr Vernon only once spilled over into outright violence, but it was an occasion that passed into pier-head folklore. The cause of the trouble was ice-cream tins.

Another of the rock shop's attractions for me, and provocations for my father, was that it sold Wall's ice-cream, in those days a brand with prestige unlike any other in Britain. The pale blue and cream Wall's pennant outside a confectioner's – with its slightly self-righteous slogan, 'More than a treat, a food' – was comparable to a Rolls-Royce dealership in the car trade. Doubtless by his usual contemptible method of sneaking around behind people's backs, Mr Vernon had won the right to display a Wall's ice-cream banner outside his shop, whereas we at the Pavilion sold only Eldorado, a local make devoid of Wall's addictive creaminess and crunchy with unassimilated shards of ice.

At that time, ice-cream was delivered to retailers in oblong tins, about two feet high. The spirit of wartime economy still prevailed, and shopkeepers were under strict obligation to return their empty tins to the supplier for re-use. Wall's eminence in the ice-cream world, and the feverish competition for its dealerships, made this responsibility all the more pressing. Mr Vernon, however, preferred to throw his empty Wall's tins into the Triangle, that enclosure of sea overlooked by the rear of his shop and by the Pavilion. Spotting empty tins afloat, my father took to retrieving them and using them as receptacles for the pennies he emptied from his machines.

Wall's were as protective of their tins as Rolls-Royce of the 'Spirit of Ecstasy' mascot. Realizing that the supply of empties from Mr Vernon was deficient, they sent an undercover investigator – yes, an undercover ice-cream investigator – to Ryde pier-head to look into the matter. This sleuth found his way into the Pavilion, discovered my father scooping pennies from an opened slot-machine into one of the sacred tins and accused him of misappropriating Wall's property. With disingenuous astonishment, my father replied that his neighbour at the rock shop had thrown the tins away into the sea and that he in all innocence, not liking to see good containers go to waste, etc. etc., had salvaged them and put them to their new use.

The undercover ice-cream investigator fetched Mr Vernon from his shop to answer this charge, so bringing the enemies into confrontation at last on the strip of concrete car-park that separated their premises. The resentment and rancour pent up so long in their loudspeaker announcements boiled over in an instant. My father took hold of Mr Vernon's shirt at the front and wrenched it completely off his back, a feat almost worthy of the music-hall stage that left his alpaca jacket and jazzy tie still in place but with only an undervest beneath. Mr Vernon's response was to rush to that contentious line of his and my father's slot-machines overlooking the Triangle. In what also was no mean feat, especially for so large a man, he dragged the 'Caley' cup-and-ball machine from its wooden shelf and heaved it over the rail into the water.

The pier had no security staff as such, apart from a few porters and ticket collectors who watched the spectacle with huge enjoyment as a welcome break from everyday routine. My father was notoriously prone to using his fists, and might well have gone on to turn Alfie Vernon into an alpaca-jacketed punchbag had not the approach of another packed Portsmouth ferry caused them both simultaneously to break off the confrontation and hurry back inside to their respective microphones. In a moment, their voices were chorusing forth once again, with only a slight breathlessness to indicate the desperate struggle that had just occurred:

'Morning coffee and biscuits, tea, minerals and light . . . and light refreshments can be obtained on the sun-roof or in the . . . the restaurant upstairs . . .'

'Good morning, ladies and . . . gentlemen, now just across here at the . . . at the shop, we'll serve you straight away . . .'

Spiv or not, Mr Vernon played the more gentlemanly part in the affair. Next day, he sent his auburn-haired wife across to the Pavilion with a cheque to pay for the drowned machine. My father cashed the cheque. Then at low tide, when the sea under the pier was only a couple of feet deep, he climbed down a long, seaweedy iron ladder into the Triangle, tied a rope around the submerged machine and hauled it up. Victorian leisure-engineering was more than proof against a little salt water. The machine was back in working order by the following morning.

Two

DURING SCHOOL HOLIDAYS and at weekends, I would
spend all day on the pier-head while my father and (for a time)
my mother were running the Pavilion. You might think it a
heavenly existence for a boy, out in the sun and open air with
the sea all around and fun things like ice-cream and candyfloss
and lettered rock and sailing boats and slot-machines close at
hand. For another kind of boy, it would have been. But for the
kind of boy I was, those brilliant summer days among festive
noise and pleasure-bent crowds were weary and lonely and
barren of amusement.

Our earlier years, in a London pub first, then a country
hotel, had accustomed me to a separate existence from my
parents' as they worked the long, unsocial hours of the
licensed trade. On Ryde Pier, those hours became longer and
more unsocial than ever previously. There is no business so
frantically busy as seaside business, where you can earn your
living only for a few short weeks each year. It came down to
about three months, between Easter and mid-September,
when we had to earn enough from the holidaymakers to
sustain us through the whole shuttered-down and incomeless
winter.

I have known other people in the catering and pub trade

who managed to have some private and family life as well as making a good living. No doubt we, too, could have had such a life if my father had had the will to provide it. But under his rule, there was never any respite from the unremitting hard labour of 'the season'. As long as the ferries kept coming and the crowds kept surging ashore, my mother could not leave her post – or posts. And, powerless though I was to help, I had to be there also, all the time, to show loyalty and solidarity.

Consequently, in the three years since we'd come down to the Island, I'd seen fewer of its beauty spots, landmarks and curiosities than the average week-long holidaymaker. I'd never been to Carisbrooke Castle, where King Charles I was imprisoned before his execution, nor to Osborne House, where Queen Victoria lived and died, nor to Cowes regatta. I'd never seen the Needles lighthouse nor Shanklin Old Village nor Blackgang Chine, where you could sit inside the bones of a whale and make a wish, nor Keats Green nor the Roman villa at Brading. The famously beautiful West Wight, with its rolling downs, chalk cliffs and echoes of Alfred Lord Tennyson, was a region as remote to me as the Himalayas. Even Ryde itself, where we lived and where I went to school, was still largely unknown terrain, apart from our well-worn routes to and from the pier-head.

I was – for the time being – an only child, but not in any way the indulged and domineering character that usually denotes. From my earliest toddlerhood, my father had impressed on me how utterly unimportant were my personal wishes and pleasures against the selfless life-or-death struggle in which he and my mother were engaged. I was used to the idea of being a burden and a distraction to them in their labours; both insignificant and threatening to the highly tuned commercial mechanism he had created. For my whole day on the pier was ruled by his stern edict not to bother him, my mother or our staff by any manifestation of unthinking child-ishness.

From outside, the Pavilion may have resembled a pleasure dome but for me, during summertime, it was a complex mental map of prohibitions and no-go areas. Except at our own irregular and unpredictable family mealtimes, I was barred from the upstairs restaurant and the sun-roof, where my mother worked as cashier as well as supervising the food-ordering and preparation and coping with the onerous paperwork entailed with restaurant-operation in these days. Any modern health and safety inspector would have con-demned her working conditions as wholly unacceptable, shut away as she was on a stool in her narrow, airless office with only the high cashier's window connecting her with the outside world, and only Melody, her liver-and-roan cocker spaniel, for company.

Of course, I was not allowed to communicate with her while she was engaged at this vital task. Nor was I allowed into the extensive kitchen and serveries, where an antiquated potato-peeling machine clanked like a steamroller, and women in white overalls laboured at stoves and fish-fryers and long marble slabs, wiping their sweaty bare arms and upper bosoms, and sometimes their sweaty bare legs, on clean drying-up cloths.

The kitchen staff had the friendliness of most Isle of Wight people and were pleased enough to see me, greeting me, with their special inflection, as 'Phil-op'. But you never knew when my father might come up from the Pavilion floor to 'watch points', as he put it – which process always included detailed and sceptical checking of my mother's cash-desk records. 'Are you sure that's right, Irene?' he would ask her with narrowed eyes, as if giving her a chance to admit that she fiddled some of the takings (which, alas, she never had the sense to do).

He walked very rapidly everywhere, on near-noiseless shoes, with his shoulders hunched and his head thrust forward as if perpetually smelling out dilatoriness or deceit. He would unfailingly materialize with a look of grim triumph just as I was doing something I oughtn't – showing my drawings to waitresses in the restaurant, perhaps, or playing hide-and-seek with the younger stillroom maids in the bread-store. '*Don't* worry people when they're busy, Philip,' he would tell me in the tone of flat disillusionment that used to cut me almost worse than did his anger. 'People are here to work, not to skylark around with you.'

My movements in his personal domain, the ground-floor amusement arcade, were almost as strictly circumscribed. I was not allowed to ask for money to play on the machines, nor even to play on them with my own money, when I had any. 'These machines aren't put here for your benefit,' he reminded me many times with weary patience. 'This is a place of business. A place of *business*, Philip.' I did play them sur-reptitiously, of course, but never without a deep sense of wrongdoing at thus amusing myself while he and my mother battled with the day-tripper hordes. My guilt was even worse if I lit on a machine (like the yellow-sparkly 'Caley') which showed more inclination than others to let you win on it. How could I have deliberately exploited a weak spot in our business for my personal gain, and pocketed winnings that should have gone to help feed us or pay for my education?

Even with the weather outside at its most brilliant, the arcade always managed to be a gloomy place. Its only illu-mination came from the lights in the machines themselves, and whatever sun managed to filter through the dado of red and yellow stained-glass diamonds above the main doors. Large as it was, my father always seemed to be everywhere, mending, emptying or servicing machines, his rapid footfall accompanied by the clink of a long chain of machine-keys and identification-discs that he carried slung on one shoulder like a tarnished silver fleece. The moment I put in a penny, or slyly twisted a 'Coin Return' handle to see if the last player's prize had gone unclaimed, I could depend he would come round the nearest corner and catch me red-handed. 'This is a place of *business*, Philip.'

I counted as a trivial annoyance, however, compared with Meatball. Meatball was a small boy from the tenements which in those days still existed a few yards from Ryde's sea front. He haunted the Pavilion arcade, on the lookout for any chance to extract money from our machines, either by stealth or violence. Aged no more than about seven, he was a tiny ragamuffin with a shock of dusty fair hair and a trumpet-shaped mouth that seemed made to protest outraged innocence. My father hunted Meatball among the twilit aisles like a destroyer tracking a U-boat, sometimes catching him shaking or rattling vulnerable machines, sometimes bent double under a pinball game to unplug it from its fragile electrical socket. However many times my father led him from the premises by one ear (no hyper-sensitive child assault laws in those days) he would always soon be back again.

Guilt racked me, too, for having inherited none of my father's multi-faceted mechanical aptitude and sharing none of his insatiable curiosity about how things worked. Between ferries, he would generally be repairing some broken-down or seized-up machine, a process I could only impotently stand by and observe. I can see him now with the glassed front of a ball-and-cup machine swung open, revealing its works glued on behind. I can see his forehead wrinkled in concentration below the peaked hairline, his tongue protruding a little way and clamped against his upper lip as he probes rods and chutes and cogwheels with an index finger or twists a miniature pocket screwdriver with a busy 'click-click-click'. I remember the reassuring glow of the one great certainty he communicated to me: that there was no mechanism in the world he could not understand and, sooner or later, restore to perfect working order.

I would sometimes help him empty machines, standing beside him with one of Mr Vernon's ice-cream tins – always keeping a weather eye out for Meatball – as he scooped pennies from one unlocked cabinet after another with quick, definitive hand movements. Of course, I'm talking about old pennies that used to be twelve to an old shilling – big, dull-brown discs with thick milled edges that weighted the pocket like stones. I remember the sight of them en masse, filling ice-cream tins to the brim; how their grime got under your fingernails and the sour reek of them on to the back of your tongue. In the fifties, some pennies still survived from the early reign of Queen Victoria, black and worn thin and smooth, with a likeness one could hardly see. We lived among seas of pennies that, somehow, never managed to turn themselves into pounds, or at least enough to make our fortune.

Not that my father did not seek to fleece the holiday-making crowds with every means at his disposal. None of the slot-machines gave its winner a prize any more munificent than their penny back and another free go. On the pinball games, the winning score was well nigh impossible; anyone with the dexterity and freakish luck to punch up the requisite hundreds of thousands was rewarded with a small cardboard box containing a single toffee. (Another of my occasional jobs was to sit in the Amplifier Room, fold the boxes into shape from rectangles of white cardboard and slip that affronting solitary sweetmeat into each one.) In our crane-grab machines, packets of ten Woodbine cigarettes reared enticingly from thick beds of liquorice comfits. The crane's jaws flopped indecisively on to this treasure-trove, never even disturbing the half-buried packets of Woodbines, picking up maybe two or three liquorice comfits which it invariably dropped again as it swung back to the chute by which prizes were delivered. Those liquorice comfits, I believed, even predated my father's management of the Pavilion: they were so ancient that their original bright colours had faded into a uniform mildewy green.

Thanks to my Grandma Norman, I was already fascinated by the Victorian age, and in the twilit aisles of slot-machines, I could fancy myself almost living in it. Stilt-legged Mutoscope peep-shows showed comedies from the dawn of silent pictures on hand-cranked frames as thick as medieval vellum. An iron sailor figure offering trials of strength – you had to try to push his outstretched hands together – wore the pale blue tunic and white bellbottoms of the First World War dreadnought era.

I spent hours gazing into glass-fronted cabinets at the little iron figures which the insertion of a penny would briefly bring to life. Many of these machines had names, etched on mirror-glass pediments, as if they were miniature films or plays. In 'The Uninvited', a miser counted out blocks of gold while ghosts flew out of chests and grandfather clocks behind his back. In 'Sweeney Todd', the barber's customer vanished through a trapdoor, and a man appeared to one side with a tray labelled HOT PIES. In 'Domestic Scene', a man rocked a baby in his arms and a cradle with his foot as his wife lay in bed, her lacy bosom twitching up and down. In 'The Automatic Palmist', a veiled gypsy woman traced a penholder back and forth above a blotter as if writing out your fortune for you. The italic-script cards the machine dispensed were the same as had been in use fifty years earlier. ('You are the possessor of exceptional qualities, but owing to excessive modesty, you have never received your rightful reward . . .')

When window-shopping slot-machines grew wearisome, I would roam around the pier-head, where everyone but myself seemed to have so energetic a role in summer's teeming canvas. Here were the brisk men in blue jerseys and squashed peaked caps who caught the ropes from the incoming ferries, looped them around iron stanchions and slid the wooden gangways forth and back. Here were the white-jacketed attendants for the car-park and the clumps of green deckchairs. Here was majestic, hook-nosed Captain House who ran pleasure cruises from a jetty a few yards back down the pier in his launch, *The Wight Queen* – and whose fat son of my age helped him cast off and tie up as I could never hope to help my father. Here were the two white-suited photographers who walked backwards in front of putative clients, exhorting them to say 'cheese' while snapping off rolls of imaginary film. Here were the 'Pier Master', Mr Smith, in his formal grey suit, and Leo, the porter who'd been an American GI, and Hilda from the station buffet, and Jack Watts, the famously dapper tram-driver who left an immaculate bottle-green sports car on the Esplanade when he came to work, and made every journey up and down the half-mile with his little white dog on the seat beside him.

Inside, I may have been subject to continual paternal surveillance but outside I enjoyed a lack of supervision that would make any responsible modern parent tremble. No one restrained me from going right to the edge of the unfenced ferry berths as the paddleboats docked, their wheels beating up avalanches of blue-black foam. No one stopped me playing on the tram station, whose twin platforms gave on to naked girders and sea. No one forbade me to descend the stone stairways to the jetties under the pier-head, which revealed themselves on lower and still lower levels as the tide went out. The bottom level, where I often went by myself, was an eerie, sunless place, with grey timbers like a forest all around and black water lapping up through concrete girders as weed-slimy as green silk. Living as I did with deep sea all around, it might have seemed an elementary precaution to teach me to swim as soon as possible. But nobody had. I realize now there were dozens of times when I could have slipped on a barnacled, green-slimy cross beam, and never been seen again.

If I couldn't swim, why didn't I fish? On summer days, scores of fishermen would be at the pier-head, stationed beside its wooden boundary posts or along its lower plat-forms with glistening rods and sandwich boxes and Oxo tins of thick pink ragworms dug up at low tide on the sand-flats to the east. Schools of smelt flickered just below the surface of the sunlit green water; mackerel, bream and dogfish and conger eels were pulled up, wriggling and twisting, on every hand; lobsters, crabs and prawns crowded the deeps around the pier's legs. You couldn't walk far without stepping over a piscine corpse of some kind, shrouded in putrefying weed and broiling on the hot concrete – a crushed hermit-crab, a liquefied jellyfish, the frilled white-papery fillet of an inkless cuttlefish.

My father was a passionate angler, albeit of the genteeler dry fly persuasion. His numerous rods and gaffs and landing-nets (by Hardy of Pall Mall) even now waited patiently in their green canvas rolls for that happy future day when he could put all this seaside vulgarity behind him and become the country gentleman he believed nature had always intended him to be. One rod he kept permanently set up at the sun-roof rail, where it looked across open sea to the Pavilion's main body. There, a ladies' lavatory produced a permanent over-flow that dropped about thirty feet vertically into the sea. The agitated water used to attract grey mullet, which would swirl around with bellies upturned as though in a ticklish ecstasy. From time to time my father would succeed in hooking one, but usually it struggled so much as he hauled it up that its soft mouth separated from its body, and all he would land was a pair of lips.

Once, he sorted me out a small rod of my own, showed me how to use it and set it up for me at the railing near the plank walkway. But I soon got bored and wandered off. While I was gone, some boys attached a dead tiddler to the end of my line and put it back into the water, hoping I wouldn't realize it was dead. And, to be truthful, I didn't. So that was another way I found of disappointing him.

Each day, as the crowds surged ashore, I would look into thousands of faces bewildered by sunshine and holiday excitement; catch passing glimpses inside thousands of families amid the stress of luggage and young children and finding their correct route to shore. Most daytrippers were London cockneys, horribly over-dressed even in that pre-leisurewear era, the men in blue or brown chalkstripe suits and thick boots, and wearing knotted white handkerchiefs on their heads in lieu of sun-hats. Many got no further than the Pavilion's built-in pub, the First and Last. I would loiter outside its wide-open doors, savouring the foghorn London accents and scraps of indigenous song that floated from within. London was the place where I was born and where I always longed to be. For it was the home of Grandma Norman, the person whom I loved – and who loved me – more than anyone else in the world.

The day's arrivals by sea were not exclusively pleasure-bent. Occasionally, a gleaming dark blue and white Royal Naval launch from the Portsmouth dockyard would put in at a side jetty, and a nameless VIP – sometimes rumoured to be Royalty – would step ashore through an honour-guard of ratings in full dress. Half a dozen times a year, a black police van would back up close to the relevant ferry disembarkation point and a convict in handcuffs would be hurried down the gangway, bound for one of the Island's celebrated prisons, Albany or Parkhurst.

Through the Pavilion's long row of pinned-open double doors I could hear the snap of Remington .22 rifles; the soft electronic punch as pinball scores racked up; the splash of pennies dropping inside wooden cabinets; the brief whir of 'Sweeney Todd' or 'The Uninvited' coming to life. We also had a jukebox, the first I ever saw, a domed marvel of chromium and sculpted pink plastic, with an outsize arrow suspended overhead and pointing downward so that no one could possibly miss it. Consequently I knew every hit song of that pre-rock 'n' roll era: Nat King Cole's 'Mona Lisa', Tex Ritter's 'High Noon', Tennessee Ernie Ford's 'Sixteen Tons', Hank Williams's 'Hey, Good Lookin' ', Rosemary Clooney's 'Come On-A My House', Frankie Laine's 'Jezebel', all murmured incessantly at the edge of my consciousness until I knew each note and vocal inflection by heart, although without the slightest idea what most of their words meant. The all-time smash of this summer was 'She Wears Red Feathers' by Guy Mitchell. So many times without a break did the jaunty, husky voice sing:

> She wears red feathers and a hoolie-hoolie skirt
> She wears red feathers and a hoolie-hoolie skirt

that finally, unable to stand it any more, my father opened the jukebox, took out the record and hurled it into the sea.

Always, I would be guiltily magnetized by Mr Vernon's rock shop, in particular by the two revolving racks of 'saucy' postcards he kept outside. Many of these were still being

printed from plates drawn in the twenties: the men had spats
and walking-sticks, and the women wore cloche hats. There
were jokes about henpecked husbands and spinsters and
chamberpots and wind ('I hear you've had a lot of wind on
the coast, Auntie') and about the endlessly recurring newly
married couple whose goings-on were for me still cloaked in
impenetrable mystery. One I remember showed a bridegroom
leaning from his hotel bedroom window and calling to a uniformed pageboy: 'I say . . . what time is it?' 'Ten o'clock, sir.'
'Thank you and . . . er, what day is it?' Did people on their
honeymoons really sleep in for as long as that?

*

IN MID-AFTERNOON came a brief period when the pier-head
suddenly went quiet. All the day's trippers had arrived, and
were down in the town, overflowing the pubs and gift shops
or packed in a glitter like massed flies' wings along the beach.
The ferries paused in their assault; the pier trams no longer
came banging over sea-borne rails to meet them every few
minutes. As if by tacit agreement, British Railways, the rock
shop and the Pavilion ceased their loudspeaker announcements. It was like a pause for breath before the start of the
evening exodus, when homebound queues could extend for
the full half-mile of the plank walkway.

I have special cause to remember one such afternoon
hiatus, late in that summer of 1952. It must have been around
a quarter to five. As often happened at that time of day, a stiff
breeze had arisen, making flags strain madly from their poles,
deckchairs blow inside-out and sun-blinds chafe in their
frames. Far out in the Solent, clusters of dim white racing
yachts were still strung out for miles, but every other kind
of endeavour seemed to be in suspense. Empty Brickwoods
beer-bottles stood like sentries outside the shuttered doors

of the First and Last. The car-park was almost deserted; the ticket-collectors had withdrawn inside their hut to brew tea. Fishermen dozed beside rods whose miniature bells no longer tinkled, as if the very fish were participating in the general siesta. Even Guy Mitchell seemed to be taking a breather from 'She Wears Red Feathers'.

My aimless wanderings had taken me into the Pavilion through its tram station entrance and up the main staircase, which had been rather grand in its former days as a theatre but was now closed to the general public, unlit and dusty. Half-way up on the right was a door into the kitchens, bearing a plastic white-on-black notice in my father's unmistakable voice:

STRICTLY NO ADMITTANCE
Except to staff

At the top of the staircase were glass-paned double doors giving on to the high balcony which ran around the Pavilion's whole circumference from either side of its stage. Above the balcony windows yawned the great hollow dome, contoured with iron girders painted a dull yellow. Far up there at its summit was a small extra dome with a glimmering frieze of red and yellow glass, traversed by two criss-crossed supports. It was said that during the war, when the Royal Navy had commandeered the Pavilion, a cache of black-market cigarettes had been hidden on that inaccessible cross-shaped ledge and never subsequently recovered. I used to imagine how it would feel to climb up in search of them – the unspeakable terror as arching girders put ever greater strain on my arms until I was hanging completely upside-down, fifty feet or more above the city of slot-machines.

Opposite the balcony entrance, on the left, was a narrow stairway leading up to non-public areas of the Pavilion roof.

As a rule, it was used as an overflow kitchen-store, and the doors at its bottom and top ends were both kept locked. On this particular afternoon, to my surprise, I found the bottom door ajar, the steps not obstructed by boxes of tinned goods or sacks of potatoes, and an inviting rectangle of blue sky at their summit. So up I went.

I emerged through a door like a ship's companionway, on to the level immediately above our public sun-roof. Below me, white umbrellas fluttered, and I could hear the clink of afternoon teas being served. The marine panorama of soft grey ships and crowding yachts looked intriguingly different from this higher perspective. To my right arose the fish-scaled immensity of the dome, embedded in broad swathes of newish-looking tarmac. My initial view of this area was blocked by some kind of water-tank, set in a wooden housing. I remember thinking it might be feasible to scale the dome from outside, peep in through the stained-glass frieze at its summit and see if the black-market cigarettes really were still there. Only at this point did I realize I wasn't alone.

A little way around the seaward side of the dome's perimeter, a man's cream linen jacket and a woman's sky-blue cardigan lay strewn on the tarmac. My first thought was that someone must be, very dangerously, swimming from up here. Then I realized two people were lying there, one of whom was my father. I remember the sight of his pale forehead with the dark widow's peak – the sight that always made my heart lift and plummet simultaneously.

With him, or to be more precise underneath him, was a woman whose face I could not see. All I could see was that she had a mass of fluffy auburn curls like Mrs Vernon's, from the rock shop.

There was time only for a brief glimpse before I shrank back again behind the water-tank, unnoticed by either of them. I couldn't be certain the woman really was Mrs Vernon. On balance, it seemed hardly plausible that she would leave her always-busy shop to venture thus into the territory of her husband's sworn enemy. Yet her auburn curls seemed unmistakable, as did her blue-and-white cotton dress and general air of tolerant good humour even in that uncomfortable posture on the almost bare tarmac. Balanced so needlessly on top of her, in his green Old England shirt but not his trousers, my father wore his usual look of almost tragic concentration. He could just as well have been working on a broken machine with his tiny ratchet screwdriver, or waiting to assail the next ferry crowd with doleful intelligence about buttered buns and doughnuts.

All my life since, I have regretted I didn't step out from behind the water-tank and demand to know what was happening, or run and fetch my mother from her cashier's window, or make any use of the power that suddenly had been put into my hands. Had I done so, the years to come might have been very different. But I was not that kind of boy. The kind of boy I was felt riven with guilt at having gone somewhere he shouldn't and seen what was not meant to be seen. The kind of boy I was tiptoed back down the dusty stairs with his unsayable secret, and wandered out again into the sun.

Three

THREE TIMES in my childhood I knew the experience of having a dream come true. The first was when I wished Grandma Norman would run a sweet shop – and she did.

Not least among the qualities that made Grandma Norman unique in my family was her ability make money at anything she turned her hand to. Yet it was, paradoxically, a talent that remained hidden the greater part of her life. Like most females born into the late Victorian era (in her case, 1889), she never imagined having an independent career of her own, least of all one at the homelier end of the retail trade. Until she reached the threshold of old age, business was something to be turned to only in emergencies and in a spirit of familial self-sacrifice.

Her initiation had come way back in 1918 when her husband William Norman – a man twenty years her senior, mildly celebrated as the Royal Naval Reserve's oldest lieutenant – went down with his ship courtesy of a German submarine in the Irish Sea. Still only in her mid-twenties, Grandma Norman was left with two small sons to raise on a naval widow's pension. Unconventionally for those days, she became a travelling saleswoman, first for Singer sewing-machines, then for the Waverly Book Company, which peddled literary classics in showy leather bindings for display in lower-middle-class front parlours. It was a role ideally suited to her striking good looks and almost hypnotic powers of persuasion. I guarantee that had she ever appeared on your front doorstep, you would not have been long in purchasing a treadle-operated sewing-machine or a morocco-bound set of Dickens or Mrs Henry Wood. She spent most of the 1920s in this occupation, earning enough to give her sons a comfortable home life and a private boarding-school education.

Her transition into shopkeeping would not happen for another fifteen years or so, until almost the end of the Second World War, when her elder son, my Uncle Phil, suddenly had need of her. Uncle Phil was still in the army, serving with its Field Security Police, but as a sideline had acquired a small newsagent's shop in Hornchurch, Essex. His wife, my Auntie Lorna, had two young children to cope with and, besides, was of a 'nervous' disposition, so Grandma Norman stepped in to run the shop for them. She always spoke nostalgically in her West Country burr of 'when we were down at Horrunchurch', recalling how she used to make ice-lollies using eggcups for moulds, but omitting the most interesting episode. During the war and its long, chilly aftermath, clothes were as strictly rationed as food, and subject to the same system of coupons from a ration-book. While at the Hornchurch shop, Grandma Norman was prosecuted for dealing in black-market clothes-coupons. Apparently it was only the exercise of her charm and persuasiveness to their utmost in court that saved her from prison.

To me as a small boy, she was a figure nothing less than miraculous. I lived for the times when I could go up to London and stay with her in her house in Clapham Old Town, and sleep with her every night, just the two of us, in the huge, jingling brass bed that dated back generations even before long-dead Grandpa Norman. There was no joy to compare with the moment when she would meet me off the train at Waterloo, her tall figure emerging from the crowd, arms wide outstretched; her face like some benign Maori or cannibal chieftain with its deep brown eyes, upturned nose and wide, humorous mouth, and the grey mole high on her right cheek that had two white hairs waving from it. I lived to be scooped into her embrace, to feel the kisses smacking all round my face and head, and hear the strings of West Country endearments that were for me alone: 'Hello my little lamb, my little precious, my little duck, my little bit o' fluff, my little bit o' fat, my little bit o' all right . . .' She had a wonderful smell that was all her own, compounded of leather handbag, Jaeger coat, peppermint and grey hair that might not have been shampooed for six months or more. Her skin also had a distinctive odour which, for me, was simply the scent of being kissed and which I would not until years later identify as the 'B.O.' that soaps like Lifebuoy and Lux had been invented to neutralize. For, like so many Victorians raised before the days of hot running water, Grandma Norman was not over-fond of washing.

Staying with her meant understanding the Chinese conception of children as little gods. It meant being put to bed at night wrapped in a shawl, with a stone hot-water-bottle wrapped in another shawl at your feet, and being awoken next morning with a cup of tea and a Rich Tea biscuit. It meant having the saucer held steady for you as you lifted the teacup and being allowed to lie in the massive brass bed as long as you liked, reading *Mary Mouse* or Enid Blyton's *Sunny Stories*, and to use a chamberpot (which Grandma Norman called the 'Po' or, sometimes, the 'Edgar Allan') from under the bed instead of having to go all the way downstairs to the proper toilet. It meant being fed only your very favourite foods – Puffed Wheat, fried eggs, fried potatoes and chips –

and leaving as much as you liked on your plate without being ordered to 'eat up'. It meant trips on the number 88 bus from Clapham Old Town to the London Zoo and the Natural History Museum and Apsley House, followed by what she called a 'mooch round' the West End, visiting news theatres (which actually showed non-stop cartoons), looking into shop windows, poking around in interesting-looking dustbins and eating ice-creams in the street, whatever the weather. It meant not having to worry about washing, combing your hair, being tidy or any of life's other more tiresome obligations. Above all, it meant a wonderful, incessant shower of sweets.

Her fondness for sweets equalled any child's in that still-rationed, restricted era when the monthly quota of 'points' from your ration book allowed purchase of only a pound and a quarter's weight. Grandma Norman, however, always had sweet coupons enough and to spare (a fact which would have surprised me less had I known of that earlier brush with the law in Hornchurch). While other adults tended to eat sweets shamefully and in secret, her attitude was that of a connoisseur. There were a select few brands that she bought in preference to all others and exalted in terms more suited to haute cuisine or château-bottled wine. Barker & Dobson's Butter Brazils, for instance, which were whole Brazil nuts encased in buttery hard toffee. And Meltis New Berry Fruits, which were soft jellies in fruit shapes with liquid centres. And Peter's Original Milk Chocolate, still in its brown and gold Victorian wrapping with the signature of 'D. Peter, Inventor'.

To think of her was automatically to think of white or pale pink peardrops, clotted together and smelling like nail-varnish; of Keiller treacle toffee, and Terry's All Gold chocolates, and Callard & Bowser's butterscotch, and Maltesers (which she pronounced 'Maltesies') and oval, buttery Murraymints, 'the too good to hurry mints'. In our long talks together in her big brass bed, she would tell me about sweets in her Victorian childhood in Somerset, the greatest time and place there ever had been. She told me how, in those days, ice-cream was known as 'hokey-pokey' (a name which, to me, seemed far more likely her own invention) and not sold in wafers or even cones, but ladled from the barrow into a glass you brought with you from your house. She told me how sweets in Victorian times used to be sold in cone-shaped paper bags, like dunces' caps, and how you could buy a halfpenny worth or even a farthing's worth of sweets, or eight aniseed balls for a penny or giant acid drops for a halfpenny each. As she spoke of giant acid drops, her face would wince in half-painful ecstasy and one eyelid would flutter up and down as if one of the sour monsters were still in her mouth. 'I'd take a whole morning to suck one of those,' she'd say. 'It left the whole inside of my mouth feeling like it was in ribbons.'

Even so, she never intended to start keeping a sweet shop at her age – she was in her early sixties at the time I'm talking about – and certainly never intended to migrate to the Isle of Wight. The remarkable enterprise she developed there was the result of a complicated chain of circumstances which for everyone else involved turned out somewhat less happily.

The business on Ryde Pier, at which my father was to labour so long and painfully, belonged in the first instance to his elder brother, Uncle Phil. To be precise, it belonged to two men named Parkinson and Cooper who ran it in the immediate post-war years when multitudes flocked back to formerly prohibited coastal resorts in joy and relief, and fortunes could be made by any caterer with a few tables and chairs and a ready supply of Spam. After a couple of bonanza seasons at Ryde Pier Pavilion, one of the partners, I think Mr Parkinson, decided to take his profits and pull out. To replace him the remaining partner, Mr Cooper, lit on Uncle

Phil, a man whose knowledge of seaside catering was zero and capacity for the requisite hard work even less. A short while afterwards, with the post-war holiday boom now starting to tail off, Mr Cooper wisely followed Mr Parkinson's example and pulled out, leaving Uncle Phil to run the Pier Pavilion on his own.

He immediately turned to his younger brother, who was then managing the Cross Keys Hotel in the sleepy East Anglian market town of St Neots, and who possessed all the practical skills Uncle Phil so sorely lacked. Although I was barely four at the time, I distinctly remember Uncle Phil's repeated visits to the Cross Keys and the lengthy conferences behind the closed door of the hotel office as he tried to persuade my father to join him in his enterprise.

It was by no means a pushover. In St Neots, my father had been as happy and settled as he was ever capable of being. Even my mother gave him credit for long holding out against Uncle Phil's pleas that he should give up the Cross Keys and go off to a pier on the Isle of Wight.

The decisive factor was Grandma Norman, to whom he had always been in absolute thrall and who at this moment was less concerned with his and his family's welfare than with succouring her inept firstborn. Not that she applied any kind of outright pressure – the old rogue was far too clever for that. She merely observed, wistfully and in the abstract, that it had always been her dearest wish to see her two boys in business together.

*

ONCE SHE HAD GOT her two boys into business together, it was only a matter of time before she was in it, too. The seaside empire which Uncle Phil now divided with my father included a building at the top of Ryde's hilly High Street, with a small café called the Creamery on its ground floor and two vacant flats above. The second summer we were there, Grandma Norman came down from London to run the Creamery. Since we lived in the first-floor flat upstairs, I had her in glorious proximity every day. I'd forget she was there, then remember with a surge of disbelieving joy as I saw her behind the café counter, winking at me and mouthing – she kept up her West Country accent even when mouthing – 'D'you want a ice?'

Another outpost of the empire, at that time seemingly its least significant, was to be found at the entrance to Ryde Pier, where an iron and glass canopy sheltered the 'In' and 'Out' turnstiles and the double gate that admitted motor vehicles. Flanking the entrance were a pair of octagonal brick kiosks, which once had sold tickets for pier-head amusements and boat trips. The left-hand of these now served as a recreation room for the ticket collectors who manned the turnstiles. The right-hand one had been adapted for the sale of confectionery and tobacco, and pre-emptively named 'the Kiosk'.

For some reason, the lease that Uncle Phil and my father had with British Railways for the Pier Pavilion also encompassed the Kiosk. To begin with, they employed a manager there; a man named Vic Strowbridge who was helped by his attractive, fluffy-haired wife, Bobbie. During Grandma Norman's season of running the Creamery café, she naturally was shown the Kiosk and introduced to the Strowbridges. I remember her exclaiming what a charming couple they were and that Bobbie Strowbridge was 'a nice little person'. With hindsight, I think that must have been roughly comparable to a kiss from a Mafia don before one is garrotted. By the following year, the Strowbridges had vanished and something I always knew in my heart was only sensible and logical, although too wonderful to imagine, actually came to pass. Grandma Norman took over the Kiosk.

After losing her sea-captain husband in the final months of the Great War she had never remarried. Though her dark-eyed good looks and magnetic charm attracted many suitors, she always had a distaste for sex, declaring she'd 'rather have a nice, strong cup of tea any day'. She used to say she never married again because it would have terminated her naval pension and because she couldn't bear the thought of 'anyone ordering my boys around' (something that would have done both a power of good). In fact, as I have only recently learned, Grandpa Norman's will stipulated that she must remain single for the rest of her life or else forfeit his whole estate.

Since the late thirties, she had lived with a man named Walter Hall, a gently irascible, grey-moustached government clerk of about her own age, known in our family as Uncle Wally. He had started out as her lodger, but was now her husband in all but the conjugal sense: they occupied separate bedrooms but were otherwise inseparable.

Uncle Wally, perhaps fortunately for him, was an un-assertive figure who went off to some vague Whitehall job each morning in a grey Homburg hat and each evening sat at the green baize-covered kitchen table, shredding out the tobacco from his day's used cigarette-ends to be rolled into fresh cigarettes tomorrow. He called Grandma Norman 'Gerrydear' – her first names were Edith Geraldine – she called him 'Wallydear', and they treated each other with elaborate politeness and consideration. After supper, for instance, there would be the most tremendous tussle as both insisted on doing all the washing-up at the tiny corner sink that, along with the gas-stove, was concealed by a floor-length curtain. 'I'll do it, Gerrydear . . .' 'No, *I'll* do it, Wallydear . . .' In the end, the two of them would be almost wrestling in their desire to spare the other the slightest touch of soapy water or damp dishtowel.

Uncle Wally came down to Ryde with her when she began running the Kiosk, although he took no part in the actual business. In this first era, 1952–6, the Kiosk opened only during the summer season, from May to September. Grandma Norman and Uncle Wally would stay in rented rooms in a pub called the Eagle Tavern in Green Street. Each autumn – on a day when I thought I could actually feel my heart breaking inside me – they returned to London for the winter.

An eye far less acute than Grandma Norman's could have spotted the Kiosk as a potential goldmine. Two of its four canopied serving-windows faced on to the wide pavement in front of the pier-gates, the busiest spot on Ryde's extensive seafront. The other two windows faced into the Esplanade railway station, which also was the main exit from the pier tramway. To the right lay 'The Western', Ryde's single soft sand beach, to which were attached ornamental gardens and an open-air theatre presenting live concert parties. To the left, beyond W.H. Smith's, were the massed bus stops of the Southern Vectis Company and bays for motor coaches offering scenic tours of the Island. The nearest rival confectioner and tobacconist was way across the busy Esplanade road, near the corner of Union Street. A dream site, in other words. If Uncle Phil and my father had concentrated their efforts here, rather than on that huge wooden folly at the pier-head, all their business worries would quickly have been over.

For Grandma Norman, the Kiosk was more than a money-making concern, or a distraction from the drab south London life of the early fifties, or even a way to be near her two 'boys'. It was, from the very start, her consuming passion. The four serving-windows required a sizeable staff, varying between three and five, but hers was always the foremost and dominant presence. She was there every day of the week, for every moment the place did business. She opened it personally every morning and closed it every evening. In all her years on the Island, first as a temporary then as a permanent resident, I never knew her go outside Ryde or have any kind of real leisure or social life or even any home she cared about a millionth as much as she cared about the Kiosk. In the end, as I had to accept, she came to love it more even than any of her grandchildren. More even than me.

Like my father, she was considered strangely upper-class to be engaged on Ryde's seaside battlefront, although, unlike my father, she never put on the slightest airs. Quite the opposite: she was fond of characterizing herself as 'Old Mother Riley', the farcical dame of thirties and forties cinema who was in fact portrayed by a man. In deference to the unrigorous hygiene laws of that time, she wore an overall, usually in semi-transparent pink nylon. But this was left gaping open at the front to reveal a tailored grey flannel 'costume' with (none too clean) white or cream blouse and the cameo lapel-brooch that was her one ornamental vanity. Her iron-grey hair was worn pinned up behind, with a few trailing side wisps. On her feet she wore dark blue canvas shoes with rubber soles that she called bumpers ('bumpurrs').

The richly warm, humorous personality I knew so well, and adored so much, was distributed in small portions along with the cigarettes and sweets. Everyone she served, child, woman or man, received a passing endearment in that affectionate West Country burr... 'What can I do for you, dear?'... 'Twenty Seniors, love?'... 'Here's your change, thanks very much, my duck...' Just as in her personal sweet-hoard in London, everything that the Kiosk sold became for me an expression of her character and appetite for life – the boiled sweet and toffee brands, Pascall, Sharp's, Palm, Trebor,

Clarnico ('Clarr-nico') and Needler's ('Needlurrs'); the boxed chocolate selections, Cadbury's Vogue, Caley's Fortune, Rowntree's Dairy Box, Terry's Spartan; the cigarette names, Gold Flake, Turf ('Turruf'), Ardath, Greys, Kensitas, Woodbines, Weights, Passing Cloud, Craven A and Capstan Full Strength; even the pipe tobaccos, Four Square, Gold Block, Digger Shag, St Bruno and Old Holborn.

It had been from Grandma Norman chiefly that I acquired the view of Wall's ice-cream as more wholesome as well as more delicious, with its buttery aftertaste, than any other brand. She had a way of rolling her tongue around the phrase 'a Wall's ice-cream' that made you salivate for one even out of doors in midwinter. So it was no surprise that the Kiosk under her management should instantly have been awarded one of the sought-after Wall's dealerships that had eluded her two 'boys'. (Fortunately, the company's undercover ice-cream investigator was never sent to check on her discharge of this sacred trust. I doubt he would have approved her practice, when she sold a threepenny brickette, of charging an extra halfpenny for the wafer biscuits that sandwiched it.)

On the broad pavement outside the Kiosk's windows, a crowd of men in peaked caps stood waiting to intercept each outpouring from the pier tramway. These were taxi-drivers from the rank in the middle of the Esplanade, and employees of motor coach companies (Paul's, Read's or Pearce's White Heather) brandishing leaflets about the various tours of the Island they offered. In their wait between boat-arrivals, they constantly came to Grandma Norman's windows for cigarettes or sweets. She knew them all by name, just as she knew the ticket-clerks and porters from the adjacent Esplanade railway station and the custodian of its ladies' lavatory, where she enjoyed the privilege of a key to save her and her staff from paying a penny on each visit. She knew the tram-drivers and conductors, and the staff from W.H.Smith's bookshop, and the man who sold newspapers next to the giant weighing-machine at the entrance to the Western Gardens and who also illegally conveyed her daily horse-racing bets to a bookmaker in Union Street.

Though no one could have been cleverer, craftier or more utterly self-sufficient, she presented herself as a helpless old lady, endlessly reliant, like Blanche DuBois, on 'the kindness of strangers'. The Kiosk's counters, for example, had sash windows, so wide and stiff that two people were needed to haul them up and down. Yet at opening and closing times, Grandma Norman would invariably be alone in the place. Morning after morning, evening after evening, she would find some bus-conductor, coach-driver, booking-clerk or other Esplanade worker to help her haul the windows up and down, rewarding him with ten Weights or a bar of chocolate and her supreme accolade, 'You're one of Nature's gentlemen.'

Nature's two greatest gentlemen on Ryde Esplanade were the uniformed ticket-inspectors who manned the pier's 'In' turnstile on the Kiosk's right side (below an archaically spelt notice reading ALL TICKETS TO BE SHEWN). One of these inspectors was a round, jolly-looking individual who could have doubled for Mr Pickwick and was known as 'Mister Reg'. His colleague, tall and stooped and haggard, was addressed with full formality as Mr Bennett. Grandma Norman and 'the men on the gate', as she called them, were devoted to one another. She plied them continually with cups of tea and bars of chocolate; at longer intervals, they would respond with British-Railways-monogrammed cups of the pale khaki fluid they brewed up in their own kiosk beside the 'Out' turnstiles. When the haunted-looking Mr Bennett disappeared from his turnstile, and afterwards died in obscurely tragic circumstances, it upset her for weeks. 'Poor

Mr Bennett' became all but canonized, with his black peaked cap, his hollow eyes and the ticket-clippers that would clip no more.

Uncle Wally, as I have said, took no part in running the Kiosk. One had the impression that Grandma Norman wished to shield him from the rough-and-tumble seafront life she herself so much relished. He would spend all day hanging around the Esplanade gardens in his grey Homburg hat, staring pensively out at the string of dark seaborne forts that guard the approaches to Portsmouth harbour. He had been stationed on one of them with the army during the 1914–18 war, but never spoke about it – nor indeed about anything very much. When Grandma Norman shut the Kiosk, which she did comparatively early in those days, she and Uncle Wally would repair to one of the Esplanade's several pubs, the King Lud, the Wellington Tavern or the Marine. There she would smoke a Churchman's No.3 cigarette and – for medicinal reasons only, as she always stressed – drink a number of glasses of Guinness. I can see her now, holding each dark, creamy-capped glass up to the light like a superior vintage, taking a long pull that leaves perhaps a third of it empty, then smacking her lips with a blissful 'Aah!'

With each generous swallow, her face would grow even rosier, her chuckle even readier and richer. The staid Uncle Wally thawed under her influence, sometimes singing snatches of music-hall songs from his far distant youth that made a reluctant little smile appear below his moistened moustache. 'I think she likes me . . . I know she likes me . . . Because she said so . . .' 'Come on now, Wal,' Grandma Norman would break in with mock severity, lifting the black Guinness bottle again, 'Pass your glass. Or should I say "Pass your glass, you silly arse"?'

*

TECHNICALLY, I was not her only grandchild. Uncle Phil had a son and a daughter, both only slightly older than I, in whose lives she also was a towering presence. She always loudly proclaimed that she made no distinction between me and my cousins, Dina and Roger, loving us all in exactly the same inordinate degree. But I knew she was only saying what she was obliged to as a conscientious grandmother. In those days, I knew I was the one she loved far and away the most, even though she could never publicly admit as much. It was an understanding between us; an occasional murmur of the unsayable for my ears alone, in the third person she reserved for super-colossal adoration. 'Bless him! Bless his little heart, the little lamb! Still top favourite with his old Gran, he is.'

In the developing chaos, which beset my family life from 1951 onward, the Kiosk became my principal refuge. I can see and feel myself now as a perplexed eight-year-old, knocking for admission at its green side door under the pier-gate's glass canopy, with homebound holiday crowds streaming past me and Mister Reg and Mr Bennett at their turnstiles shouting, 'Have all your boat tickets ready, please!' The door had two opaque glass panes side by side, with wire mesh behind the glass. On the right-hand pane was a faded poster of the musical-comedy star Sally Ann Howes rapturously biting into a still-rationed Mars bar. 'I buy Mars every week,' the caption said, 'because Mars are marvellous.'

In high summer, with all four windows in operation, the Kiosk's interior reminded me of the Alamo, its white-coated garrison holding back hundreds of money-waving Mexicans from behind ramparts of bottled boiled sweets. Below each window jutted forth a glass display case full of rock, in six-penny, shilling and half-crown sizes, like heaped-up sticks of pink, orange and lime-green dynamite. The serving area was bisected by a crude wooden unit whose sloping surface displayed chocolate bars: Cadbury's Dairy Milk, Fruit and Nut, Sliced Nut, Bourneville and Milk Tray Selection, Fry's Five Boys, Lyons' Nut Milk, Tiffin, Milk Motoring, Crunchie, Banjo, Mars, Punch, Crest and Bounty. There was no cash register, only a compartmented wooden tray. Directly inside the door was the ice-cream fridge, a chest-high contraption with a black rubber lid. Jammed in between the display unit and the furthermost window was a whirring candyfloss machine.

Wasps were everywhere. Trapped inside the counter display-cases, they gorged at leisure on the stacked-up rock, sucking it as full of holes as Gruyère cheese. Mice were another chronic problem. Directly underneath the Kiosk was an ancient cellar workshop connected with the pier tramway. The mice came up through a floor grating to their nocturnal feasts. I remember Grandma Norman's bewildered exasperation as she showed me a handful of sixpenny Dairy Milks with the chocolate and silver foil half gnawed-away. 'I wouldn't mind,' she said, 'if they'd only eat the whole thing instead of wasting it like this.'

Her main assistant through many seasons was a small, friendly woman named Dorothy, who wore her white overall cinched with a black elastic belt, and had one of those broad smiles that consist more of gums than of teeth. There was an Irish girl named Maria who had an artificial leg, and a darkly sunburnt older woman named Doreen who had a gigantic bosom and the lugubrious expression that so often goes with it. Doreen's physique was a source of endless interest to the taxi and motor-coach men waiting about the pavement outside. I remember one taxi-driver, a man named Brownie, celebrated for his Victorian muttonchop whiskers, eyeing her with something like devoutness as she served him a packet of nuts and raisins. When he had gone, Doreen turned to

Grandma Norman with an expression of glum outrage. 'He said, "You've got a lovely pair there, dear," ' she complained. 'Take no notice, love,' Grandma Norman replied soothingly. 'He's only jealous.'

There also was Mrs Dunwoody, a widow who lived near Grandma Norman in Clapham and who came down to Ryde for a couple of months each summer, partly to help at the Kiosk, partly on holiday. Mrs Dunwoody hailed originally from South Shields on Tyneside and so was known as 'Geordie' or, to me and my cousins, as 'Auntie Geordie'. She was a fat, greedy, flatulent, good-hearted woman who wore gold bangles on her upper arms, used a toilet preparation called White Shoulders, and spoke with the singsong lilt of her native region, often placing a hand on her heart and exclaiming, 'Ee, dear me!' Her pampered brown Pekinese, Sue-Sue, spent each day with her at the Kiosk, reposing on a cushion atop an ice-cream-wafer carton and growling at anyone who came near. After lunch, as an emphatic mark of her non-employee status, Auntie Geordie took Sue-Sue off on an extended walk. As she left, she would lean over Dorothy or Maria at the busiest window and tear a handful of paper bags from the string-threaded block hanging on the wall. 'I'll just take these to wipe Sue-Sue's bottom,' she never failed to explain loudly.

The Kiosk had a small back room, screened from its customers' view by a partition of plywood display shelves. On the right of this narrow inner space, brown cardboard rock-cartons were piled against the wall, five or six feet high. On the left, below a net-curtained window, were a minuscule wash-basin, an Ascot water-heater and a shelf bearing a single gas-ring. Here, Grandma Norman studied horse-racing form, prepared tea and snacks for her staff and her beloved 'men on the gate' and entertained the various travelling reps from the sweet and tobacco companies.

For me, that tiny cockpit among the rock-boxes became a re-creation of her kitchen in London, which itself had re-created a West Country kitchen in the glorious Victorian age. On the shelf, among cartons of chocolate and cigarettes, she kept a bread-bin, a tea-caddy, crockery, cutlery, butter and a cutlery-box. I'd sit at the iron-legged table, wedged in to the right of the doorway, and she'd give me thick slices from a crusty cottage loaf with Cheddar cheese and Branston pickle, and a cup of strong, sweet Twinings Nectar tea, her invariable brand. Amid the rough-and-ready squalor, she maintained stray fragments of Victorian gentility, always insisting on a spoon for the jam or pickle and a separate china bowl for one's teacup dregs which must never be referred to as a slop-bowl but a 'tea-bowl'. In the early mornings, after she'd opened for business, she would cook me huge breakfasts of bacon, fried potato and fried bread on the single gas-ring. The sizzling aroma wafted over the partition to the serving-windows and the Esplanade beyond. 'What can I get you, my duck?' I heard her ask one customer who temporarily interrupted her cooking. 'Bacon and egg, please,' was the wistful reply.

The Kiosk's increasingly hefty takings were left on the premises each night, not in a safe but in a black tin box that had belonged to some Victorian lawyer or stockbroker forebear of hers. Once a week, I had the job of paying in the accumulated loot at the National Provincial Bank in Union Street. No one then thought twice about sending a small boy through Ryde's busy streets with a brown canvas bank-bag containing several hundred pounds.

Each afternoon, Grandma Norman would withdraw into her back room for an hour's rest in a deckchair squeezed in among the piled rock-boxes. First she would read some historical romance, like *Mary of Carisbrooke* by Margaret Campbell Barnes or *The Remarkable Young Man* by Cecil Roberts; then she would doze. But, although her eyes behind their horn-rimmed glasses might appear shut, she remained intensely aware of the business going on over the partition; the tinny whirr of the candyfloss machine, the thump of the rubber fridge-lid, the rustle of sweets on weighing scales, the chip of coins being thrown into the open till. Her staff fully realized this, calling out queries like, 'How much are the quarter-pounds of Terry's Spartan, please, Mrs Norman?' Now and again, she would shout what her mode of speech could never make quite into a reprimand: 'Maria, dear! Count the change back to the customer the way I showed you, love!'

Often I would be sitting there beside her, eating a choc-ice or 'Maltesies' from a one-and-sixpenny box, and enjoying the same long confidential chats we'd always had in her big brass bed in London. She'd tell me yet again how wonderful it used to be in Victorian times; about the bustles and horse-drawn buses and hokey-pokey and giant acid drops. She'd tell me again about her life amid the Chelsea artists' colony in the twenties, and how she'd known a painter from New Zealand whose mother had been a cannibal, and how she'd been to the Chelsea Arts Ball, and what fun it was in the General Strike of 1926, when London's buses were driven by undergraduates from Oxford and Cambridge, and you could travel anywhere you wanted for the same flat fare of sixpence.

What seemed like distant history to me was, for Grandma Norman, still a matter of personal involvement and strong emotion. She was still outraged by the shooting of 'poor Nurse Cavell' in the First World War, still fulminated against the coterie led by 'that Cosmo Lang and that Lassles [which I eventually deciphered as "Lascelles"]', who in 1936 had prevented King Edward VIII assuming the throne with Mrs

Simpson as his queen, and so turned him into 'the poor Duke o' Windsor'. Having been conditioned to it by lethal official propaganda in two successive wars, she loathed all Germans, believing, as many still did, that 'the only good German is a dead German'. A lifelong Tory, she read Lord Beaverbrook's *Daily Express* like a religion; her great hero outside her own family was Winston Churchill, Britain's saviour from Hitler, who – after the grim post-war tenure of 'Attlee and those horrible Labour people' – was triumphantly back as Prime Minister again. When, for all his great services, Mr Churchill received the rather modest and belated reward of a knighthood, I remember Grandma Norman reading out the *Express*'s banner headline as if she were conferring the honour personally: 'Arise, Sir Winston!'

Confined to the Kiosk and dedicated to its customers, as she was, she still took a keen interest in her surroundings, especially where they evoked her own beloved Victorian age. She knew, for instance, of an old man in a leather merchant's shop in Union Street who remembered when Queen Victoria would drive in to Ryde (along Queen's Road) from her summer palace at Osborne. 'Ryde for Pride' had been the borough's regally inspired slogan in those days, she told me. It was from her too that I learned of a magnificent edifice named the Royal Pier Hotel, which had once stood at the bottom of precipitous Union Street, where the Western Gardens were now. 'They had to knock it down when the motor-car was invented,' she told me. 'Coming down Union Street, the cars couldn't manage the turn at the bottom, so they'd keep crashing into the hotel.' Thanks to her, I could never look at the Western Gardens without feeling the vanished hotel's ghostly presence.

Although she had no competitors, on either a commercial or a personal level, she liked to imagine a deadly business rival in Dinelli's Café, on the Esplanade's opposite pavement, which was locally famous for making its own soft ice-cream. 'Ugh, horrible stuff!' she would say, pulling her cannibal face. 'I tried one one day, and just threw it down on the ground.' She savoured the thought of Mr Dinelli, a hard-working, taciturn Scots-Italian, fuming with comic-opera rage at the Kiosk's success, and waged a constant battle of wits with her unsuspecting foe over their premises' respective closing times. 'That ole Mr Dinelli shut at half-past six last night,' she would report triumphantly. 'Then at seven he looks across here and sees us still doing a roaring trade.'

She would talk with pride of the Kiosk's escalating results ('Took eighty pounds yesterday') and how she was on course to sell sixteen tons of rock by the end of this current season. 'And I've got it all on sale or return, y'know,' she would add with a wink, as if gloriously putting another one over on the unsuspecting Mr Dinelli.

Sooner or later, we would get on to the subject of my father, the only person on earth I could allow her to love as much as she loved me. She would tell me yet again what a dear little boy he had been at my age, with his dimples and square-necked jerseys and the slight speech impediment that gave his almost every utterance a babyish charm. ' "My Mummy's honey tarts!" he used to say. "They're *ludley*!" ' She would recall his solicitude when she was prostrated with a migraine headache (which she pronounced 'mugrain', causing me to imagine some penitential kind of breakfast food). 'Terrible, those mugrains used to be,' she would recall, closing her eyes devoutly. 'I was in such pain that if the *whole* of the German army [First World War, she meant] had come marching through my bedroom – with fixed bayonets – I wouldn't have cared. Your Uncle Phil used to complain about having to do the washing up, so your Daddy would do it all by himself.

"Poor ting," he used to say in that sweet little voice of his. "No wonder she's got a headache wiv' all this washing up." '

She talked endlessly of the wonderful man that dear little boy had become – his kindness, gentleness and thoughtfulness which, where she was concerned, were, indeed, inexhaustible. 'He got me in a whole lot of new stock from the store today and put it away all by himself, bless him. But he always was a tremendous worker. When he was a little boy, he used to help his Uncle Alf Lark, who had a livery stable in the City o' London. Uncle Alf couldn't believe it! He said your Daddy would be standing behind the horses with a dustpan and brush before they'd even had a chance to do their business.'

She would tell me something else that it was not always possible to deduce in everyday life – how very much my father loved me and how his life's whole energies were employed for my benefit and mine only. It seemed that even at times of his greatest seeming indifference where I was concerned, he spent hours expatiating to Grandma Norman about his pleasure and pride in me. 'Only yesterday, he was sitting on that same stool you're sitting on, and telling me what a lot he thinks of you. Talking all about what a clever little boy you are and what a fine man he thinks you'll grow up to be.'

I always felt both profoundly moved and seared with yet another kind of filial guilt. Moved because I had no idea he felt that way about me; guilty because I'd been too unperceptive to realize it myself. Next time I see him, I thought . . . I'll let him know that I know . . . And I'll *deserve* it.

Four

JOAN CAME INTO our lives in the winter of 1951, when my father turned Ryde Pier Pavilion into a roller-skating rink. I was eight years old, she must have been around twenty-seven; nevertheless, in those days, I never called her anything but 'Joan'.

She attracted notice first of all as a brilliant skater, streets ahead of the unsteady multitudes who banged and racketed around the Pavilion's wooden floor. Although in fact no more than a gifted amateur, she cultivated the aura of a professional. Whereas everyone else made do with our ratty strap-on issue skates, Joan wore her own white boots with small silver wheels and green india-rubber plugs, for sudden stops, under each toe. Unlike any other female customer, too, she had her own special skating outfit, a one-piece grey wool dress with long sleeves and a high neck. The effect would have been modest, even severe, but for the shortness of the grey pleated skirt and the bare legs that tumbled out underneath it.

With hindsight, I doubt whether the skirt-hem could have been more than an inch or two above her knees. But, bear in mind, these were the early fifties, when respectable women's bodies were scarcely less well hidden than they had been in Edwardian times. Until this moment, women's legs for me had existed only in the fantasy world of films, pantomime and my father's *Lilliput* magazines. This was the first time I had ever met them in the flesh, pale, naked and unashamed.

I remember standing and watching Joan circle the rink on what must have been one of her earliest visits. She was, as always, somewhat apart from other skaters, moving on her superior course with unsmiling absorption as if engrossed in some self-imposed training regimen. Her tall white boots swept so lightly over the Pavilion floor, you would have thought them mounted on ice-blades rather than wooden wheels. Her trim grey silhouette was bent slightly forward; her skirt flowed back with the slipstream, uncovering still more uncharted areas of upper thigh, showing an occasional flash of matching knickers.

What struck me at once was the contradiction between this daring, almost brazen physical presence and the face that went with it. For her features were as thin and uncertain as her limbs were ample and confident. She had wide-set, unexpressive eyes; clamped-tight lips; a longish nose with a suspicion of redness at its tip. Her mousy hair was pinned back above each ear with Kirbigrips, creating a faintly Scandinavian effect. Her expression was at the same time shy and grim, as if the big, bare legs had nothing to do with her, and she feared their shameless flaunting of themselves could not end other than badly. She was suffering from a slight cold and, in mid-flight, with no sacrifice of speed or grace, pulled a handkerchief from her sleeve and dabbed at her nose with it. To look at her big, cold legs and reddened nostrils together was like feeling a sudden draught of the winter sea-air from outside.

Flipping round from forward skating to backward, she suddenly realized I was watching her. But she did not call out 'Hello' or smile, just gave me a tight-mouthed look that let me know she knew I'd been looking at her legs. I, for my part, stared down at my own bare knees, which suddenly seemed grimy and dusty beyond endurance. Such was to be the tone of our relationship over the next twenty years.

*

FOR ANY LESSEE of Ryde Pier Pavilion who made the mistake of staying there, the great problem was the off-season months when the pier-head grew as remote and unfrequented as a concreted desert island but a whopping rent still had to be paid to its owner, British Railways. Turning the Pavilion into a roller-skating rink for the cold half of each year was the best idea my father ever had as an impresario. (It may have come from his partner, Uncle Phil, but I somehow doubt it.) The circular wooden floor of the old theatre auditorium was as spacious as any purpose-built rink. Its horseshoe-shaped promenade balcony provided an aerial view to non-skating spectators. Refreshments could be sold from the same tea bar that served the summertime penny arcade. All he had to do was buy a job lot of skates, make some minor adjustments of seating and lighting, and find a place on shore where he could billet 300-odd slot-machines until the day-tripping crowds returned.

Apart from three cinemas and innumerable pubs, Ryde offered its populace desperately few amusements during the long, wave-lashed winter. From the moment our skating-rink first opened its doors, it was a sensational hit. I remember my first amazed sight of the throng streaming around the Pavilion's interior; the deafening rumble and roar of wooden wheels; the queue for admission stretching through the entrance-hall and spilling out on to the tram station. Part of that same memory is hearing my father's voice for the very first time over a public address system. With so large and unsteady a crowd, there had to be continual safety announcements, chiefly about the necessity of all skating in the same direction. 'Please keep to the right,' he repeated in a tone of what to me seemed rising exasperation. 'Ladies and gentlemen . . . please keep to the RIGHT.'

Our main public was the youth of Ryde and its environs – but not exclusively so. In that pre-television, pre-eating-out era, whole families used to come skating together. I remember seeing a boy of about my own age being pulled along by his mother and father and laughing with his head thrown back like one of the idealized children in advertisements for Ovaltine or Chilprufe underwear. Nor was there the same class barrier that existed around our hot-weather entertainments. Even posh yachting types from Cowes and Seaview turned up, with their oilskins and blazers and barely intelligible accents, to have a go. One of the rink's most faithful devotees was a local accountant named Wellesley Butt, a little beaming bird of a man who always wore a three-piece suit with his black skating boots, and practised endless curves and figure-eights alone in a secluded corner in front of a full-length mirror.

As I have said, the Pavilion's amenities also included a pub, the First and Last, so named because it could offer ferry-passengers their first drink after landing on the Island and their last one before departing. Though contiguous to our domain, it was not operated by my father but by Burt's brewery of Ventnor. It consisted of just one room with a veined marble counter, smoked Victorian mirrors and a coke stove with a blackened pipe that disappeared into the ceiling. Its barmaid, a chain-smoking woman named Marje, was rumoured to disdain the pier-head ladies' lavatories and to lift up a trapdoor and urinate directly into the sea.

The First and Last stayed open all winter, mostly for the benefit of the few pier-head porters who huddled around its stove. When bar-trade was slack, Marje would don a pair of skates and join me on the rink's beginners' bars, still wearing her barmaid's white blouse and black gabardine skirt, and with her eternal Gold Flake hanging from her lower lip. It never occurred to me that she was 'tiddly', not even when she sank to the ground and stayed there with her wheeled feet stuck straight out in front of her, showing dusty and laddered knees – which were not at all the same as legs – brushing cigarette ash off her bosom and chuckling secretively deep down in her throat.

I can feel myself there now, on a winter Saturday afternoon just after dark. I can see the string of coloured lights around the promenade balcony, and the dark, hollow dome above. I can see through the shoreward windows the glowing lamps along the pier, and the distant, chilly sparkle of Ryde. I can smell the raw leather of my lace-up toe-pieces, the mangy straps across my insteps, the brown wooden wheels with HAMOCO printed around their rims, the grime from the wooden floor that coats my hands and bare knees and makes my tongue taste of metal. I feel again the elation of first leaving the beginners' bars and rolling unaided to one of the balcony-posts a few feet away. I can feel the faint breeze in my face, and the soft thwack as my wheels hit the green canvas jacket which all the posts wear at the bottom to save their sculpted woodwork from being battered to splinters.

To start with, the rink's only supervisory staff were two men in maroon rollneck sweaters who stood motionless on skates in the centre of the floor, glaring balefully at the multitudes circulating around them. It therefore seemed a stroke of luck to find a young woman customer whose skating expertise was complemented by such a riveting physical presence.

Within a few weeks of Joan's first appearance at the Pavilion, my father invited her to work there as a supervisor-cum-teacher. Her grey wool skating outfit was exchanged for an official one in maroon velvet, high-necked and long-sleeved, with a skirt that seemed to reveal even more of the big, pale legs. Pinned to her front she wore an oval red badge saying 'MC'.

What we learned about her in those early days was pretty much all I was ever destined to know. Like us she was a recent immigrant to the Isle of Wight, having been born and brought up in Birmingham. Her voice had the distinctive accent known as 'Brummie' or 'Brummigan' which always seems to be articulating a grievance and which pronounces 'i' as 'ee', so that 'is' becomes 'ees' and 'it' becomes 'eet'. Her face, with its pointed nose and pursed lips, certainly looked capable of scolding and complaining in abundance. But, in fact, her voice was so small and quiet as to be barely audible. Her personality was almost entirely expressed in strong physical action – skating and dancing and acrobatics. Except on very rare occasions, she spoke only when spoken to.

An air of mystery and ambiguity clung to her from the very start. She was one of a family named Salsbury which had moved down from Birmingham after the war to take advantage of the Island's rock-bottom property prices (would that my family had done the same). Her parents owned a beachfront mansion named Wellington Lodge, on Ryde's westerly shore, which they ran as a seasonal 'private hotel'. She was married – or so it appeared – to a big flaxen-haired man named George Goldring who was not from Birmingham but, rather, looked as if he had just leapt off the deck of some ninth-century Viking ship. Now and again on the rink she would be seen with a little girl of about five or six, whom she introduced as her little sister Lynette (or 'Leen').

It was puzzling to me that someone in her late twenties should have a sister so very much younger than herself. Still more bemused was I upon first seeing her mother, Mrs Salsbury, a corpulent woman in her late forties, with all the Brummie plaintiveness Joan herself lacked. How could so ancient a figure possibly have a daughter three years my junior? Of course, it was all a fiction, common enough in that era when unmarried mothers were social outcasts. Lynette was Joan's daughter by a father who had been killed or had decamped during the war. She lived at Wellington Lodge with grandparents whom she called 'Mummy' and 'Daddy', while Joan and the Scandinavian-looking George Goldring lived together elsewhere in Ryde. Although Joan in those days gave her surname as Goldring – even signing herself so in our rink visitors' book – George was just her boyfriend.

Almost everything I knew about her came from my mother, who seemed to like her well enough during this initial period. It was my mother who told me that, in fact, Joan hadn't been roller-skating for all that long, but had previously been an accomplished ice-skater. If you could do one, you could usually do the other.

*

ALMOST SINCE first coming to consciousness, I had known that my parents were locked in a struggle, that my mother was on the losing side and that I was powerless in any way to affect its outcome. One of my earliest memories is overhearing an exchange between them one evening after I had been put to bed. I remember the contrast of the reassuring light through my half-open bedroom door with what was being said in the hall outside. My mother had accidentally broken something of my father's – some sacred component of his fishing or shooting tackle, I couldn't make out exactly what. 'You're going to suffer for that,' I heard him tell her, not with his usual explosive anger but in an ominously quiet, almost thoughtful way. 'I suffer when I've done nothing, Clive,' she answered with a kind of numb resignation. 'You're going to suffer and *suffer*...' he repeated in the same pensive tone, as though choosing the manner of her suffering gave the same reflective pleasure as picking a decorated fly to cast for a trout.

From the earliest age, I was aware that my father 'ran after' other women, though what he did when he caught up with them remained shrouded in mystery. The West End pub that he and my mother managed, the Porcupine in Charing Cross Road, stood almost directly opposite the Hippodrome theatre, in those days the home of Ivor Novello shows, those romantic stage musicals which had kept London singing and dancing through the worst of the wartime Blitz. The Porcupine was the Hippodrome's stage-door pub, providing my father with a large and willing seraglio from its singers and 'ballet girls'. At least those affairs were generally of short duration. Generally, my father would go to my mother and make a hurried confession just before the arrival of an enraged husband or boyfriend on their doorstep. Very often, his explanation would be that the female concerned had misconstrued what was intended as no more than kindness and courtesy. He'd been driving along, he'd say, minding his own business when suddenly at the side of the road he'd seen a poor girl, crying...

Unassertive and crushed though my mother was, she always had her champions, who appreciated her rather sad-eyed prettiness, her refinement and her selfless hard work. One of them was the great Ivor Novello himself, for whom she would cook fish and chips after his evening performance, before he walked home to his flat in Aldwych. Concerned that – unlike my father – she never seemed to go out or have any fun, Novello one evening spirited her away from the pub and took her to supper at the Savoy.

Running the Porcupine alone should have been enough to make my father's fortune. The soldiers of every nation who thronged London in that final phase of the war didn't care how much they paid for drinks or for the little food that was available. The Victory Parade in 1945 passed beneath the Porcupine's windows, allowing him to sell grandstand seats at hugely inflated prices. Suspending his officerly scruples – as he always could suspend them at will – he was involved in black-market dealings in whisky, butter, eggs, even cigars purloined from the famous Dunhill shop in Jermyn Street. One day in the Porcupine's bar, he offered my mother's mother – unshakably straight and respectable Grandma Bassill – £5 for the watch she was wearing. Then, under her outraged gaze, he strolled to the opposite end of the counter and sold it for £20.

Instead of retiring from the Porcupine as a millionaire, however, he left it prematurely and under a cloud. The brewers who owned the pub, a firm named Levey & Franks, required their managers to be old-fashioned 'guv'nors'; models of sobriety and propriety, dressed like City stockbrokers in black jackets and striped trousers. My father was already in bad odour for ignoring his employers' dress requirements and also for the most public and near-disastrous of his extra-marital affairs – with Ivor Novello's own female personal assistant. He then sealed his fate by getting fighting drunk one night at the New Arts Club, just round the corner from the Porcupine, and assaulting a moderately famous American film actor named Bonar Colleano.

Our subsequent brief stay at the Cross Keys Hotel, in St Neots, Huntingdonshire, was our golden time as a family. St Neots in those days was a small, sleepy riverside market town in a community of old-fashioned gentleman farmers.

My father could indulge in his cherished pastimes of fishing and shooting to his heart's content. More like one of the local squires than a mere hotel manager, he drove around in a pony and trap, bought an island on the River Ouse, even began building a dream thatched cottage in the nearby village of Great Staughton where, he said, we were going to live one day. Our hotel life remained in my memory in a set of glowing postcard images – the sign of crossed golden keys above the archway to a medieval courtyard; the low-timbered rooms, the log fires in open grates, the twinkling huntsmen's horns and horse-brasses.

Yet I knew that even at the Cross Keys my mother had suffered and suffered. That was where I overheard the exchange between them, through my half-open bedroom door in the corridor reputedly haunted by the ghost of a medieval monk. And the 'running after' had gone on just as busily in the country as it had in London. My father ran after a hotel maid named Ena, whom I remember polishing brass in the lounge and singing 'Cherry Ripe'. He also ran after various female hotel guests, the wives of several local landowners and the town's summer Carnival Queen.

It was at the Cross Keys that I first became aware of the frequent trips away he would make on his own, leaving my mother to cope with the business single-handed. I never had any idea where he went, and she never told me. In my trusting mind, these mysterious journeys had a romantic, almost noble air, as if he were still flying off with 57 Squadron to help save Britain from Hitler. I remember standing under the hotel's archway, gazing towards the river bridge, torn between dread and excitement. Dread because I feared him; excitement because he always brought me back some marvellous present. On that occasion, it was a toy sabre in a scarlet tin scabbard wound around with gold cords.

His effect on the small, unsophisticated seaside community that Ryde was in the late forties and early fifties can well be imagined. The glamour-icon of the hour was the gentleman officer, fresh from wartime heroism, as portrayed by keen-jawed movie heroes like Jack Hawkins and John Mills. My father played the part with an understatement that could not have rammed home its message more powerfully if he'd gone around beating a drum or wearing outsize sandwich boards. The words 'officer', 'gentleman' and 'hero' shrieked from his soft green tweed sports jacket with leather-patched elbows, his striped tie, unstiffened shirt-collar, mid-brown suède shoes, and the Dunhill briar pipe he always filled with Log Cabin tobacco ('Sweetened in Bond') from a yellow oilskin pouch.

Like all such figures in films, he drove a vintage car. In his case it was a giant black Wolseley saloon, dating from around 1920, whose grey plush rear compartment included a speaking-tube from passenger to chauffeur and a built-in umbrella stand. Like many such screen heroes, too, he was followed everywhere by a black Labrador, a huge, gentle old beast he had acquired for his shooting days in St Neots. It was called Nigger, a common name for black dogs in those cosily racist times, and one imbued with further echoes of RAF glamour. Guy Gibson VC, who led the Dambuster raids on the Ruhr Valley – and whom my father claimed to have taught to fly – owned a black Labrador with the same name.

His own service career, as I understood it, could have been lifted straight out of some film. After crashing his Blenheim in Alsace-Lorraine, he had been declared unfit for further operational flying and had instead been offered an administrative job – possibly in one of those so-familiar control-rooms, seated on a high dais, watching WAAFs move flags around a board to denote 'Bandits' coming in over the

Channel. But – just as a character played by Richard Todd or Leslie Howard might have done – he said he couldn't continue serving if he was no longer able to fly. An admirably romantic decision in a movie, but one which in real life changed his destiny from youthful Air Marshal with decorations, prestige and a pension, to flailing showman at the end of a draughty seaside pier.

Our tiny flat above the Creamery Café was dominated by mementoes of the countryman's life my father had sacrificed to move to the Island and work with his beleaguered older brother. On the sitting-room wall hung a painting by Peter Scott of wild geese flying in a triple skein over yellow marsh-land. Fishing and shooting reference works lined the single bookcase, and the bay window-seat displayed copies of the *Field* magazine in an overlapping line. Against the facing wall stood a walnut linen-press in which – unlocked and unsecured – he kept his various guns, including a flintlock blunderbuss with a razor-sharp bayonet that flew out at the touch of a spring.

The running after people must have begun directly we arrived in Ryde. I had seen the process unwittingly for myself, that day on the Pavilion roof when I found him lying on top of an auburn-haired woman. I often turned the memory over in my mind, wondering if I really had seen it rather than just dreamed it – the figures on the hard, inky tarmac, the back-drop of sea and racing yachts, the woman's good-humoured smile. With a child's literal-mindedness, I imagined it to have concluded some actual chase; a grown-up game of 'He' that ended in this uncomfortable-looking and irrational posture, stacked directly one above the other even though there was room and to spare on either side.

But none of us in those days ever dreamed that Joan was destined to be added to his list. She was more than a decade his junior and out of a markedly lower social drawer; something that burningly mattered in the Britain of the early fifties. He would often mimic her accent, exaggerating the stretched-out vowels and lugubriousness which the city of her origin seemed tailor-made to demonstrate at their most comic. 'Ooo!' he would exclaim with his dimpling grin, *'Bairming-gum!'* Joan never took offence, never answered back, just smiled her same shy, wintry half-smile.

In those early days, his sole interest in her seemed to be for the expertise of her skating and the distinction she brought to the rink as its 'MC'. As she circled round and round in her trim official uniform, my father would stand and watch her, filling his pipe from his yellow oilskin tobacco-pouch with that air of wisdom and foresight in which I used to believe so boundlessly. For incidental music we broadcast 78 rpm gramophone records of Mantovani and his Orchestra playing waltzes like 'The Blue Danube', 'Tales from the Vienna Woods' and, of course, 'The Skaters' Waltz'. The predominant effect was of violins, lush and melancholy and seeming to waft over the rink from a great way off. The music to me became indivisible from Joan's sharp face as her big, pale legs carried her on their faultless course.

Even when her employer was not visible, his careful surveillance continued. Behind the Pavilion's stage and along its two flanking walls hung a plasterboard frieze of crudely-painted figures, seven or eight feet high, intended to represent the world of compulsive roller-skating that lay beyond the Isle of Wight. The cavalcade included a skating Zulu with assegai and shield, a skating Red Indian chief, a skating Cossack, a skating French gendarme, a skating gorilla and a skating Scotsman in a kilt and tam o' shanter, brandishing a knobbly stick in one hand and a whisky bottle in the other. Directly behind the panel where the Scotsman cavorted was my father's office and Amplifier Room. To help him 'watch points' on the rink, he had drilled a spyhole through the wall, using one of the Scotsman's eyes as camouflage. If you studied the figure closely while Joan was practising below, you would see a sudden change come into its expression. The Scotsman's left eye remained, as usual, a blank, woozy cross but the right one, at its centre, glinted with human deadly seriousness.

*

COMPARED WITH the chill vault it would become in later years, the wintertime Pavilion then always seemed busy and cheerful. There were skating sessions every afternoon and evening, with a deafening, chaotic children's 'matinée' on Saturday mornings. At Christmas and on New Year's Eve, my father put on special gala dances and 'Krazy Nites' which I was too young to attend and which always left the rink intriguingly strewn with paper streamers, shrivelled balloons and wheel-flattened and grimy cotton-wool snowballs. He also began a skating club, which convened on Sunday afternoons. The membership consisted mainly of local teenagers – although no one at the time employed that word. Young people in the early fifties had no fashion, music or culture of their own, but were just spotty, gauche facsimiles of their parents. The boys who joined our club wore sleeveless Fair Isle jerseys and thick grey flannel trousers, and had names like Johnny and Lofty. The girls styled their hair with Toni home perms, and wore shapeless flowered dresses, hand-knitted cardigans and ankle socks in white or beige. For reasons mysterious to me now, I used to hero-worship a boy named Johnny Brading, who had a ginger-coloured sports jacket and a patch of livid colour in either cheek. I was entranced by his deep Isle of Wight accent and the way his Adam's apple strained against the skin of his long neck and jerked up and down as he talked. He only ever spoke to me once, when he was speed-skating and I happened to wander across his path. 'Moind yerself,' he cautioned me gruffly.

As an attraction for club members only, my father introduced roller-netball, putting up professional nets and marking out a pitch on the Pavilion floor. We had our own mixed-gender netball team, called the Ryde Redskins and uniformed in dark red sweaters bearing the hand-embroidered profile of a Red Indian chief. We would travel to play rival teams at other rinks on the Island or even on the mainland. Joan was the team captain and its star player. How I used to cheer and clap as her scarlet shape flashed through the enemy's clumsy interceptions, and the ball juddered yet again into the net.

To the skating club, my father was a figure of unending fascination. I picture him behind the counter in the Pavilion's entrance hall, where admission tickets were issued and skates given out from a wall of rough-timbered shelves. He is repairing a faulty skate, turning it this way and that with a clatter of its wheels on the counter's metal surface. I am just one of an admiring crowd who watch him as he works, and hang on to every word he says. What will he be telling them about today? Possibly about flying missions from France in Blenheims in the first days of the war. About the time he had acted as escort to a fifth-columnist undergoing court-martial (accompanying the accused even into the toilet), or the wild horseplay in the officers' mess after dinner in which even the station CO would join in rugger scrums like a schoolboy. 'At every mess night,' he tells the enraptured Patsys and Loftys – and, of course, 'MC' Joan – 'you could be sure of ruining a dress-shirt.'

Now, two girls skate out of the Ladies', which, with Victorian delicacy, lies along an angled corridor off to the right. They are dressed alike in white boots, short skirts (though nowhere near as short as 'MC' Joan's) and carnival peaked caps with tissue paper crowns. Each holds a short wooden cane, musket-fashion, on her shoulder. They have worked up a song and skate-dance routine in the hope my father will let them perform it as some kind of rink cabaret. He auditions them in front of his skate issue counter, watching them with an impresario's inscrutable wisdom and puffing clouds of fragrant blue pipe-smoke. Their wheels clatter in unsteady tap-rhythm as they flourish their canes and sing:

> Make way, oh make way
> For my eastern rose . . .

They forget the words, giggle helplessly, jam their paper caps more firmly on to their curls, skate off into the Ladies' corridor, whisper together for a moment, then skate back and begin again:

> Make way, oh make way
> For my eastern rose.
> Men crowd in dozens
> Everywhere she goes . . .

A sizeable crowd, almost always including 'MC' Joan, would be invited to stay to tea before the evening session. We had it in the servery behind the Tea Bar, where three or four tables would be pushed together to form one long one, covered with a red and white gingham cloth. We had beans on toast, sardines on toast or tinned tomatoes on toast, the latter one of my mother's few visible pleasures. At the head of the long table, some distance from both of us, my father would be at his most jovial as he explained to his rapt audience some new mechanism or structural improvement he had in mind for the Pavilion. In a familiar and – to me – heart-warming ritual, he would take an empty Player's cigarette packet, remove the white cardboard tray, pull out its silver paper lining, bend it flat and tear off the side panels. On the remaining white rect-angle he would sketch an explanatory diagram with rapid strokes of his Yard-O-Led propelling pencil.

As well as his fly-fishing rods, he always kept a sporting gun or two down at the Pavilion, even though there was nothing to shoot but seagulls. One Sunday just before tea, at Heaven knows what prompting, he produced a rifle and a box of orange cartridges, then threw an empty mustard pickle jar out of the servery window and took shots at it as it bobbed in the grey sea, forty-odd feet below. I remember leaning from an adjacent open window with Johnny Brading and 'MC' Joan – the wind tearing my hair; the 'crack-crack' of the gun; my triumphant joy when, after four or five shots, the jar exploded in a faint yellow cloud and sank beneath the waves. At the time, I thought how lucky the skating club was to be provided with this spectacular extra amusement. Looking back, I can see it was designed to impress one person only.

*

BY NOW, I had come a long way from struggling up and down the beginners' bars with Marje the barmaid. I could do running starts, skate backwards at speed as comfortably as forwards, come to an instant dead stop by standing on my toes, even crouch down and go along on just my right skate, holding my left leg out in front of me. I had my own black skating boots with rubber toe-stops, and a pair of brown corduroy long trousers, made by my mother, in which, in my own eyes, I cut a supremely dashing figure. My rock-steady balance gave me a delicious feeling of power and superiority whenever a grown-up put on skates for the first time and felt their feet trundling away in all directions. I'd guide them around with an air of huge self-importance, giving helpful advice, like 'Keep steady, now. Just keep steady.'

My father alone was unimpressed by my progress. He himself skated only in a rudimentary way, stepping along, pipe in mouth, like some movie war hero learning to walk with artificial legs. But about the theory of skating – like the practice of repairing and maintaining skates – he was, as always, omniscient. Since opening the rink, he had subscribed to a magazine called *The Skater*, which published news of roller-skating events at rinks all over the country and contests for figure-skating and exhibition dancing every bit as glamorous as their counterparts on ice. Often in *The Skater* there would be a photograph of some boy or girl, only a little older than myself, who had won a bronze, silver or even a gold medal in figure-skating tests set by a central examining body in London. He would point out these prodigies to me with a meaning air that needed no words. Such awards lay within my compass, too, if only I would stop merely enjoying myself on skates and apply myself to the discipline of formal figure-eights like Mr Butt the accountant in front of his full-length mirror – and, of course, like Joan. For, with our rink's sponsorship, Joan was now formally in training to take her bronze medal figure-skating test.

He was particularly disapproving of my turns. When I changed from skating forward to backward, I still did it in the way beginners are first shown, turning my toes outward and swivelling around in an arc. The more deft and difficult way was a step called the Mohawk. Without slackening speed, you lifted your right foot and placed it at a ninety-degree angle behind your left. As your right skate carried you backwards, you twisted your body around and brought your left foot into alignment with a little toe-pointing kick. What connection this had to North American Indians with tufts of hair down the centre of their scalps, God only knows.

Turning around the easy way felt somehow shaming and unmanly whenever I saw my father watching me from the sidelines – especially if Joan also happened to be on the rink, executing half a dozen flawless Mohawks with each circuit. One day, when she had no pupil under instruction, he suggested that I should ask her to teach me the step. Even then, he seemed to demand a kind of reverence for her. 'If you were to go over and ask her nicely,' he said, 'I'm sure Joan would very kindly teach you the Mohawk.'

I went across and asked her nicely, and together we skated to the side of the rink where the rifle range stood in summer. Holding my hands above my head, Joan took me through the Mohawk's simple procedure – left skate forward, right skate angled behind it, turn and kick. But I could think of nothing except how horrifically close I suddenly was to the maroon velvet of her skating outfit, the trim waist, the matching knickers beneath the pleated skirt, the big, bare leg falling out below. I found myself suddenly bereft of all dexterity and coordination. My skate-wheels tangled together. I lurched forward and, with a flailing hand, briefly touched one of the legs. It was as smooth as marble, and ice-cold.

Joan corrected my balance by pulling both my hands high above my head. I saw her face looking down through the roof of our arms with a grim half-smile; as if she suspected that touching her leg had been my only object all along. The soft little Brummie voice told me what I already, agonizingly, knew – what would be my fate whenever I felt her unrejoicing eye on me.

'Well,' she said. 'You made a nice mess of *that*, didn't you?'

Five

ON NEW YEAR'S EVE during the mid-fifties, the landlord of the Star Hotel in Ryde High Street would amuse his customers by dressing up as a woman. He took great trouble with his impersonation, borrowing an ankle-length black chiffon gown that gave him the appearance of a widowed Spanish noblewoman; and donning a curly auburn wig and full make-up including a black beauty spot on the right cheek. During the night's rowdy festivities at the Star he would dance cheek-to-cheek with a succession of male partners, slapping them playfully with an ivory fan if any greater familiarities were attempted. Such was the humour of my father's brother, my Uncle Phil, a man with the dubious distinction of making his younger sibling at times seem almost normal.

The fact that I had been named after him might have been expected to create special bonds of affection and empathy between Uncle Phil and me. Grandma Norman always intimated that it did, often reminding me that Uncle Phil's birthday on 18 April fell only five days after mine and three after hers; metaphorically drawing the three of us close in one of her Mafia chieftain hugs. In her wishful vision of a happy, united Norman family, he was 'Big Phil' and I 'Little Phil', like full-grown and cadet versions of the same Canadian beaver trapper or atom-bomb. But in reality, the only other person named Philip Norman I've ever met was a mystery to me, as to pretty much everyone.

Lying in the huge brass bedstead I used to share with Grandma Norman, I would often muse on the very different characters of her two adored 'boys' as evidenced in their two photographs on the dressing-table. My father, in his RAF uniform, looked almost heartbreakingly handsome with his long, dark widow's peak, his faraway eyes, cupid's-bow mouth and dimpled chin. Uncle Phil by contrast wore a tunic vaguely like army battledress but with no identifying insignia. He, too, had a widow's peak, although a less pronounced one than his brother's. In looks he was closer to Grandma Norman and, even more, to the sea-captain father who had perished in the final year of the Great War. His face was vaguely oriental, unsmiling and, even then, starting to develop jowls and a double chin. His eyes were dark and of a curious intensity; in the old art-gallery cliché, they seemed to follow one around the room.

Grandma Norman was fond of reciting the elaborate names she had given both her sons, commemorating revered ancestors in London and the West Country, yet also subtly suggestive of a typical Grandma Norman joke. 'Your daddy's name,' she'd tell me, 'is Theodore Clive Hummerston Norman. And your Uncle Phil's' – making even more solemnly uproarious big eyes – 'is Philip Patrick Philippeaux Norman.'

Her tall, dark house in Clapham Old Town had not been rearranged (and not often cleaned) since Uncle Phil and my father had left it to go out into the world at the start of the 1930s. On my visits she would give me their old toy soldiers and half-built model boats to play with and their *Tiger Tim* and *Pip, Squeak and Wilfred* annuals to read. She still kept their first teddy bears – small, close-shaven, yellowish specimens with limbs now secured by only the frailest threads, and mouths like black-darned harelips. Comparing their expressions with the two photographs on the dressing-table, I fancied I could tell which had been my father's bear and which Uncle Phil's. There was also a larger, darker bear on iron wheels with a leather tab on its back. If you yanked hard on the tab, it uttered a faint, protesting 'Ur!' The bear's face, with its blank button eyes, seemed to me somehow like Uncle Phil's, its slow, somehow dignified progress on its iron wheels like Uncle Phil's gait, its guarded monosyllabic grunts like the little I ever overheard of Uncle Phil's conversation.

To me, it felt no time at all since the 1920s, when my father and Uncle Phil had inhabited these same rooms as small boys with Grandma Norman; when she had told them the same jokes and sayings, pulled the same funny faces and done the same comic dances she did for me now; when she'd cooked them eggs on fried potato and cabbage with pepper and vinegar, and imbued them with her own disregard of the outside world and its tiresome constraints of morality. Not that she ever saw it that way, of course. To her, whatever unspeakable things they might do, her 'boys' were always paragons of manly virtue. She would tell me how, at Manor House School on nearby Clapham Common, they had won all the speech day prizes between them, and then been asked to give some back so that other less brilliant boys could have a chance. 'Both their school reports always used to say the same: "Work – excellent. Games – excellent." And "Conduct – excellent." ' The latter was not an assessment with which their respective future wives would have agreed.

My father's practical talents naturally fitted him to become an apprentice at an Oxfordshire aerodrome, then to go into the peacetime RAF. The more cerebrally clever Uncle Phil, however, pursued an erratic course only explained in later life by his reluctance, as my mother once put it, 'to stand when he could sit and sit when he could lie down'. Fluent in French, German and Italian, he spent some time living with a family in France, then joined the staff of a language school kept by a distant relative of Grandma Norman's. In the later thirties, in an uncharacteristic burst of energy, he joined the 'International Brigade' of young intellectuals who volunteered for the Communist side in the Spanish Civil War. By Grandma Norman's account, he only just escaped with his life, catching (as she put it in her Edwardian idiom) 'the last dreadnought' to leave Spain with the Brigade's shattered remnants.

In the world war that followed, Uncle Phil's role was a mysterious one. Although Grandma Norman always firmly maintained that he was 'in Intelligence', his only known posting was to the army's Field Security Police, an equally apt use of his talent – later so abundantly revealed to his family – for snooping and spying. He also seems to have been in Italy during the fall of the Fascist regime when, according to Grandma Norman, 'he saw Mussolini hanging up by his heels'. I had no idea what this meant, yet still recognized it as a typical Uncle Phil moment: half-sinister, half-farcical.

His wife, my Auntie Lorna, was also my godmother (a further bid to unite the family's two hemispheres, which had Grandma Norman's fingerprints all over it). Auntie Lorna – who, in later years, was usually referred to as 'Poor Auntie Lorna' – had dark-eyed, large-nosed, faintly Spanish looks, and spoke with the softened r's that often go with that type. She and my mother had been close friends before they met Uncle Phil and my father, who in their late twenties were as alike as devastatingly handsome twins. Indeed, my mother initially went out with Uncle Phil, and at some subsequent dance or party struck up a conversation with my father under the impression he was his older sibling. Not long afterwards, Auntie Lorna met Uncle Phil, and the brothers and two best friends started going around together. Even at that stage, however, the foursome was often fractured by sudden, cataclysmic disagreements between the brothers for reasons never explained to their respective girlfriends. One Saturday night, they would all be pubbing together; the next, my father would come into their local, see Uncle Phil and Auntie Lorna there, and grimly but wordlessly steer my mother to the opposite end of the bar.

Before meeting Uncle Phil, Auntie Lorna had been going out with a professional wrestler who fought under the name Norman the Butcher. One night as Norman the Butcher was driving them somewhere, he'd crashed his car, injuring Auntie Lorna's right wrist so severely that plastic surgery had to be performed on it. Plastic surgery was still rudimentary then and the operation was botched, leaving a hump of alien new skin just above her wrist that she sought to camouflage by tying a piece of coloured chiffon – usually black or green, to match her dress – around it. The nervous winding and unwinding of this coloured chiffon (which would increase the longer she stayed married to Uncle Phil) only drew greater attention to the disfigurement it was meant to hide.

While my father and mother enjoyed undeniably happy times in their initial courtship, that of Uncle Phil and Auntie Lorna seems to have been troubled from the beginning. I often heard the story of how, during their betrothal, he so hated a certain hat she was wearing that he snatched it off her head and jumped up and down on it. A source of bitter dissent from the outset was that Auntie Lorna had been brought up a devout Roman Catholic. Although Grandma Norman and her 'boys' were essentially godless, all three could quote Anglican scripture piously when it suited them. Before Uncle

Phil could marry Auntie Lorna, however, he had to visit the local Catholic bishop and promise that their children would be raised in her faith. My mother was a witness of the furious row that ensued when he returned from the bishop to Auntie Lorna's family home on Clapham Common's North Side. Auntie Lorna took off her engagement ring and threw it back at him but missed, and the ring fell into a bowl in which her old mother was enjoying a hot water and mustard foot-soak.

Their wedding, in 1939 or thereabouts, was not auspicious. The group photograph of them and their respective families, taken in Grandma Norman's back garden, was dominated for some reason by Auntie Lorna's old flame, Norman the Butcher. There was an awkward moment, too, when one of Auntie Lorna's female relatives entered a room to find Grandma Norman holding court to a group of elderly aunts and cousins from her own side of the family. All were wearing capes of lynx fur which had not been properly cured and thus emitted a pungent feral odour mixed with that of mothballs. On seeing this conclave, Auntie Lorna's kinswoman drew back in horror. 'I'm not going in there,' she loudly declared. 'It's full of a lot of old crows.'

Following the accident with Norman the Butcher's car there had been a court case, as a result of which Auntie Lorna was awarded several hundred pounds in compensation for the injury to her wrist. She was no sooner married to Uncle Phil than he persuaded her to invest this capital in the first of his business ventures; a company called the Chelsea Marble Works. Uncle Phil, of course, knew even less about producing marble than he later would about seaside showmanship; the company soon failed and Auntie Lorna's money was lost. The question of what she always termed, in reproachful initial capitals, 'The Compensation' was to remain a rankling, never-resolved one throughout her years with Uncle Phil – the first pillar, as it were, in a whole Parthenon of wrongs.

Their daughter, three years my senior, had been named Geraldine after Grandma Norman but was always known as Dina. Tall and slender, she had the same slant-eyed, cheek-dimpled beauty one saw in girlhood pictures of Grandma Norman and babyhood ones of her father. Her brother Roger, eighteen months older than I, had inherited his Latin nose from Auntie Lorna and, from Uncle Phil, a pair of intense brown eyes and an early tendency to corpulence. As a toddler, he had pulled a saucepan of boiling water off a stove over himself, and his left arm remained scarred white from wrist to elbow. He and I had the usual small boys' warring, competing relationship and Roger, being bigger and stronger, tended to win most of our arguments. Dina would always be my protector, enfolding me in her arms so that my nose pressed hard against the buckle of her school raincoat. Whenever the three of us had to share a bedroom, Roger would tell me that a huge hand was coming through the darkness to kill me, then Dina would calm my fears by singing 'Greensleeves'.

My father, their Uncle Clive, was always good to Dina and Roger, often better than their own father (which, admittedly, was not very difficult). But even in the era when our family was ostensibly at peace, Uncle Phil never became a strong presence in my life. I can remember only once ever sitting on his knee as he told me a mysterious and slightly frightening story that depended on repeated exclamation of the word 'Bones!' While not understanding it, I recognized the whimsical humour that more often found expression in the rather cruel as well as egotistical form of practical jokes. These were often recounted by Grandma Norman with almost reverent appreciation of his wit and inventiveness – how he had once lined up empty chairs as a silent protest outside a too-long occupied lavatory; how, on another occasion, he'd cut his toenails over a meal waiting to be served to Auntie Lorna.

At the war's end, as I have already mentioned, Uncle Phil made his unlikely transition from military policeman to running that small newsagent's shop in Hornchurch, Essex, which Grandma Norman eventually took over on his behalf, making ice-lollies in eggcups and suffering her near miss with the law over black-market clothes-coupons. That Uncle Phil could not cope even with a small newsagent's should have cautioned him against any more grandiose commercial ventures, but of course it did not. By means never fully documented, he then found his way to the Isle of Wight and got to know two men who wanted to offload a giant pier-head pavilion, having milked it of most of its profitability. By 1949, he was running Ryde Pier Pavilion on his own and already importuning his more practically minded younger brother, with their mother's irresistible support, to come to Ryde and help him.

It was always phrased so: that my father was 'helping' Uncle Phil rather than running things with him on equal terms, even though in those earliest summer seasons I cannot recall Uncle Phil's being directly concerned with managing any department of the Pavilion; not its restaurant, its arcade, its bars or skating-rink. His main contribution seemed to be a revival of his late role in the Field Security Police to apprehend others in dereliction of their duties. My mother had passionately not wanted move down to Ryde and had only agreed – and contributed her savings of £100 to the new venture – on the brothers' making her a solemn promise that she wouldn't have to work on the pier. Of course, she instantly found herself working there up to her neck. One summer day, she dared take an hour off from the kitchens and cashier's desk and have her hair done at Jack's Beauty Shop in Union Street. As she sat under the dryer, she saw Uncle Phil's face glowering through the shop window at her. The misdemeanour was instantly reported to my father, who hit her for her disloyalty.

To his mother in her mobbed sweets and rock kiosk at the pier-gates, Uncle Phil was equally far from a tower of strength. The maintenance of Grandma Norman was left entirely to my father, who did everything from ferrying in fresh stocks of confectionery and cigarettes to buying her the deckchair in which she took her afternoon rests and the gas-ring on which she cooked her morning fry-ups. Uncle Phil's labours at the Kiosk were limited to serving the occasional customer with ten Weights cigarettes or a Crunchie bar in a deliberate, slow-breathing way as if he were simultaneously working out an abstruse problem in quantum physics. Sometimes, as I stood with Grandma Norman at the main serving-window, we would see him making his dignified way along the Esplanade's opposite pavement. 'See how he always goes by on the other side of the road?' she'd say with no diminution of love in her voice. 'That's because he's afraid I might see him and want him to do something for me.'

To be sure, my father had no sooner begun 'helping' him than Uncle Phil detached himself completely from the Pier Pavilion and its management to plunge off at yet another surprising commercial tangent. He became landlord of the Star Hotel at the top of Ryde's precipitous High Street, not far from our flat above the Creamery Café. Unlike the Creamery, however, the Star did not belong to the brothers' joint property holdings but was Uncle Phil's private and personal fiefdom. Situated as it was far from the sea and pier and holiday crowds, its purpose seemed to be not so much to generate much-needed extra income as to induce amnesia.

Ryde in those days had scores of pubs, most of them

owned by the Island brewery Mew Langton. The Star was an undistinguished specimen, tall, narrow and gloomily faced in grey concrete with woodwork of faded dark blue. Its public bar gave on to the High Street; its 'bar parlour' (where more genteel customers sat and had drinks served to them on a tray) was reached through a side door around the corner in Star Street. On the first floor were Uncle Phil and Auntie's Lorna's private sitting-room, their bedroom, a bathroom and kitchen; on the second were Dina's and Roger's bedrooms and a couple more spare ones. I particularly remember the bell at the side door, a rusty lever protruding from a sort of ornamental concrete bowl. You pulled it once or twice, and nothing would happen; at the third or fourth pull, a maniacal jangling would come faintly from within.

The Star's interior, which I remember most in a brooding twilight, displayed many reminders of Uncle Phil's special humour. Up the long, straight staircase from the ground floor to his private quarters hung a series of French coloured prints showing dogs in men's clothes, poodles, spaniels and Dalmatians, walking on their hind legs, queuing up at kerbside pissoirs or urinating jocularly against walls. In Uncle Phil's and Auntie Lorna's bedroom hung a larger study of a little boy urinating in a high arc into a pond, from which a scandalized frog was leaping. 'Ne buvez jamais de l'eau', ran the caption beneath. Dimly I grasped the principle that urination in French had a subtlety of humour it could never aspire to in English. Auntie Lorna's only decorative touch was a small wooden plaque with a defiantly non-French motto on it, hanging in the first-floor lavatory. 'Don't worry,' the motto ran. 'Stick a geranium in yer 'at and be 'appy.'

Many pubs euphemistically style themselves 'hotels', but in the Star's case the term had some substance. Its next door neighbour in Star Street was the Commodore, largest of Ryde's three cinemas, a magnificent place decorated on a Napoleonic naval theme where you bought your ticket at a pay-box like a stern gallery of Nelson's flagship HMS *Victory*. As well as a film programme that changed three times weekly, the Commodore presented regular variety shows, a lavish annual pantomime, classical music concerts, opera and once even a stage-adapted circus. From long tradition the Star Hotel was its appointed theatrical 'digs'.

In those times, when film stars were stratospherically remote, television barely existed and rock 'n' roll music was still half a dozen years away, the chief household gods of the British were radio stars. Radio, of course, meant the monopolistic BBC, whose Light Programme pumped out ceaseless comedy sitcoms and variety shows, providing catchphrases used throughout the nation and punctuated by laughter that was genuine and spontaneous rather than the modern engineered, overdubbed kind. The cream of these audio legends appeared at Ryde's Commodore cinema and put up at the adjacent Star Hotel – Dick Bentley, Joy Nichols and 'Professor' Jimmy Edwards from *Take It from Here*; Charlie Chester from *Stand Easy*; Richard Murdoch and Kenneth Horne from *Much-Binding-in-the-Marsh*; harmonica stars like Larry Adler, Tommy Reilly and the Three Monarchs; impressionists like Peter ('The Voice of Them All') Cavanagh; pianists like Winifred Attwell and Semprini, who introduced his light classical repertoire with a Transylvanian croon of 'Old ones . . . new ones . . . loved ones . . . neglected ones . . .'

I envied Dina and Roger their proximity to such super-stars-in-residence and their growing collections of autographs and signed photographs. I, too, acquired an autograph book with pale pink, green and orange pages, which kind-hearted Dina would present to Richard Murdoch or Avril Angers along with her own. When soliciting a photograph, she would usually request 'one for my little cousin as well'.

One of the most fascinating of the Commodore's attractions – who, alas, did not put up at the Star Hotel – were a 'mind-reading' act named Pharos and Miss Radar. Radio variety featured several such duos with essentially the same schtick: that one of the pair possessed supernatural telepathic or mind-reading powers. He (or she) would be elaborately blindfolded, then the other member of the team would go into the audience, pick out a series of people at random and put questions about their sex and personal appearance which the blindfolded one would answer as if by thought-transference or second sight. In fact, it was all done by a code concealed in the questioning: 'Can you tell me if this is a lady or gentleman?' meant it was a gentleman, 'I wonder if you know what colour his tie is?' meant a green one, and so forth.

The exotic spin put on this old formula by Pharos and Miss Radar was that Pharos, the questioner and alleged thought-transmitter, had the black-bearded dignity of some Spanish grandee, while Miss Radar was a refined-looking woman whom Norman Hartnell himself might have arrayed in her silver cocktail dress, though Hartnell might well have jibbed at the final decorative detail. Attached to the top of her head was a short metal pole surmounted by a lozenge-shaped radar scanner, identical to the ones that embellished the newer Portsmouth ferries. Before starting to question her on the gender or tie-colour of an audience-member she had positively never met before, Pharos would command 'Scan!' And, by no mechanism visible to the naked eye, the radar scanner on her head would begin slowly revolving.

Because Uncle Phil knew the Commodore's manager, Roger and I saw Pharos and Miss Radar several times from complimentary seats in the front row of the stalls. At one matinée, Roger was even called up on stage to assist in the ceremonial blindfolding of Miss Radar, which was not done with a conventional white handkerchief but with two large slabs of baker's dough. She never fluffed an answer and never smiled, not until she had correctly identified every detail of the last subject. 'And finally,' Pharos would say, knitting his fierce black brows, 'can you tell me, please, where this gentleman was born?' 'In bed!' Miss Radar would reply with the faintest quirk of her mannequin's mouth.

Unable to get their autograph at the Star, Roger and I tracked them all over town, finally running them to earth one sunny afternoon in Abell's Gift Shop on the Esplanade. Miss Radar, we were disappointed to see, did not wear her radar scanner outside the theatre. 'Please may I have your autograph?' I asked Pharos, feeling a gust of sheer terror as his bearded face looked up from the eggtimer with coloured sand from Alum Bay that he was examining. 'By all means,' he replied, snatching the book out of my hand, then staring at me with knitted brows as though I were a thought-receiver whose scanner had failed to revolve. For I'd forgotten to bring a pen.

*

I CAN ONLY PRESUME it was the stimulus of finding himself a theatrical landlord that prompted Uncle Phil to dress as a woman at the Star on New Year's Eve. The concepts of 'drag' and transvestism were unfamiliar ones then, at least among the pub-goers of Ryde, and the imposture was felt to be closer in spirit to pantomime dames who put up at the Star. I never saw the spectacle at first hand, but I remember being shown a set of photographs of Uncle Phil in his Spanish duenna's gown and beauty spot, looking rather like an inflated version of his daughter Dina, dancing cheek-to-cheek with successive male partners, including at least one

amorous-looking sailor. It was the only time I ever heard
Grandma Norman voice even faint criticism of her adored
firstborn. 'All this dressing as a *woman* . . .' she murmured,
wrinkling up her nose in distaste, but then left it at that.

The Star Hotel also accepted a few non-theatrical residents. One was a red-faced man called Arthur who came
down from London each season to sell newspapers on the
Esplanade with a monotonous cockney bellow of 'StarNews-
Stand-*erd*!' (and who also once had his picture taken, dancing
with a dragged-up Uncle Phil). Another regular seasonal
boarder was Mr Ross, to whom Auntie Lorna introduced me
one summer's evening just as he was sitting down to cauli-
flower cheese from a card table in her private sitting-room.
On learning that my name was Philip, he jumped up again and
offered me a large, warm, fleshy hand. 'Philip just like Prince
Philip!' he said in a foreign-accented voice. 'I'm sure you're
just as clever as Prince Philip.' As I moved off, somewhat
bewildered, he stabbed the air with his forefinger as if making
an incontrovertible point. 'And you *look* just like Prince
Philip, too,' he added.

Mr Ross came originally from Holland. He was a squarely
built man of about sixty-five with grey hair standing up
slightly around a bald head, and a large, squashy nose. His
invariable costume of well-cut sports jacket, long silver tie
with tie-clip and suède chukka boots, combined with his
extravagant way of expressing himself and raining fulsome
compliments on all around him, suggested some émigré
impresario like the movie magnate Sir Alexander Korda.
In fact he was an antique-dealer who came to the Island
each summer from Bridgewater in Somerset to scour its still
unplundered second-hand shops.

A cut above the usual type of summer visitor, unde-
manding, obliging and fulsomely appreciative, Mr Ross was

rather adopted by Auntie Lorna and, even more, by Grandma Norman, for whom he answered every requirement of a 'Nature's gentleman'. He became one of the chosen few outside her own family allowed to sit beside her as she reclined in her deckchair in the Kiosk's back room, sharing the odd box of 'Maltesies' or glass of Guinness. I remember her repeating with amusement the life-story he must have told her during these sessions – how he'd come over from Holland to join the British army during the 1914–18 war and had been given the name 'Harry Ross' because his real one, Van Stratton, sounded too German. His solitariness and evident loneliness touched her heart and she implied that at the private hotel in Bridgewater where he spent the rest of the year he was not nicely treated. 'I think it's one of those cases,' she told me in her portentous way, 'where Familiarity breeds Contempt.'

Mr Ross's equation of me with Prince Philip, the dashing young Duke of Edinburgh, was none the less dazzling for being patently inaccurate. He seemed to find me more fascinating than any adult ever had before, listening with close attention to everything I said then exclaiming loudly at its cleverness and maturity, praising my drawings as of a young Leonardo. He treated both Roger and me like equals, asking us what we thought about grown-up matters like Mr Churchill and the Korean War, never teasing or belittling us in the usual adult way. On learning, for instance, that I collected model soldiers, he expatiated at length on how it wasn't at all a childish hobby, telling me of all the grown-up soldier collectors he had known. He would take the two of us with him on his journeys across the Island in search of what he jokily termed 'anti-queues'. Travelling by green Southern Vectis bus, we would visit Godshill, Haven Street and other Island beauty spots where our parents never had time to take us. We would look at a few antique shops, Mr Ross would treat us to lunch at an hotel, then allow himself to be inveigled into a toy or souvenir shop, where he'd shrug with mock reluctance, wave a hand and say, 'If there's anything you vouldn't like . . .' Each time Roger or I said 'Mr Ross?' he'd tap his bulbous, veiny nose and reply: 'With the very big noss.' Grandma Norman mysteriously counselled us never to go into public lavatories at the same time he did. But at such moments Mr Ross would say, 'I'm just going to make myself comfortable,' and disappear inside on his own.

This pleasant and profitable era ended one summer day at the pier-head when my father called me into his Amplifier Room, shut the door carefully on the noise of the arcade outside and turned to me with an expression both grim and knowing. 'You're not to go on any more of these outings with Mr Ross, Philip,' he said tersely.

I was mystified. 'Why not, Dad?'

His eyes became very wide and staring, the way Grandma Norman's always did when she was making a joke. But with him, it was never a joke. His irises, usually hazel brown, paled almost to yellow with a horror and disgust I still found totally unfathomable.

'You know exactly what I'm talking about, Philip.'

'I don't, Dad. Honestly.' And I honestly didn't.

'Yes, you do, Philip,' he said quietly. 'And it's something very filthy.'

I had half an idea now what he meant – and, at the same time, realized that I rather than Mr Ross was on trial. My father treated my silence as an admission of guilt, acknowledging it with a grim nod. 'It's very filthy,' he repeated. 'You do know what it is, Philip, so don't pretend you don't. And

I'm not having any son of mine mixed up in anything like that. So the next time Mr Ross asks you to go anywhere, say you're very sorry but you can't. All right?'

'Yes, Dad,' I replied, full of shame.

Six

THE YEAR 1952 began with a national catastrophe that temporarily blotted out the growing unrest within our family circle. On 6 February, King George VI died. I heard the news at school, just as my class was settling down for a double singing period in the senior assembly hall. It was passed to me as a whisper, '*The King's dead*'; I passed it on to the next boy, still not sure whether to believe it. Then our elderly – and useless – singing teacher, Mr Monk, rose into view from behind his upright piano and surveyed us with a look that seemed close to nausea. 'The King . . . is . . . *dead*,' he confirmed, stressing the words like metronome beats.

That of course was an era when unquestioning love and respect for its royal house ran through all classes and age-groups in Britain, barring a few peripheral lunatics. To me, the King was a figure only a little less benignly remote than God. I knew from Grandma Norman (who called him 'George the Good') how courageously he had taken on the throne after the abdication of his brother, Edward VIII, and what a steady light he had been throughout the war, sharing his people's hardships even down to taking only the regulation fuel-economy five inches of hot water in his bath. The strain of that time still seemed to haunt his haggard profile on stamps and postal orders and the brown envelopes bearing the words 'On His Majesty's Service' that brought my father's income tax demands. I used to think these were a personal appeal to rally to the King's service, by returning to the RAF – possibly even undertaking some vital secret mission. It shocked me that he always tore such envelopes furiously in half without even bothering to open them.

With the King's death, a shroud of blackest mourning fell on the whole country for what seemed like months. Theatres and places of entertainment (including our skating rink) shut down as a mark of respect, and music and variety shows on the radio were cancelled indefinitely. The mourning sound I remember most strongly is of naval ceremonial pipes, whose eerie, atonal squeal seemed like a sound almost from beyond the grave. Cinema newsreels endlessly showed that lean, sad Windsor face in its final days when, as one commentary said, 'The King walked with Death . . .' There was also footage of the King's pretty older daughter, Princess Elizabeth, returning from an African visit with her husband, the Duke of Edinburgh, to attend her father's funeral, then face the ordeal of being transformed into Queen Elizabeth II. She looked drawn and sad as she came down the staircase of the Comet airliner to be greeted by grim-faced statesmen. Yet I remember feeling a twinge of envy – for her future, unlike mine, was clear, secure and unchangeable.

*

THAT SPRING, with Britain only just out of mourning, my mother persuaded my father to leave our cramped little flat above the Creamery Café and move to the more salubrious easterly part of Ryde. A friend of hers named Mrs Hull was leaving a large rented flat in Trinity Street, which also included a garden, and suggested that we might like to take it on. My mother jumped at the chance, hoping that better surroundings might revive my father's waning interest in domestic life.

Our new flat occupied the whole ground floor of a rambling yellow-and-vermilion-brick mansion called Dunraven. Like most houses thereabouts, it had been built as a holiday home for some wealthy family in the days when Queen Victoria summered on the Island and Ryde was very nearly as grand as 'royal' Cowes. It had been divided into four flats – two at basement level and one above us whose occupants, a married couple named Allen, had to come through our front hall to reach the covered staircase to their quarters. Our portion of the communal garden included an expanse of lawn with a walnut tree in its centre, and a red-brick air-raid shelter whose sunless rooms some previous tenant had filled with rows of small, shrunken apples.

If we had set out to find the loneliest part of Ryde, we could hardly have done better. Trinity Street was a narrow lane leading nowhere in particular, its pavement cobbled and sprouting with weeds. Dunraven stood alone at the far end, opposite a stone wall that screened the mossy and dusky graveyard of Holy Trinity church. In those days before loud radios and hi-fi, the silence was absolute. Sundays alone brought disturbance in the form of church bells, rung at deafeningly close quarters for up an hour at a time

Our move took place amid circumstances of high drama. It was characteristic of my father that, little regard though he might have for my mother, he could still be consumed by fits of proprietorial jealousy where she was concerned. In particular it irked him when friends they had in common showed a preference for her and even dared overtly to disapprove of the way he treated her. The worst offenders in this regard were a man named Peter Dorley Brown, who ran the Esplanade Garage, and his wife, Brenda. To me, they seemed a wonderfully privileged and fashionable fifties couple, Mr Dorley Brown with his scarlet and beige Ford Zephyr car, Mrs Dorley Brown with her bubbly red hair and and leopard-skin trews. Both were Londoners who, it emerged, had grown up in the vicinity of Clapham Common as my father had, though he'd never met either of them in that earlier time. Mr Dorley Brown, indeed, was somewhat like my father in his pugnacious good looks, and also in his omniscient way with machinery and motor-cars. But in the way he ran his business (successfully) and treated his family (lovingly) the resemblance ended.

The night before we were to move to Trinity Street found my mother in distress of an unspecified though familiar kind, so that evening the Dorley Browns invited her to go out for a drink with them. My father was out elsewhere in different company and himself, as usual, drinking heavily. As the evening wore on, he conceived the notion that she must be with another man. The obsession grew with each double Scotch until finally, at around 10.30, he set out to hunt her down in his 1920 Wolseley limousine with the grey plush interior and built-in umbrella stand.

By now very drunk, he made his way to a place called the Starboard Club in Seaview, a mile or so east of Ryde, where both he and the Dorley Browns were members. It was, for that time, a fashionable spot, with a bar composed largely of mirrors. Finding my mother not there, he flew into a rage and accused the club's owner of complicity in a plot to cuckold him. There was an altercation which ended with him smashing most of the mirrors in the bar. The owner called the police, but before they could arrive my father dashed outside, jumped into the Wolseley and headed back to Ryde again.

The coastal route back between Seaview and Ryde includes a beach-side road called the Duver which in those days was owned privately. Every vehicle that used it had to pay a toll of three old pennies to a white-coated man with a leather satchel over his shoulder. At the Ryde end of the Duver, my father was greeted by the familiar sight of the tollkeeper with arm extended in a 'slow down' sign. Still incandescent with rage and the exhilaration of vandalism, he did not slow down but, instead, jammed his foot hard on the accelerator. The toll-keeper was an elderly man, but proved to have a greater zeal for duty and quicker responses than anyone could have imagined. As the Wolseley surged past him, he jumped on to its running-board, thrust his hand into the open driver's window and repeated his demand for threepence. My father gave him an impatient shove that sent him sprawling into a clump of stinging nettles.

Next morning, as my mother awaited the removal men's arrival, she got a call from Ryde police, informing her that her husband had been arrested for being drunk in charge of a motor vehicle and had spent the night in a cell. She had to go to the police station and get him out, whereupon he vanished to the end of the pier and drank a bottle of whisky on his own, leaving her to cope with the move as best she might. He subsequently appeared before Ryde magistrates and was heavily fined – although not, surprisingly, disqualified from driving. The story appeared as a page lead in the *Portsmouth Evening News* under the headline 'Ex-Wing-Commander's Expensive Night Out'. A few days later, the paper forwarded him a letter from an elderly woman living on the other side of the Island. She told my father that *she'd* always wanted to push the Duver toll-collector into the nettles, and enclosed a £5 note towards his fine.

I knew nothing about any of this until a boy named Michael Rooke came up to me at school and, without pre-amble, announced, 'Your father's been to prison, Norman.'

He was a heavily-set boy with a Hitleresque forelock of black hair and unnaturally dark-ringed eyes. I remembered him in the early days of the skating-rink, trundling towards his mother with outstretched arms and shouting, 'Catch me, Mummy.' 'Oh, Michael,' she replied, fending him off in disgust. 'Your hands . . . they're *filthy*!'

'Your father's been to prison,' Rooke repeated more firmly and loudly for the benefit of other boys standing nearby. 'I read about it in the *Portsmouth Evening News*.'

He was only referring to my father's night at Ryde police station, but – having no access to the *Portsmouth Evening News* – I pictured a real prison with convicts in black-arrowed suits and manacles on their legs. Looking back now, I marvel at the numb stoicism with which I accepted the idea; the fatalism mixed with absurd trustfulness. Certainly, my father was often absent from home for periods equivalent to a short prison sentence. But, for the man of utter moral rectitude I knew him to be, such a thing was obviously inconceivable. He'd once told me how, when we lived in a pub in the heart of London's West End, he'd persuaded a friendly tube-train-driver to let him drive a train between Leicester Square and Charing Cross stations. I imagined something similar happening at Ryde police station, with the police offering him a night in a not-too-uncomfortable cell so that he could experience what happened to real criminals when they were incarcerated.

Being the kind of boy I was, I didn't breathe a word of what I'd been told, either to him or my mother.

*

WITH US TO Trinity Street came Nigger, my father's old black Labrador, and Melody, the little brown and white cocker spaniel bitch who followed my mother everywhere with an involuntary wiggle of her hind-quarters. Two summers before, she had fallen from the pier-head into the sea, bouncing off a transverse girder and breaking her pelvis, yet somehow surviving in the water until she was picked up by two fishermen in a rowing-boat. We also had a Siamese cat, pedigree-name Louis Armstrong, who was the first to realize the deficiencies of the new household. In the flat directly below ours lived a man named Mr Cass who worked at Johncox's, Ryde's leading fishmonger. Louis quickly took to calling on Mr Cass and his family and thereafter was seen less and less in our part of the house.

The flat was a gloomy place with big, high-ceilinged rooms that made our furniture seem small and inadequate, and expanses of black floorboard that all but swallowed up our few bits of carpet and coconut-matting. The front hallway had only the faintest glimmer of light, filtered through a glass-paned door from the cavernous porch beyond. The doors to the sitting-room and bedrooms had china knobs hanging out loosely on rods that one had to twist and jiggle before they would work. My room was at the front, overlooking Holy Trinity churchyard and the clump of high plane trees that grew there. It had evidently always been a child's bedroom, for there was veiny green linoleum on the floor and the front panel of the built-in washbasin bore a coloured transfer of Mickey Mouse. In the whole flat, that was the only light-hearted or festive note.

To begin with at Dunraven, we still had some semblance of family life – at least during out-of-season months. I can remember sunny winter Sunday mornings, with Holy Trinity's bells ringing endlessly and deafeningly across the road, and my mother and father together in their low divan bed, covered only by a sheet and with their backs turned resolutely to each other like ill-matched bookends. He would occasionally busy himself in our portion of the garden, or go pheasant-shooting over farmland near Ryde with a man named John Russell whose family owned Stainers Dairies. One day, he brought back a live barn owl that had fallen out of a tree, stunned by the combined roar of the guns underneath. He kept it for a few days in the big, unfurnished back bedroom, but it seemed no happier at Dunraven than anyone else was destined to be.

In the long run, however, Dunraven's better location and garden proved no better at anchoring him than the Creamery Café, the Cross Keys Hotel and the Porcupine pub had before them. He continued to live a good half of his life in the same mysterious other world he always had, frequently going off on solitary trips for days, even weeks at a time. If I asked my mother where he was, she replied, 'Away on business,' with a curtness that discouraged all further inquiry. I knew the business must be serious and presumed it must be connected in some way with my welfare, present or future. Meantime, thank goodness, only she was there in the dim, brown flat with our two dogs and, sometimes, Louis the fickle Siamese.

Looking at myself at age nine, I saw little to compel any greater interest or attention on his part. I saw a small, puny boy with a golden fringe and an unsmiling face that looked at the world in oddly sidelong way, like a parrot but less wisely and knowingly. My turn-out was the same as every boy in that pre-fashion era – porous Aertex or Achilles shirts, grey flannel or khaki shorts fastened by an elastic belt with a metal S-clasp, sandals made by the Birthday company (a name falsely implying that it did something or other to celebrate its customers' birthdays) with patterns of circle and diamond shapes on their toes. In any assembly of those sunnily innocent, obedient and law-abiding fifties children, I would always have been among the least conspicuous.

My precise position in the social scale puzzled me, as it always had – and still does today. I knew that, despite the downmarket nature of our business, my family rated technically as 'upper class'. As well as my father's RAF officer background and mannerisms, there were all those stories of my genteel West Country ancestors endlessly told to me by Grandma Norman. ('Your great-grandfather Hanham owned a manor house and broad acres in Trowbridge. And *his* father was a Freeman of the City o' Bath . . .') Yet we'd never had anything to do with the Isle of Wight upper class, their yachts and yellow oilskins and substantial white houses in Bembridge and Seaview, and blessed immunity from the chaos of each summer season. I knew I should give thanks for not being like Meatball and the other unruly boys who haunted the beaches and pier-head, with their ragged clothes and nasal Island accents. Yet, for all their humble homes and rough, un-uniformed 'council schools', their lives seemed to have a crude warmth and security mine did not; if it hadn't been so disloyal to all my supposedly illustrious nineteenth-century forebears, I could almost have envied them.

I had one talent only, or so it seemed then: I was good at drawing. For as long as I could remember, other children had looked admiringly over my shoulder as I worked, and grown-ups had taken my studies of cowboys, medieval knights and Crimean War lancers away to exclaim over among themselves. Part of what made me so ridiculously quiet and untroublesome a child was my ability to amuse myself for hours on end with a pencil and paper. Even when prevented from drawing, as on my summer days at the Pavilion – when such an activity would have been the height of disloyalty to my father in his labours – I generally had some new project or quest on my mind. How did one reproduce those extra, fur-collared jackets that swung from the shoulders of Napoleonic hussars? Or the stern of a ship like Nelson's *Victory* under full sail? Or the long holster for a rifle on a cowboy's horse? Looking back from here, I see more than just an ever-reliable hiding-place from the world's unpleasanter realities; I recognize also a small but unquenchable glow of ambition.

Without white cartridge paper before me and a dark green Venus or red Royal Sovereign pencil in my hand, I seemed to myself to be without any distinction whatever. At school, I was good at history and English though, somehow, never quite as good as the class brainbox, a Baptist minister's son named Stephen Edgar Alexander (S. E. A.) Green. What did not come easily to me, I wrote off as beyond my power; I had no sense of what could be achieved simply by trying. I there-fore resigned myself to being 'no good' at maths and science and PT, and being still the only non-swimmer in my class. Even my drawing had these stubborn blind spots: I could do you people in any costume and with any weapons from the whole span of history, but was resolutely 'no good' at animals, scenery or still-life.

My parents, preoccupied with the season and disliking each other, took no interest in my schoolwork and never commented on my end-of-term reports, if they read them at all. The only person I remember ever trying to set me straight was my form-mistress, Miss Turner, a woman whose enor-mous mouth and helplessly projectile salivation had earned her the cruel nickname of 'Spitfire'. She was also kind and conscientious, and one day took me aside to tell me I was 'a bright little boy' and that, if I put my mind to it, I could do just as well in the subjects I didn't happen to like. But, intimidated by the hails of spittle that accompanied these encouraging words, I hardly listened to her.

Mine was a universe completely without culture as it was defined in the early fifties. No one ever took me to an art gallery or classical music concert; the only music I ever heard came from the radio and our arcade jukebox, the only humour from seaside comedians and the saucy postcards in Mr Vernon's outdoor rack. My attitudes became the cheerfully philistine ones of Grandma Norman – that opera was 'a lot of fat women screeching', that ballet was 'all ballyhoo'. I realize now that I had a strong aesthetic sense even when I was no more than a toddler. In the late forties, you still saw pony-drawn Victorian milk-carts from which the deliveryman ladled milk straight from the churn. I remember, aged three or four, seeing one of those carts, with its fancily fretworked wooden sides, and thinking to myself that I liked the way it looked. Even to today's over-attentive adults, a child would have difficulty in articulating pure visual pleasure; in the fifties, even had I had the confidence or willing listeners, such a thing was unimaginable.

The only place where I could gratify such nascent, inexpressible impulses was the cinema. At Ryde's three picture-houses (the sumptuous Commodore, the historic Theatre Royal, the fleapit Scala – pronounced 'Scaler'), programmes changed at midweek, with an additional one-off show on Sunday nights. I saw every film I legally could, which is to say those with a 'U' certificate ('Suitable for Universal Exhibition') or an 'A', which children could see provided they were accompanied by an adult. If no grown-up in the family were available, it was common for children to stand outside the cinema and ask total strangers to take them in. The usherettes were up with this dodge, and during the performance conducted frequent checks to ensure that children were still seated with the adults they had hijacked. One afternoon, I persuaded a young couple to act as my passport into a gripping 'A' Western, then unwisely moved several rows away from them. The film had reached its most exciting moment –

some US cavalrymen, trapped in a Mexican pueblo village, tensely awaiting an Apache night-attack – when an usherette's torch beam triumphantly illuminated me and an officious female voice ordered me out into the street.

The reason I loved Westerns so passionately was not the incessant violence between cavalry and Indians or rival gun-fighters, but the sheer stylishness of everything – the huge white Stetsons, the black leather waistcoats, the neat, small Winchester rifles, the shiny-spurred boots, the long-barrelled Navy Colts. Hollywood musicals came next in my affection, with the richness of colour and texture that existed nowhere in Britain then. I saw *Show Boat*, with Howard Keel and Ava Gardner, five or six times: at the end, as the great paddle-boat dwindled away down the Mississippi to the strains of 'Ol' Man River', I felt I had passed through a profound and draining experience. I sat just as entranced through black-and-white American films of modern times, detective and love dramas, despite having only the haziest understanding of their plots. It was enough to be in that parallel world where people lived in long, low white houses, and drove long, low white cars, and drank black coffee (pronounced 'cor-fee') with meals, and said, 'I object, Your Honour,' and spent half their lives in night-clubs, and where so many darkly handsome but unpredictable heroes bore such a striking resemblance to my own father. No feeling was quite so dreary as coming out of the cinema at five or so in the afternoon; leaving behind that magic, smoke-filled darkness for the bright sunshine and mundane slow motion of reality.

With my cousin Dina's encouragement, I had become an avid reader of *Photoplay* and *Picturegoer* magazines – the latter still produced in 1920s-ish dark sepia – which gave purportedly intimate glimpses into the domestic life of Hollywood stars much like *Hello!* today: ' "I'm a rebel at heart," says Barbara Bel Geddes . . .' 'Ida Lupino enjoys a fresh Californian salad on the patio of her lovely Beverly Hills home . . .' 'Roy Rogers' children have a Wild West birthday party, and Trigger comes, too . . .' 'Dinner at home with Larry and Betty Parks . . .' 'Doris Day frolics in the pool with her little boy, Terry . . .' 'Rosalind Russell reads a story to her sons on the night before Christmas . . .' For aesthetic reasons I could not begin to fathom, I was besotted above all with Jane Russell, the huge-bosomed, scowling star of *Son of Paleface* and *The French Line*, described on her posters as 'Mean, Moody, Magnificent'. In the *Daily Mirror* I'd read how, while making a film in Britain, she had met a little orphan boy named Tommy whom she now proposed to adopt and take home with her to Hollywood. Could any boy in the universe be luckier?

*

MY FATHER'S SPELLS at home were uneasy times for me, deepening my awareness that I wasn't the kind of son he wanted or deserved. I was guiltily conscious of being nothing like him to look at – not dark and almost gipsy-handsome like the Norman side of the family, but fair-haired and pale like my mother and so, presumably, the inheritor of every quality that made him treat her with such angry, even violent disdain. I knew how much it pained him that I skulked indoors with my pencils and paper even on beautiful days and shrank from all the athletic pursuits in which he had once excelled ('Victor ludorum' at his school sports, year after year). I could not catch the easiest throw, climb a tree, build bridges and cranes from Meccano sets or, most culpably, tell one end of a screw-driver from the other.

Whereas he had a marksman's perfect 20–20 vision, I had been found to have a 'lazy' left eye while we were still at

St Neots, and now wore National Health-issue spectacles with black wire rims and pink nose-pieces. That confirmed me as a weed and a drip whose only force of character lay in obdurately resisting all his efforts to make me manly. When he cut my fingernails to manly short length with his silver clippers, shearing off each nail far below the quick, I struggled and cried for the horrible numb-pawed feeling of it until finally he let me go with a sound I can reproduce only as 'Grr!' The word for me in his era – one that still returns to haunt me in Graham Greene's *Brighton Rock* – was 'milky'.

The countryside sports which he loved so much, and to which I remained so indifferent, brought his manliness into bleakest relief against the unmanliness I felt in myself. As well as dexterity, strength, disregard for personal discomfort and infinite patience, they also demanded a sensitivity, a soulfulness, to which I could never aspire. For I knew that shooting birds and catching fish were not activities pursued for their own seemingly brutal sake but as expressions of love for the countryside, even for the creatures fated to be annihilated. Unenlightened and shallow as I was, I felt it cruel for a gorgeous-hued pheasant to be pumped full of shot in mid-air and flutter pathetically to earth to be picked up in a dog's jaws, or for a trout or salmon to be hooked in the mouth.

In my solitary cowboy-and-Indian games, whenever I levelled a toy pistol at him and said, 'Stick 'em up,' he would always answer solemnly, 'Never point a gun,' which I dimly recognized as the first and most essential law of the adult firearms-user. Yet surely, I said to myself – only ever to myself – it wasn't a gun: it was a toy. And what did he do with guns other than point them?

I knew I could not measure up to him in any way: not his good looks, his strength, his athleticism, especially not the code of honour and chivalry by which he professed to lead his whole life. Above all things, he hated 'deceitfulness' – which, in time, I would realize applied only to deceitfulness in others. He always knew, as if by some psychic power, when I was being deceitful. Before the false denial even rose to my lips, his eyes would stare at me, boring into my very soul with their mixture of anger, incredulity and fresh disillusionment.

Even during these periods of domesticity, there were times when he did not seem to occupy my mother's and my world at all; when he would lie for hours on his elbows in the bath, staring down the length of his black-hairy chest, or sit in the chintz armchair by the sitting-room window, tapping his right-hand fingers in endlessly changing patterns on its arm. The hazel eyes found no fault with me then: I was not sure whether they even saw me.

He could be physically affectionate – far more so than my rather reserved, self-conscious mother. At unpredictable moments, he would draw me into a bear-hug like one of Grandma Norman's, calling me 'Phil-o' and 'my old cocka-lorum', enveloping me in a world of tweed and pipe-tobacco and manly strength which, just for that moment, seemed the safest place on earth. With that same unpredictability, he would buy me things – munificent non-birthday and non-Christmas presents for which I never dared ask him and which I'd only mentioned longingly and theoretically to my mother. Without warning, the Wolseley would stop; he would disappear with his round-shouldered stride into the toy or stationer's shop, then return and brusquely drop the longed-for model stagecoach or sub-machine-gun water-pistol or Dinky Talbot-Lago racing car into my lap.

Sometimes he could seem almost like a boy himself, reading my *Eagle* and *Knockout* comics with as much enjoy-ment as I did, sharing my enthusiasm for films like *Shane* and *Annie Get Your Gun*. Without warning, he would snap out of his sad reverie, sweep me on to his lap and read to me from a book called *Round the Year Stories* or from *Oliver Twist*, or tell me the story of how King Midas changed his own daughter into gold. Seized by high spirits as inexplicable as his melancholy, he would sing out loud in a high, unselfconscious voice, drawing on what I presumed to be a largely RAF repertoire including 'Phil the Fluter's Ball', 'The End of Me Old Cigar' and 'Oh Dear What Can the Matter Be', jokily saying 'three old ladies locked in the *conservatory*' instead of 'the lavatory'.

In 1952, the film *Ivanhoe*, starring Robert Taylor and Elizabeth Taylor, reached the Commodore. It was considered a film of such historical interest that a party from my school was taken to see it. Afterwards, the playground came alive with knights swinging imaginary swords and maces, and we were encouraged to make weapons and armour in our handiwork classes. At his skate-repair counter at the Pavilion, my father made me a magnificent helmet from an old biscuit tin, somehow beating it into a semblance of chain-mail and adding a movable visor and black feather plume.

The many times when I thought he was God made all the more burdensome the dark secret I had buried in my heart. In my mother's presence, I was merely afraid of him. But if ever circumstances left the two of us alone together, I was terrified of him. My constant fear was ever having to sleep alone with him, for in bed he never wore pyjamas, only a skimpy white singlet. I knew it was unthinkable that so manly a man could be guilty of 'filthiness' – that he himself loathed and detested such filthiness when he suspected it in others, like the Dutch antique-dealer Mr Ross. But this didn't lessen my dread of his infinitely powerful black-hairy body coming into contact in any way with my pale, puny one.

Once when we'd shared a bed alone together – it was still

at our old High Street flat – I awoke in the early morning to find his fingers playing with me, twiddling rapidly and impatiently as with the neck of an uninflated balloon. I remember in my barely-awake state being not in the least bit surprised; just vaguely thinking, 'Oh, well . . . it's happened at last.' And knowing I could never mention it to another living soul.

Part Two

'HAPPY CELEBRATION,

DING-DONG-DING'

Seven

WE NOW DID roller-skating all the year round. In the summer of 1952, my father opened an outdoor rink in Ryde Esplanade's Western pleasure gardens, running it through the season in tandem with the arcade and restaurants at the pier-head. In the centre of the gardens – locally known as 'the Western' – stood a large oval-shaped enclosure with a covered stage, formerly used for brass band concerts and variety shows. Removal of the deckchair rows that had filled it revealed a concrete floor that made an ideal skating surface. The encircling canopied wall had continuous windows, through which passers-by could view the freewheeling spectacle within.

I was exhilarated to hear that we were expanding on to the Western, but not particularly surprised. At that time, it seemed to me logical and inevitable that, having established a beach-head at the Pier Pavilion so to speak, my father would eventually take over every major entertainment site on Ryde seafront. The previous summer, the Western enclosure had seemed an alien place to me and my cousin Roger as we sat in front-row deckchairs, watching the Ryde Municipal Orchestra ('Director: Henry Jolliffe'). Now, by a familiar miracle, its oval concrete floor, its no-longer-used stage and the iron sea serpents that supported its encircling canopy turned into yet another extension of home.

Accustomed as I'd become to the quantum leaps of my father's imagination, I was equally unsurprised to learn that, as well as offering general free-skating, our new onshore outdoor rink would feature a nightly roller-cabaret act, Edna and Jimmy Webster. A brother–sister partnership from some-where on the mainland, they gave a show that was part-ballet, part-Apache dance routine. Jimmy, a Latin-looking young man in a grey bolero jacket, spun his red-haired elder sister around at incredible speeds, holding her supine over his head or swinging her by one arm and one leg, round and round, up and down just inches from the concrete. The finale was a whirlwind rotation by Jimmy with both arms flung wide, while a horizontal and independently spinning Edna clung by her teeth alone to a mouthpiece attached to harness on his chest.

Second in importance – a close second – to the rink's cabaret stars was the young woman I still knew and referred to as Joan. As at the Pier Pavilion's wintertime sessions, Joan was employed at the Western rink as a combination of supervisor and teacher. In addition, she had her own featured performance spots, between shows by Edna and Jimmy Webster, when she would give demonstrations of figure-skating or roller-dancing.

She was, indeed, now something of a local celebrity. That previous winter, accompanied by her 'husband', George Goldring, she had gone up to London to take the bronze medal in figure-skating for which she'd trained so long at the Pavilion rink under my father's watchful eye. I remember the late-night telephone call from George to our High Street flat telling us that she'd passed, and how the relief I felt was mixed with despair. For if Joan with all her smooth-footed skill was still only at bronze medal stage, what hope could I possibly have?

It still was no more than faintly mystifying to me that, among all the people we knew, the dozens of employees, drinking companions and hangers-on whom my father magnetized with his good looks and charm and RAF-ness, he should have singled out someone like Joan for such particular favours and attention. As I accepted everything, I accepted that, not only in our business but also in the limited family life that went on behind it, Joan always seemed to be there. Winter and summer alike, I was used to seeing her angular face, framed by fluffy brown hair, with its wide-set eyes and narrow mouth, its rather rueful expression as if someone somewhere was being very unkind to her but she had resolved to endure it without protest. Whichever skating-rink the season demanded, there would be Joan circling it in her one-piece maroon skating outfit and red MC's badge, with effortless sweeps of her big, bare legs.

At that point, employing what I now see was fairly elementary camouflage, my father seemed to have made a friend of George as much as of Joan. They were always out together, with my mother making up a reluctant fourth, at more genteel local watering-holes like the Starboard Club in Seaview (where my father had evidently been forgiven for smashing all the bar's mirrors) or Spencer's Inn in Union Street, which had bow-windows with distorted glass like an illustration from Dickens. At our High Street flat, I often used to be woken by late-night laughter and crashes from the adjacent sitting-room, indicating that Joan and George had been brought back after pub closing time for an RAF-style party. At one such session, my mother later told me, talk turned to Joan's girlhood prowess as a gymnast and, with George's encouragement, she did a handstand in the middle of the carpet, covering her face with her skirt and underslip and revealing her legs all the way up to stocking-tops and knickers. I could picture how, even upside-down, her face would still have been tight-tipped and disapproving

Another night, the two couples attended a dance put on by Ryde School, where I had not long since become a pupil. Afterwards, I heard my mother tell her friend Mrs Dorley Brown that Joan had worn a white satin gown which made her look 'like a Christmas tree fairy'. What she failed to add – I suppose out of sheer embarrassment and humiliation – was that my father had ignored her throughout the whole evening and danced every dance with Joan, cheek to cheek.

Nor did his generosity towards Joan and George limit itself to rounds of drinks. Above our flat at the Creamery was a set of attic rooms, unoccupied since our arrival from St Neots, which he now offered to them at a modest rent. The café below, which had been run for Uncle Phil and him by various people, never very satisfactorily, was also currently in need of a manager. It seemed no more than a sensible tying up of loose ends for George to give up his barman's job at the Crown Hotel and take over running the Creamery. With George busy in the café all day and most of each evening, my father became concerned that Joan might be lonely, so whenever we went anywhere as a family, she'd come along as well. I remember how his usual melancholy terseness on these occasions used to vanish whenever Joan was with us. He'd be full of jokes and observations and anecdotes, and would always hurry to open the car door for her with an old-fashioned courtly bow.

However much I saw of Joan, she remained as remote and uncomfortably fascinating to me as ever. What today I recognize as extreme shyness – possibly mixed with some embarrassment at the pedestal on which my father so publicly set her – seemed then a chilly and rather grim impassivity. Not that she was ever directly unpleasant to me. Even on the rink, where she held supreme authority, she never bossed or reprimanded me. On the rare occasions she spoke to me, in that faint, plaintive little Brummie voice, it was in a totally unassertive, even respectful way – I can still hear the half-embarrassed dying fall on which she used to say 'Phil'. Yet her presence always made me feel uneasy and clumsy; I knocked things over, blurted out absurdities, got my words mixed up. At moments of my worst, burning-eared humili-ation, I always seemed to see Joan's face watching me with the same wintry, knowing look as when she'd caught me staring at her legs, and when I'd actually touched one of them while making such an abysmal mess of that Mohawk turn.

My mother was not the only one to whom being friends with Joan brought disagreeable experiences. For it meant I, in my turn, had to be friends with Lynette, the small daughter Joan cast in the role of her 'little sister'. As close as she now was to us, the pretence continued in all its implausibility, with eight-year-old Lynette kept in the care of Joan's aged parents, Mr and Mrs Salsbury, invested with their surname and trained to call them 'Daddy' and 'Mummy' (or 'Moomy') while treating her real mother as an oversized sibling whom she saw only for occasional outings and sleepovers.

I hated Lynette as only a boy of nine can hate a girl of eight. It does me no credit, but that's the way it was. I hated her brown skin and her little squashy nose and the high-pitched nasal giggle that was her response to almost every-thing that anyone said to her. I hated the smell of wet pants that always seemed to hang around her, and the way she said 'Give it me' when she meant 'Give it *to* me' and 'Loose eet' when she meant 'Let go of it'. I could not fathom why adults seemed to find her cute, and why even the more sympathetic and enlightened of them still joined in the game of saying I had a crush on Lynette, and that we were 'lovebirds'.

That she, too, had learned to skate, and was gaining in prowess each day, made me seethingly jealous. '*You* can't skate,' I'd whisper to her when we were out of grown-up earshot, relishing the dismay it always brought to the little brown face. 'I *can*,' she'd protest with a wail. 'No, you can't. You can't even stand up on skates, let alone move forward . . .' If we were both given ice-lollies or a packet of crisps, I'd challenge her to a race, wait until her teeth had credulously crunched through her lolly or crisps, then wave mine at her in triumph with everything still to enjoy.

Eventually, she told on me to her supposed 'Mummy', Mrs Salsbury, a pale-skinned woman with a mouth shaped like a daffodil and all the Brummie aggression that Joan so conspicuously lacked. One evening at the Western rink, I found myself cornered by Mrs Salsbury, who was wearing a dress and coat in the same nubbly cream colour with high-heeled shoes to match. ''Ere,' she said in Midlands dialect so thick I could barely understand it, 'Oi've got a bone to pick with yow. Yow've been getting-gon at Leen, haven't yow? You're not to do eet, do yow hear?'

Unexpectedly, Joan came to my defence, or at least minimized the enormity of my crime, while Lynette smirked triumphantly beside her. 'Oh, Mum,' she protested in her small, passionless voice. 'You *know* what kids are . . .' But Mrs Salsbury was not to be put off. 'He's not to gow on getting-gon at her, and Oi've told him so . . .' I skated away in a trance of mortification, wishing beyond words that we didn't have such people for friends, and that Grandma Norman had been there to defend me.

Each year, like other Island resorts, Ryde concluded its summer season with a carnival week in which the high point

was a procession of decorated floats representing organiza-
tions and businesses in the town. In the 1952 Ryde Carnival,
my father decided to enter a float representing our summer
and winter skating-rinks. I was to appear on it in fancy dress,
a prospect that filled me with excitement until I learned two
things. Firstly, I was not to be dressed as a cowboy or Ruri-
tanian hussar as I wanted, but as a Scotsman in a kilt like the
one in the Pavilion's wall frieze; secondly, that Lynette also
would be taking part.

We were not the Carnival procession's most exciting entry
– a Bedford lorry (driven by my father) with its tailboard
perfunctorily swathed in orange crêpe and crude side-placards
that said RYDE ROLLER SKATING RINK. The theme was the
same one of worldwide skating as on the Pavilion frieze,
though this time the supposed eight-wheel mania was not seen
as extending beyond the British Isles. Joan portrayed an Irish
girl in a green beret and matching sash, and Lynette was a
Welsh girl with a conical black hat and a broomstick. All three
of us wore skates with their wheels locked to stop us rolling
off the back of the lorry as it made its slow progress through
Ryde's main streets and along the Esplanade to the parade's
terminus beside the Canoe Lake. The one consolation offered
to me for having to wear a kilt was that it would include a
real Scotsman's sporran made of leather. But in the event
the leather sporran did not materialize; instead, I wore a small
pelt of rabbity white fur secured by elastic. It was the lowest
point of my life until then.

*

MY MOTHER had never worked harder in the business, or for
fewer thanks. Seven days a week all through the season, she
was at the Pavilion, supervising the kitchens, running the
cash-desk, doing the books and the onerous official paper-

work still necessitated by food-retailing, and acting as my father's private secretary. When the restaurant closed, at 6.30 or thereabouts, she'd cycle down the pier-planks on an old black bicycle with a shopping-basket on its handlebars, to spend the evening helping him at the open-air rink.

On its seaward side the Western enclosure had a small glassed-in booth which my father used as an office and to keep watch on the circulating multitudes. It was in there that Edna and Jimmy Webster would wait to perform, red-headed Edna clutching a man's jacket around her skating dress, which was shorter than Joan's ever had been, and fringed with white like a cowgirl's buckskin. There was also a hand-microphone, connected to half a dozen-odd Tannoy-boxes around the canopied perimeter. When my father wasn't around to make the evening session's various announcements (please all keep to to the right, lucky ticket-numbers and so forth), my mother would step in and do that, too. She got rather good at it, though – of course – never receiving any word of commendation from him.

Midway through the Edna and Jimmy Webster spot, Jimmy would invite one of the spectators to let him spin them around the way he spun his sister. One evening, to my astonishment, the volunteer who walked out from the rink-side amid a rustle of applause was my mother. As it was autumn now, and getting colder in the evenings, she wore navy-blue pinstripe slacks and her long Jaeger camelhair coat, unbuttoned, with the belt hanging down. I can see Jimmy now, in his dove-grey bolero jacket, picking her up around the waist and going into his instant high-speed pirouette. As she whirled, her pinstriped legs swung outward, but her camel coat with its hanging belt and brown silk lining still hung straight down behind her. She made a strange wailing sound that rose and fell with each revolution like the hum in a spinning top: 'WoooOOOooo! WoooOOOooo! *Wooo-OOOooo!*' You couldn't tell if she was doing it for the spectators' benefit, or really was terrified.

Another evening, Joan gave a demonstration of roller-dancing with a member of the wintertime skating club named Johnny Valvona. Round and round the grey concrete oval they swept to the familiar, crackly strains of 'The Blue Danube', Joan firstly in Johnny's arms in conventional waltz style, he forward, she backward; then the two side-by-side, Johnny's right hand holding Joan's over her shoulder, her expression more than usually grim and put-upon as if she were only with great difficulty keeping him at bay.

As they circled the rink, my mother gave a commentary about them over the PA system. I can still hear her voice from the undersized speakers around the rink-edge, competing with the evening bustle of the beach, the gardens and the nearby Esplanade. She is speaking in the breathy upper-class tone she always puts on at moments of special unease. And the uneasy task at hand is to talk about Joan – or 'Jeawn', as she pronounces it – with seeming objective admiration.

'Jeawn and Johnny Valvona demonstrate the roller quick-step to Strauss's "The Blue Danube". You may be interested to know, ladies and gentlemen, that Jeawn has recently taken her bronze medal in figure skating . . . If we practise hard, perhaps some day we *all* may be as good as Jeawn.'

*

SINCE UNCLE PHIL now had a pub with accommodation, it had been inevitable that Grandma Norman and Uncle Wally should stay there for the summer rather than in lodgings kept by strangers. I bitterly envied my two cousins, Dina and Roger, this unfair dividend of her presence, and made myself a frequent caller at the Star Hotel to ensure she gave them nothing, either by way of gifts or her big, smacking kisses, that she didn't give me, too.

On my visits, I could not but be aware of a family under as much stress as my own, albeit for ostensibly different reasons. Smouldering always like intrusive incense was the matter of Auntie Lorna's Catholicism and the promise wrung from Uncle Phil that their children would be brought up in her faith. Dina now attended the convent school attached to St Mary's Catholic church, whose bulk loomed over the narrow High Street barely a hundred yards north of the Star. Roger, though at a 'C. of E.' school, had become even more devout, often leaving notes to his mother asking her to be sure and call him in time for early-morning Mass. To add add insult to this ecumenical injury, Auntie Lorna openly consorted with the St Mary's nuns, who wore square black head-dresses with wimples that circled their faces – so I used to think – like expanses of boiled-egg white. Uncle Phil called nuns 'currant buns' and frowned most tremendously if ever he found that one had been invited into his home.

That was the external, quasi-comical source of strife between Auntie Lorna and Uncle Phil as I understood it at the time; in later years, a much darker story was to emerge. For all his seeming intellectual superiority and gravitas, Uncle Phil was as heavy a drinker as my father, and as aggressive, destructive and violent a drunk. His over-large, under-used brain gave him a talent for psychological cruelty (of which cutting his toenails over Auntie Lorna's dinner was an atypically light-hearted example) that made my father seem a novice by comparison. My mother may have 'suffered and suffered' but, I now realize, it was nothing to the extent to which my poor, cheerful, vulnerable, over-religious godmother suffered and suffered.

Grandma Norman's presence at the Star – brief as it was

between the Kiosk's opening-hours – might have been expected to moderate Uncle Phil's behaviour and give Auntie Lorna another much-needed ally. She had always been extravagantly affectionate to both her daughters-in-law, calling them 'duck' and 'my love' just as she did her grand-children and favourite customers, encouraging them to visit her in her nest of rock-boxes whenever they liked and to have no secrets from her. It had always worried me that my mother always seemed less spellbound by her than did the rest of humanity, calling her 'That *Nan*' with a decided edge, and often talking about her as if she were not the most wonderful being on earth. 'I didn't like it when Clive used to come home on leave in the war . . . she'd always say "go out and buy some food and I'll cook you a meal . . ." She could never be bothered to have food in the house . . . and the *stink* of B.O. in that lair of hers . . . She doesn't understand that if you put sweat-pads in the under-arms of your dresses, you do have to change them every so often . . . And, of course, everything I tell her gets repeated to Clive straight away . . .'

No such reservations troubled Auntie Lorna, who would greet Grandma Norman each evening with a battery of pent-up grievances against Uncle Phil, sipping unsteadily at a gin and tonic and winding and re-winding her chiffon wrist-scarf. One seldom, in fact, saw Uncle Phil around the Star, though I suppose he must have carried on the pub landlord's duties of shelf-stocking and serving and sorting out 'empties'. His misdeeds were always committed offstage, in the manner of classic Greek tragedy, and reported afterwards. Once I overheard Auntie Lorna describing a scene he'd made as they were having lunch in the first-floor lounge that served also as their dining-room. Though I caught only incomplete details, it was easy to picture his ponderous irritability, her increasingly vain appeals to reason. 'He kept saying the chair behind was digging into his back . . . I said, "Well, IF the chair's digging into you, WHY don't you just get up and move it?" . . .'

Grandma Norman listened in seemingly scandalized sympathy, now and again murmuring a 'tut-tut' or 'there-there'. But I knew, if poor Auntie Lorna didn't, whose side she was really on. It was awkward for me to visit the Star because Mr Ross was back in residence there that summer, and expected me still to go out with him and Roger – who had not been banned from his company – on antique-buying day-trips as of old. 'Ve vill take the Southern Wectis bus?' he proposed. 'Look at some anti-queues in the pretty village of Godshill?' He had no idea what had been suggested about him behind his back, and accepted my mumbled refusal with a philosophical shrug. 'You are such a clever boy . . . cleverer than the real Prince Philip. Of course you're too busy at your studies to go by bus with poor old Harry Ross.'

My cousin Roger and I had never got on particularly well, though we'd knock around together if neither of us could find better company. I remember him once coming up to me on the Western, wearing an incredulous grin and carrying – I saw to my surprise – a small black leather-bound Bible. 'Did you know that the word "piss" is in the Bible?' he said. 'So's the word "dung".' He flicked through the pink-edged pages and, sure enough, there was the Old Testament passage about 'eat their own dung and drink their own piss'.

As we hunched, sniggering, over it, a pious-looking old lady in a flowered black straw hat came up and beamed at us both. 'How *wonderful* to find two little boys reading their Holy Bible,' she quavered emotionally. 'So many children nowadays, I'm sorry to say, grow up without ever wanting to learn the stories of Jesus. You dear little boys have made my day.'

Since Roger had been living at the Star Hotel, however, a great gulf had opened between us. Despite Uncle Phil's fabled scholarship, he had not felt it worthwhile to pay for his son's secondary education, as my father was paying for mine at Ryde School. Instead, Roger was now at the free-of-charge town secondary modern, a workhouse-like building never known by its full title but, belittlingly, just by the street where it stood. I had admittedly been somewhat tactless on first seeing him in the telltale grey pullover and green tie, but, in my own defence, I was genuinely surprised. 'Oh,' I said. 'You go to Green Street, do you?' Since scalding his arm with hot water as a tiny boy, Roger had been as nervous and volatile as his mother. Like me he had an eye-complaint which, at moments of stress, made his dark brown irises quiver frantically back and forth. They were quivering at me, I saw, from a face full of weary disgust. 'Yes,' he almost spat, 'I go to *Green Street*.'

As a result, he had acquired a thick Island accent – pronouncing his sister's name, for example, as 'Deen-err' – and was seen around town with the kind of ragged, lower-class boys who hurled abuse, or even stones, at anyone, like me, with a Latin motto on his blazer-badge. To make matters worse, Auntie Lorna was always loudly praising my good manners and nice speaking-voice, and asking Roger why he couldn't be more like me. He got his own back by suggesting that, as a pathetic Ryde School boy, I was in imminent danger from his Green Street classmates, who held off from attacking me thanks only to his personal intercession. He would sidle up to me in the street, chewing imaginary gum like an American gangster, and murmur contemptuously into my ear, 'I saved your life just then, and you didn't even know it.'

Dina, lovely, dark-eyed Dina, remained my friend and ally, even though at twelve she seemed practically grown-up – and, indeed, had already been put to work by Uncle Phil in non-convent hours behind the counter of the Star's public bar. One midday, when I was alone in the upstairs sitting-room, Dina appeared, wearing a black barmaid dress and leading a pallid, sweating man by the hand. 'Poor John Freer has just been hit down in the bar,' she told me. 'He's going to stay here until everything's calmed down a bit. Would you look after him and fetch him up another gin when he wants one?'

It was Dina who tried to cheer me at the end of that summer when Grandma Norman, having again triumphantly reached the sixteen-ton mark in rock-sales, closed up the Kiosk and returned with Uncle Wally to London. Dina suggested we use the coming winter months to make our accumulated photographs and autographs of the Star's resident radio personalities into a proper collection. 'We'll do it really nicely,' she promised. 'We'll buy albums and use stamp-mounts and get cherry-red and silver crayons to write all the names with.'

Then, out of the clear, autumn-blue sky, my father and Uncle Phil had another of their cataclysmic rows. No one but themselves – and maybe Grandma Norman – ever knew its cause, although one can guess that Uncle Phil's lack of commitment to the Pier Pavilion must have been a strong contributory factor. For my mother and me, under my father's code of total war, it meant instantly severing all relations not only with Uncle Phil but with Auntie Lorna and Dina and Roger as well. I could no longer visit the Star Hotel or even speak to my godmother and two cousins. The months ahead lost the single consolation of sticking photographs of Richard Murdoch and Semprini into albums and writing their names in silver or cherry-red crayon.

And that was to be just the beginning.

Eight

THE SUMMER OF 1953 was set fair to be a doubly glorious one. Ended at last was the year-long national mourning for King George VI. On 3 June we were to crown as his successor a shy-smiling young woman towards whom the whole nation felt loyally protective. By early spring, the shops were already full of Coronation souvenirs depicting a radiant Queen Elizabeth II and her naval-uniformed Prince Consort on chinaware, tea-caddies, chocolate bars, jigsaw puzzles and dishtowels. To encourage foreign visitors to join the festivities, and bring sorely-needed cash into the country, a brand-new national identity had been created: no longer bomb-racked and drab and xenophobic, but open-hearted and welcoming. 'Come to Britain, sunny Britain, smiling Britain,' sang the bandleader Edmundo Ros to a calypso beat, 'Celebrate in this our Coronation Year . . . It's a land of milk and honey . . .' He was to be right, at least, about the 'sunny' bit.

As an additional boost to the patriotic fervour, our young sovereign-in-waiting bore the same name as Britain's greatest-ever queen, Elizabeth I, whose reign encompassed the rout of the Spanish Armada and the piratical conquest of half the world. Newspaper editorialists talked seriously of a 'New Elizabethan' age that would recreate the domestic glories of the young sovereign's great forebear and send forth modern versions of Drake and Raleigh to win fresh victories on her behalf. The whole country felt somehow reborn, with the grimness of the post-war austerity years suddenly magicked away, the dreary recent past forgotten, the present full of nothing but good news, the future bright and beckoning.

And, as if to set the seal on the new golden age, and make the nation's spirits fizz even more effervescently, Grandma Norman's distant cousins in Somerset launched Babycham.

*

THE ISLE OF WIGHT was to enjoy a front-row seat in the impending celebrations. After her crowning, in true Elizabethan style, the new Queen was to carry out a ceremonial review of her navy at Spithead, the historic marshalling-place for British warships, a few miles across the water east of Ryde. Every nation in the Commonwealth and many outside were to send ships to take part in the event, creating the largest fleet ever assembled in British waters in peacetime.

It was as if the season's-end carnival week lasted all through that brilliant summer. Strings of red, white and blue flags fluttered above Ryde's hilly streets and the lights along the Esplanade burgeoned into loyal crowns and fleurs-de-lys. The most extravagant patriotic gesture came from Teddy Hoare, owner of the Ryde Castle Hotel (or, as he styled it, 'Hotel Ryde Castle'), a battlemented, ivy-covered pseudo-château opposite the Eastern Gardens. Mr Hoare was a local showman to eclipse even Alfie Vernon; a tiny, pink-faced man who had a wife only half his age, and drove around in a silver Buick convertible as long as a bus. Under his aegis, the Hotel Ryde Castle became a miniature Buckingham Palace with a squad of outsize papier-mâché Grenadier Guardsmen stationed along its sea-facing ramparts.

Amid all the optimistic bustle, I watched my parents' relationship decline to its lowest point ever. Previously, though they had had terrible rows, there were often recovery moments, when my father would take my mother on his knee – her face often still bruised and swollen from the preceding phase – or when he'd make affectionate jokes about the way her bottom wagged from side to side when she walked. But now there were no more spontaneous pettings or jocular references to 'the old bottom'. When not shouting or screaming at each other, they communicated in the same brusque, flat tone as if grudging even this small expenditure of words.

In former times, their rows would sometimes involve me: 'Don't go on like that in front of Phil . . .' 'Don't *you* go on like that in front of Phil.' Once, at our old High Street flat, they even physically fought over me, my father pulling me by the left arm, my mother by the right. He was stronger, of course, wrenching me away from her and hustling me downstairs and into his old Wolseley limousine to carry me off to the Pavilion. Half-way along the pier I began to cry – I remember the scarlet train off to the right with its melting steam, and the seagulls perched on the hooped boundary railings. My tears so disgusted him ('Grrr!') that when we reached the pier-head he hustled me straight into the phonebox by the ferry ticket-barrier and dialled our flat, Ryde 3113. 'All right, Irene,' he said before my mother even had a chance to speak. '*You* win!' But I knew their contest hadn't really been about me, and that I certainly was no prize.

For as long as I could remember, I'd had the ability to shut myself away in my own private world of drawing and military uniforms, creating voices inside my own head to drown out the angry or distressed or drunken ones from other rooms. My parents' mutual dislike and contempt had been the normal state of things for so long that I felt almost surprised if ever

I saw another boy's parents treating each other with affection or politeness. My response – and how I regret it now! – was to try to be as little trouble as possible. When my school held summer sports or open days, we had to take the invitations home by hand. I never bothered to give my parents theirs, knowing in advance that they'd be too busy to attend. When I was cast in the end-of-term operetta as Solfarino, Master of the King's Music, I assumed without even asking that it would be too burdensome for my mother to make me the doublet-and-hose costume that was required. So, in a portent of things soon to come, I kept staying away from school with pretended illnesses until another boy was given the role in my place.

In a wider context, too, my family life presented the sharpest possible contrast with pre-Coronation euphoria. The rift between my father and Uncle Phil that had opened up the previous autumn remained still unresolved. After almost eight months, no one else in the family, not even – or, I should say, especially not – their respective wives had any idea what it was about, nor even exactly where and in what circumstances it had taken place. Though still joined together in business, the brothers did not speak nor communicate in any way. Uncle Phil confined himself to the Star Hotel at the top of town, sulking like a portly Achilles in his tent, while my father selflessly continued 'helping' him at the pier-head. Even Grandma Norman's arrival to reopen the Kiosk at Whitsun, and her prayerful pleas for love and harmony between her 'boys', had been unable to effect any reconciliation.

Our side of the family and Uncle Phil's, as a result, continued to be as grimly and uncomprehendingly divided as West and East Berlin. Under the law of unquestioning loyalty imposed by their spouses, my mother and Auntie Lorna, the former best friends, could no longer associate nor lend each other the little moral support they once had. I could no longer go and play with Dina and Roger, nor have them to play with me. Loyalty in my father's definition required more than simply not talking to Uncle Phil and his family; it meant ceasing to acknowledge their very existence. If I saw Auntie Lorna or Dina around town, I'd look the other way, making my eyes film over like a toad's. Once when I saw Uncle Phil approaching, he deliberately crossed the road to avoid me.

Without Dina and Roger, my life outside school hours became an even more solitary one. My closest to a best friend was Bobby Greenham, a darkly sunburnt boy with brilliant white teeth, whose parents kept the newspaper shop at the bottom of Union Street. My main appeal for Bobby, I knew, was my ability to get on to the pier without paying its three-penny toll. He would follow me through the turnstiles and down the half-mile of planks and, on seeing my father, begin to raise his school cap furiously. This evidence of old-world courtesy, in my father's eyes, always produced rewards in the form of cakes or pennies or free goes on the rifle-range.

Sometimes I would be asked to tea with Bobby, his older sister Stephanie and his younger brother David, whom the others by a common oddity of pronunciation called 'Davit'. Their flat, below and above the paper shop, was so small that they had to bath in the kitchen sink. As we went in through the shop, Bobby and Davit would grab a handful of new comics from the counter, then sprawl on the back staircase to read them, forgetting my existence altogether. Tea was in a subterranean living-room with a high barred window, beyond which the lightly-shod feet of holidaymakers shuffled cease-lessly to and fro. As soon as we sat down, Bobby and Davit would chorus to their mother: 'How many pieces of cake each?' 'How many Munchmallows?' 'How many biscuits?' When she told them, they would each grab their allotted portions and vanish from the table, leaving me there with only their black cat, Jezebel, for company.

On my first visit, I was unwise enough to confide in the two of them and their sister about how bad things were getting at home. Later, as we sat down to tea, Davit – who breathed heavily through his nose – turned to his mother and announced, 'Philip told us his mummy is very sad.'

'Davit . . . sshhh!' his sister Stephanie reproved him ostentatiously.

He gave her an injured look. 'What's the matter? I just said that Philip's mummy is very sad.'

'I don't want to hear about it anyway,' Mrs Greenham broke in.

'All I *said*,' Davit repeated with dogged self-righteousness, 'was that Philip's mummy is very sad.'

'I didn't say that,' I stammered, blushing. 'I meant that she's been working very hard and she gets tired and fed-up.'

'But that wasn't the only reason, was it?' Stephanie said, giving me a smile that, I'm sure, was intended to be bright with sympathy.

'I just meant she was tired . . .'

'But that wasn't the *only* reason, Philip, was it?' persisted Stephanie.

Bobby and Davit's stamping-ground was the Western, the small pleasure gardens at the foot of Union Street where we had our open-air skating rink. The beach beyond was the only part of Ryde's shoreline where incoming tides did not wash right up to the sea wall, but instead left a hummocky upper hillock of sand as powdery as the Sahara in which dog turds lurked like thickly-breaded cutlets. It was widely denounced as a risk to public health and, in fact, had taken a large share of blame for the recent child-polio epidemic and been fenced off for several months like a wartime minefield. It was nonetheless Ryde's most popular beach, every inch of its scorched, fetid, litter-covered dunes crammed with holidaymakers throughout every season. It was also where most of the town's traditional seashore amusements could be found – speedboat trips, pedalo rides, Punch and Judy, and the elderly busker in his ancient white suit and Panama hat who sang 'Shoes to Set My Feet a'Dancing' while scraping on a violin.

I sometimes roamed the Western and its beach with Bobby and Davit and a group of children whose families ran nearby guesthouses, cafés and shops. But we had little in common. Bobby's main occupation, one for which his rather distant brown eyes ideally fitted him, was patrolling the tideline, searching for money. Surprising amounts of it were washed up if you had the patience to look – pennies, three-penny-pieces, even the occasional sandy and green-mouldy half-crown. When the tide went out almost to the pier-head, exposing tracts of hard wet sand beyond the soft, Bobby and the others would fan out to play football or cricket or rounders or games of catch. My 'lazy' left eye had always made me incapable of taking any but the easiest catches, even if I wanted to. Bobby's circle called me 'Four-eyes' and did comic imitations of my pathetic under-arm throwing style.

At low tide, at the end of a concrete sewer-pipe, a rather haunted-looking man named Mr Eade gave donkey- and pony-rides in three or four trails of hoof-broken sand to a larger breakwater eighty or so yards to the west. He was helped by his wife, his son Jimmy and a group of girls of roughly my age who, in exchange for helping with children's donkey-rides, were sometimes allowed to gallop ponies across the sands. The girls wore tweed jackets and jodhpurs and carried riding-crops, and were the most enchanting creatures I'd ever seen in real life; their leaders were twin sisters, Jean and Janet Black.

Although twins, they were quite unalike in appearance. Janet was a dark-haired, exotic beauty who could galvanize even Bobby Greenham and make him forget his eternal beachcombing with the possibility that she 'liked' him. I felt sure she would like me, too, in my turn, despite my National Health glasses, and sought to impress her by using the long words I'd picked up from Billy Bunter and William books. Janet's response was to turn to the other donkey girls with a look of almost nauseated disbelief. 'He's mad,' she announced, pointing at me. '*Mad!*'

Jean had fair hair and slightly protuberant teeth, and seemed an altogether softer, more sympathetic character. At present, she liked a boy called John Jameson whose mother kept the Roseville private hotel, but I felt sure that, once she realized my qualities, she would transfer her affections to me. My daydreams about her, I now see, were coloured more by loneliness than by childish eroticism. I pictured us sharing a bedroom, as in some Enid Blyton story, and Jean's rather toothy face in the glow of an electric fire as she leaned down to switch it off for the night.

Where the pier met the sea wall, the soft sand drifted so high that one could climb up to the wooden cross-beams directly underneath the tramway station. I was up there one day, with Jean and Bobby Greenham seated side by side on the beam above mine. Jean's legs, in their jodhpurs and short rubber boots, dangled just above my head. She glanced down in response to something I'd said, then turned to Bobby with a quizzical frown. 'I think he must be a bit mad,' she said.

Bobby's white teeth flashed in the under-pier gloom. 'A *bit!*' he echoed sardonically.

*

CORONATION DAY, 3 June, came nearer and nearer. Out in the Solent the warships of all the world, awaiting review by our new young Queen, lay at anchor to east and west like faint grey eels as far as the eye could see. The Pavilion, half a mile from shore, commanded unrivalled views of the enormous flotilla. Temporarily forsaking his usual day-trippery, fish-and-chip milieu, my father devised an opulent Fleet Review Day package deal, which he advertised in local papers and even a couple of national ones. A grandstand seat in the upstairs restaurant or the sun-roof, plus a smoked salmon and champagne lunch, were offered for the (as it would prove) over-ambitious sum of £25 per head.

One could take 'Visit the Fleet' trips from the pier-head in Captain House's pleasure launch *The Wight Queen*, churning up and down the long avenues of exotically-flagged destroyers and minesweepers. Some of the foreign ships let you actually go on board for a few minutes to savour the whiff of strange tobaccos that hung around their decks and the outlandish toggles and pom-poms on their sailors' caps. They seemed to lie out there for weeks, obliterating the usual Solent view of tankers and liners and Portsmouth factory chimneys. Up on the non-public part of the Pavilion roof – close to where I'd seen my father with the auburn-headed woman – an artist sat at his easel, painting the misty spectacle in delicate brush-strokes of steel-grey and lifebelt-white. After dark, the lights of innumerable portholes and mastheads twinkled like a sea-borne metropolis.

As part of the celebrations, every schoolchild in Britain was to receive a silver spoon and a china mug bearing the likeness of the new Queen and the Duke of Edinburgh. My junior school, however, departed from this formula. Our headmistress, Miss Beavan, was an evangelical Christian who claimed to have had several private conversations with Jesus during a spell of missionary work in Palestine. Instead of Coronation mugs, thanks to Miss Beavan, we each received a copy of the Gospel According to St John, bound in pale blue paper covers and stamped 'E.R.'. A boy in my class named Tony Child unleashed hoots of laughter for thinking the initials stood for 'Elizabeth Rex'.

On 2 June came news that a British-led expedition had conquered Mount Everest, the world's highest mountain, which climbers of all nations had been vainly attempting to scale for half a century past. That the first two to the summit were a New Zealander, Edmund Hillary, and his Nepalese Sherpa did not dilute the patriotic acclamation: New Zealand was sort of Britain, and the Sherpa's name, Tensing, sounded sort of British. Loyal images of Royal Standards and Horse Guards were joined by one of snow-encrusted men in goggles and hoods, descendants of Scott and Shackleton, claiming the earth's last unreachable place as the first New Elizabethan territory. Coming as it did with perfect timing on Coronation Eve, it seemed like a personal gift to the sovereign-to-be, affirming that the whole world now really did lie at her feet.

The evening before Coronation Day was one of very few I can remember when my mother's duties on the pier and at the Western skating-rink allowed her to take me home to Dunraven and put me to bed herself. As we passed the huge Gothic front door of Holy Trinity church in Dover Street, she suddenly stopped. 'I think we should go in,' she said, 'and say a little prayer for the Queen tomorrow.' She had never seemed in the least religious, and I remember thinking how serious all this must be to penetrate her usual unhappy self-absorption. So into the gloomy, empty church we went, and knelt in a pew for a few minutes. I had no idea what to pray since, as I have said, the Queen seemed to me pretty fortunate, her future, unlike mine, secure for ever. Whatever my mother prayed, she kept to herself.

On the day itself, as history remembers, loyal sunshine suddenly gave way to unremitting, humid rain. It fell impartially on the Queen's golden coach, threading its way in London to Westminster Abbey, on Ryde's seafront, the pier and the assembled world fleet. The hours of pageantry were televised by the BBC, even though only a few thousand people in the whole country owned television sets. The lucky ones who did invited friends and neighbours in to huddle around the flickering screen that was seldom larger than sixteen inches square and glowed blue rather than black-and-white.

We did not own a set, which seemed irrelevant, anyway, since Coronation Day was the busiest I ever remember at Ryde pier-head. We spent a normal morning there, my mother working behind the restaurant cash-desk, I patrolling the sea perimeters with a large Union Jack which my father found backstage and gave me. After lunch, he magnanimously allowed us to go on shore and watch the BBC coverage with Mr and Mrs Dorley Brown, their three sons and various neighbours at their small but chic flat in Castle Street. In the endless, rainy procession of soldiers, sailors and foreign dignitaries, the new Queen was somehow the least noticeable figure, smiling diffidently from within the gold encrustations of her State Coach. The day found an unexpected star in Queen Salote of Tonga, who rode through the downpour smiling and waving from an open carriage, so inspiring another Edmundo Ros calypso:

> The Queen of Tonga
> Came to Britain from far away.
> Oh, the Queen of Tonga

Came to Britain on Cor-on-ation Day.
Happy Coronation, ding-dong-ding!
Happy celebration, ding-dong-ding!

I remember how her bulk and oriental-eyed looks and broad smile, together with the rather shabby-looking mackintosh she wore, put me in mind of Grandma Norman and made me like her even more. (The real Grandma Norman worked on at the Kiosk until closing time without even a radio, loath to sacrifice any opportunity to shift more rock.)

*

WHAT CAME NEXT that flag-waving, jubilant summer is easily explicable in terms of modern child psychology. Any child-therapist, I guess, would agree that I was subconsciously trying to win my parents' attention and re-bond their disintegrating relationship in a mutual concern for me. Unfortunately child-therapists were not thick on the ground in 1953, especially not in seaside catering circles on the Isle of Wight. Nobody had the least clue what I was up to, least of all myself.

Judge of my psychological condition that at ten years old I had two great ambitions: first to be old, second to be ill. Becoming an invalid seemed the perfect answer both to the insecurities of my home life and all the multitudinous things that worried me at school. I had been profoundly impressed by films I had seen about small boys with 'weak' hearts who were treated by all around them with reverential tenderness. Almost as pleasant, I thought, would be to have a disabled leg, like so many admired war heroes, and be obliged to hobble around on a stick. At my baby school, Partlands, the most loved and petted one among us was a little girl named Mary

Elderton who wore an iron brace around her foreshortened right leg. Mary Elderton became my role model.

To be old, with one's whole life behind one, seemed like utter heaven to me. Of course, I spent the most blissful times of my life with an old person, Grandma Norman, but that was just the start of it. Grandma Norman had always collected around her people of even greater antiquity than herself, who regarded her as a kind of deity much in the same way small children did. Back in the war, long before I could remember, she had living with her an old lady named Auntie Annie Pickard who used to think the barrage balloons moored above London had men inside them. The West Country, where she had spent her earlier years, harboured two more such figures whom she regularly visited and who occasionally came up to London to stay with her. Near Witney in Oxfordshire lived an immensely fat, rosy-faced woman named Auntie Annie Collins who had been nursemaid to my father and Uncle Phil during the First World War (and had also taken me as an evacuee towards the end of the Second). In Hungerford, Berkshire, lived her cousin Aunt May Chapman, a nervous old lady in a 1920s-ish black straw hat who was our link with the Showering family and Babycham.

Grandma Norman and these old ladies still had the Victorian habit of sharing the same bed without the least sexual query attaching to it. Since I always slept with her by inalienable right, this could mean crowded conditions between the sheets for me. Hugely fat (or 'stout' in the politer word), Auntie Annie Collins still maintained the demeanour of a servant, always addressing Grandma Norman scrupulously as 'Mrs Norman'. Yet each morning when she brought us tea, she'd climb in beside her old employer, her bulk pushing me further and further across the bed until I slipped over the opposite edge and lay suspended in a kind of hammock of tucked-in blankets. I also slept with Aunt May Chapman, minus her false teeth, in her long flannel nightie and pigtail, and, a few times, with Aunt May and Grandma Norman together. I smelt their liniments and poultices and surgical bandages and corn-plasters, heard them peeing with a hollow patter into chamberpots and emitting what Grandma Norman called 'rude below-noises'. I lay beside them or between them for hours, drinking tea and eating Rich Tea biscuits, and listening to the converse of their so-enviable world.

Old people didn't have to go to school or do long-division homework or endure PT lessons with aptly-named Mr Savage, who lashed you across the bare buttocks with a whistle on a white cord if you were the last to stand up or sit down or get undressed or dressed. All they had to do was laze around all day in their slippers in front of warm fires, pouring tea from pots with woollen cosies, eating sweets, complaining how cold it was, or how unseasonably mild, and exchanging their endless stories about friendly-sounding ailments like rheumatism and arthritis.

Even in her summers at the Kiosk, Grandma Norman somehow managed to collect her circle of subordinate older ladies around her. During her afternoon rest-periods among the piled-up rock-boxes in the back room, she received visits from a Mrs Proctor, a quavery little woman with yellow-streaked grey hair who did odds and ends of sewing work for her. She would sit Mrs Proctor ceremonially down on the wooden stool that had the fold-out step-ladder, make her Twining's Nectar tea on the tiny gas-ring and feed her chocolate or Cadbury's Snack biscuits. Mrs Proctor supplemented her seamstress work by acting as live-in nurse to an elderly man, whom she was always complaining about in a rich, quavery voice. 'There's never any froth on Fred's water,'

I heard her confide to Grandma Norman one afternoon. I had no idea if she meant the kind of water you washed with or the kind you found in chamberpots.

There was also Miss Ball, a figure destined to exert baleful influence over Grandma Norman's future domestic arrangements, but at this point just the latest and most bizarre-looking of her foundlings. Miss Ball came from Portsmouth but owned various properties in Ryde, including a café in Castle Street where we sometimes went for tea after open-air skating sessions. She had wild, frizzy hair, a soulful, beaky face and a barrel-shaped body that was always wrapped in the same dusty calf-length black coat. Behind her on a lead she trailed a poodle of the same dusty hue as herself named Monty.

Her flutingly genteel voice was of special appeal to Grandma Norman, who always relished the idea of highly born people in reduced circumstances. The oddest thing about Miss Ball was her connection with a number of Hungarian men, all much younger than herself and mysteriously dependent on her, who dogged her regular journeys from Portsmouth to Ryde and back again. 'There was another of those Hungarians waiting for her out on the Esplanade first thing this morning when she came off the boat,' Grandma Norman would report. 'Poor man, he'd got nowhere to go, so he'd had to sleep the night in a hen-house.'

Miss Ball spent the longest time with her, back among the rock-boxes, sometimes talking, sometimes staring into space in her soulful way while Monty the poodle rootled about noisily underfoot. This soulful expression never faltered, even when she reached out to take the last Cadbury's chocolate finger in the packet.

Whatever my subconscious plotting, the whole thing started purely by accident. A week or two after the Coronation there dawned a Monday morning which found me in dread of something at school: a PT class or house-badge inspection, I forget exactly what. So I decided to pretend I was ill. For want of anything that could be worked up into a symptom, I chose the old lady's favourite, cosy-sounding complaint of rheumatism. Fortunately, it happened to be one of those increasingly frequent times when my father was away from home. Without his sceptical eye to inhibit me, I put on a fine show, telling my mother in just the right key of wincing bravery that I had pains in both my legs. I remember settling in bed and looking out at the sunlit trees above Holy Trinity churchyard, exultant that I'd got away with it.

After a few days, I staged a convincing recovery, although not enough yet to go back to school. I gravitated to the Kiosk, there to enjoy the pleasures of convalescence in Grandma Norman's back room, listening to her hold forth to the confectionery and cigarette travellers and Mrs Proctor and Miss Ball, and eating crusty bread with Cheddar cheese and Branston pickle and ice-lollies and Fry's Tiffin bars and Lyons Mint Chocs and 'Maltesies'.

On about my fifth day, I was down on the Western beach near Eade's donkeys, sailing a clockwork boat in the pool at the end of the concrete sewer-pipe. To my surprise, I saw my mother coming towards me, slipping and stumbling on the hummocky soft sand. She wore her navy-blue woollen shirt with the white lateral stripes, and I was startled to realize that she'd been crying, something I'd never seen her do. She told me she'd been talking about me and my pains to Dr Sim, our family GP. He had said I must go back to bed immediately and stay there until he could examine me.

Dr Sim came that afternoon. He was a burly red-faced Scot with a knowing manner, and I supposed that the game must very soon be up. He made me take off my pyjama jacket, listened to my chest through his stethoscope, tapped me all over with large, warm fingers and asked me to describe the pains I was suffering. Drawing on bedtime memories of Grandma Norman and her old ladies, I said they occurred as sharp twinges in both my legs and, sometimes, in my right shoulder. Dr Sim left the room, spoke to my mother inaudibly in the hall, then returned and sat down on my bed again. I remember his grey bullet-head outlined against the sunlit trees, and the stupefaction with which I suddenly realized what he was saying.

'In hospital, you'll have a good time . . . There'll be a lot of other boys and girls your age . . . It's nothing to worry about . . .'

Nine

I WAS WRAPPED in a rug and taken by taxi to the Isle of Wight County Hospital, on the northern outskirts of Ryde. It was a place whose yellow-brick exterior I knew well, having passed it every morning on my walk from our old High Street flat to my former school, Partlands. On its extreme right was a domed glass roof which, I knew, marked the children's ward. As I dawdled by, I'd always look up at that dome and wonder what could be going on inside it. Now my curiosity was about to be satisfied.

Those fictitious leg, arm and shoulder pains had been convincing beyond my wildest dreams, but not, unfortunately, as rheumatism. Britain at the time was only two years on from a nationwide epidemic of polio, then known as 'infantile paralysis', which had left thousands of children of my age permanently crippled. Ryde had seen an especially virulent outbreak, allegedly incubated by the unwashed soft sand on its Western beach. What I intended to be rheumatics bore enough similarity to polio's early warning signs for Dr Sim to decide to take no chances. At the County Hospital I was X-rayed, blood-tested, then admitted for observation on 'complete bed-rest', meaning I couldn't get up at all. I was to be kept there for something like three months without once putting my foot on the ground.

Why didn't I just tell them it had all been a ruse to escape a school PT class? Things had gone much too far to start back-tracking now. Too many white-coated people were tapping my chest and listening to my heart through stethoscopes, and making me stand up against huge cream-coloured machines that felt cold against my bare ribs, and giving me little glasses of strange milky-tasting medicine to drink back in one gulp. Besides, every new procedure seemed to confirm there really was something wrong with me – not painfully or threateningly but in a pleasant, abstract way that made the white-coated people treat me with deferential tenderness and compliment me repeatedly for being 'brave' and 'good'. Everyone behaved as if I was ill, so I must be.

Initially I was put in the main children's ward, leading off the glass-domed part, which turned out to accommodate only the youngest, cot-bound patients. One of these, a boy aged about two, repeated in an incessant refrain, 'Mummy's coming... Mummy's coming... Mummy's coming in a minute...' I had to sit in a wheelchair while a bed was made ready for me and my mother returned to Dunraven to fetch my food ration-book. I divided my time between the only book I'd brought with me, *Billy Bunter's Benefit*, and an affectedly grown-up scrutiny of the ward's Victorian architecture. 'Nurse,' I heard a girl's voice say from a nearby bed, 'I think that boy must be a bit cracked.'

My first night was a nightmare. I had no idea what people on complete bed-rest did about sanitation, and was too embarrassed to ask. I read and re-read *Billy Bunter's Benefit*, trying to lose myself in its descriptions of study feasts at Greyfriars school until twilight swallowed up the print. As darkness set in, the growing simultaneous pressure on my bowels and bladder drove me out from between the sheets and further and further up my pillow until I was clinging to the iron bedhead like a flood victim waiting to be rescued by helicopter. Finally, a nurse noticed me and asked, 'Do you want a bottle? Or a bedpan?' Numb with shame, I put in an order for both simultaneously.

Later that night, I awoke to find a group of nurses standing around the foot of my bed. 'Philip Norman,' one of them murmured, showing my chart to her colleagues. 'Admitted today . . .' And I thought I heard her add, 'Acute rheumatism . . .' I drifted back to sleep with a feeling of quiet exaltation.

From then on, things went beautifully. I felt fortunate in comparison with boys and girls in adjacent beds, most of whom seemed to be recovering from something called 'a cute appendicitis'. Unlike them, I didn't have to have stitches taken out of my side or glucose drips attached to needles in my arm or humiliating injections in my backside. My only ordeal was a daily blood test that, over the weeks, would make the vein in my left arm-joint thicken into cloudy turquoise. I became friends with a bespectacled boy named Brian Trot and a bird-like girl named Hazel Slarke from Bromley, Kent – she who had loudly opined on my arrival that I 'must be a bit cracked'. All day and far into each night, the piteous little voice from the glass-domed end kept up its cry of: 'Mummy's coming . . . Mummy's coming in a minute . . .'

After a couple of weeks, I was moved from the main ward into a side room containing three beds, all unoccupied. The one allotted to me stood in a wide bay window with chequered panes, looking out on to the hospital's casualty entrance. By that time, thanks to its tenacious harvesting and analysis of my blood, the hospital had succeeded in finding something wrong with me. According to my mother, the 'count' of red and white corpuscles in my blood showed an unbalance, so they had to go on keeping me under observation. It seemed that I'd hit on the ideal malady, far better than rheumatism or a weak heart, in its combination of piteousness, painlessness and lack of disagreeable remedies. Each morning when the needle pricked that heightened blue vein in my arm, and yet more of my blood was siphoned into a minute bottle, I prayed that the magical discrepancy still wouldn't have gone away.

The ward's other two beds remained unoccupied except during late-night emergencies, when I'd awaken to bright light and a sound of screaming as some new arrival's broken arm or leg was set. But mostly I enjoyed blissful solitude, waited on hand and foot and treated like a celebrity. One day, Brian Trot from the main ward was ushered in to see me, wearing a brown plaid dressing-gown and carrying a banana. I was touched to think he'd brought me a gift, but as soon as he sat down beside me he started eating it himself.

Week followed sun-drenched week, and still they took my blood, wrote things on my chart and ordered that I should continue on 'complete bed-rest'. Hospital routine became second nature – the dawn awakenings with a bowl of hot water and a towel, the meals at impossibly early hours, the background noise of clashing trolleys, thick-soled shoes squeaking on lino, and curtains quickly drawn round a bed where something bad was about to happen; the blue-rimmed enamel bowls and acrid red mouthwash, the over-boiled cabbage, the stiff-yolked fried eggs, the pale slivers of fruit cake and almost tasteless orange juice. I grew nonchalantly adept at bedpans and blanket-baths, and learned to tell a first-year nurse (pink-and-white striped blouse) from a staff-nurse (black belt) and a sister (dark blue piped in white).

No one suggested I should keep up with my schoolwork,

so I spent hour after hour contentedly drawing. The nurses, orderlies and cleaners admired my pictures and laughed at the long words I used, nicknaming me 'the Professor' because of my glasses, and agreeing I was a 'caution' and a 'character'. The ward had a store of communal toys from which I was given a stuffed pug-dog made in Victorian times that today would doubtless fetch a fortune at Sotheby's. I remember lying with it on my chest, drowsing back to sleep after my early-morning wash, as the sky flamed pink above the hospital's opposite wing. I can smell the dog's canvasy odour as I write, and see the wisps of woolly stuffing from long ago that leaked through its broken seams.

Being next to a bay window on the hospital's forecourt meant I could have visitors at any time of day, not just in the single prescribed hour between three and four each afternoon. My mother came most afternoons, bringing me books, fresh drawing materials and, once, a friction-operated toy battleship. My father came only a couple of times, never in company with my mother and never staying longer than a few minutes, though each time he brought me an astounding present – a 5 lb tin of Sharp's toffees (which had to be shared out among the whole ward), a clockwork naval launch, a Timpo 'Cattle Drive' with longhorn steers, outriders and a miniature chuck-wagon.

One day, to my amazement, Auntie Lorna and my two cousins, Dina and Roger, appeared at the open window in blatant disregard of the continuing feud between our two sides of the family. I was touched, appreciating what it cost – and could further cost – my vulnerable godmother thus to defy the convention of Norman wifely loyalty. I quite understood when she limited the visit to only a few minutes, winding and re-winding the green chiffon scarf around her damaged wrist and glancing nervously down the drive as if she expected Uncle Phil to materialize at any moment. Grandma Norman was too busy to leave the Kiosk (something I accepted without question), but she sent Uncle Wally to see me a number of times and also wrote to me regularly from her back room, adding so many kisses and o's for hugs that they had to ascend vertically up the right-hand margin. She would also send her love, and sweets, via taxi-drivers from the Esplanade rank who had to deliver people to the hospital or collect them. One taxi-man showed me how to fold a piece of paper into a lily. Another used to wink at me and say, 'Are you going to die? Or are you going tomorrow?'

My ringside view of the casualty entrance provided virtually non-stop entertainment. One day at dusk I saw a boy from my school, 'Monkey' Hinge, unloaded from an ambulance on to a stretcher, his simian lower jaw masked by a red blanket; a further victim of a cute appendicitis. Another time, a little Austin Seven car drew up and two brawny women in civilian clothes – volunteer workers of some kind – hauled a stricken elderly man from the back seat and threw him on to a trolley in such violent haste that, I swear, he bounced.

*

IN MID-SEPTEMBER, my blood-count finally returned to normal. No polio having materialized either, I was sent home – but with instructions that I should still be kept in bed. After two and a half months on complete bed-rest, I'd almost forgotten how to walk. Leaving the bright bustle of hospital and returning to our silent brown flat was an experience of the most unutterable dreariness. I pined for the nurses and sisters and ward orderlies, the early-morning washes, the thin fruitcake and flavourless orange juice, even the bottles and bedpans. I cried for my bay window overlooking the casualty ramp, and my pug-dog with his Victorian smell and leaky straw stuffing.

It was immediately plain that my 'illness' had not had the desired effect of bringing my parents back together. If anything, it had given them the opportunity to drift even further apart. I returned to Dunraven to find only my mother in residence, with Melody the cocker spaniel, Nigger the Labrador and Louis Armstrong the fickle Siamese cat. Every morning, she set off on her old black bicycle to help my father at the Pavilion, and every evening came home by herself. After he had closed the slot-machine arcade at six o'clock, his whereabouts were a mystery.

I spent the hours by myself lying on a divan in my parents' bedroom, which had French windows to a small concrete balcony overlooking the air-raid shelter. Our downstairs neighbour, Mrs Cass, cooked my lunch and brought it to me on a tray. At four o'clock, she also brought me my tea. I drew endless pictures, read Billy Bunter and *The Gambols Annual* and made desultory attempts at an enormous circular jigsaw puzzle showing the new Queen and her Consort set about by Grenadier Guardsmen, Life Guard trumpeters and red-robed peers. The Coronation sunshine was as strong as ever. Wasps and huge, fat bluebottles sailed in from the garden below. I made clubs of rolled-up newspaper and squashed them into yellowish blobs all over the balcony window-pane. Edmundo Ros's voice floated on the breeze, still singing, 'Oh, the Queen of Tonga . . .'

The flat's side door was left open all day, a common practice in that era before casual theft, murder, kidnapping and paedophilia became ubiquitous. One afternoon, as I was bent over my sketchpad, a woman I'd never seen before walked in and sat down on the chair beside my divan. She was very short, with curly iron-grey hair and a much-wrinkled brown face whose chin stuck out like Popeye the Sailor's and even seemed to have a few grey bristles growing on it. She wore a creased pale blue cardigan over a white nylon overall, and carried a bag from which knitting-wool protruded. 'Hello, son,' she said in a whiny Scottish accent, then took out the wool and two grey needles and began to knit in silence. After a moment, she looked up, met my puzzled gaze and smiled. 'Are you going to draw me a nice picture, son?' she asked.

Her name, it finally emerged, was Mrs Kennie. She was one of that season's employees at the Pier Pavilion's kitchen, but had been deputed by my father to come and keep me company in the daytime. As always with his decisions concerning my care and welfare, I was the very last to be told.

Mrs Kennie showed no curiosity whatever about me or the malady I was supposed to be suffering from. But, between the click of her knitting-needles, she told me all about herself. She told me she came from Glasgow and had only recently moved to the Island with her husband and five children. Her sons, Ron and George, were taxi-drivers on the Esplanade rank; her daughter, Gladys, worked as a waitress at the Harbour Café (run by the mother of my father's arch-enemy, Alfie Vernon). Her husband, from whom she was separated, lived with their eldest daughter, Grace, in Gunville, near Newport. She also had a son named Robert ('Raburrt') only a couple of years older than I, who shared her lodgings in nearby Monkton Street.

Mrs Kennie had been detailed to sit with me and that is what she did for hour after hour, endlessly knitting as I drew or read or slid one or other of my two Dinky Land Rovers up and down a tilted wooden tray, muttering race-track commentary under my breath. Sometimes she would describe the succession of terrible operations which, she said, had taken almost her whole stomach away, leaving her like this little shrunken brown leather purse with almost nothing inside it. She could invest post-operative vomiting with the melodrama of grand opera. 'Och, you shoulda' seen what came up that time . . . greet big lumps, the colour o' beetroot . . . That time when I come home, ma daughter Grace makes me a beautiful dinner . . . pork, roast potatoes, green peas . . .' She always said 'green peas', presumably so as not to confuse them with the orange or magenta kind. 'But as soon as I took it down, back it all came up again . . .'

To help the little invalid through these long daytime hours, my mother rented a television, a Ferguson model with a seventeen-inch screen and twin frontal knobs set in a strip of gold mesh. But it was an inconstant companion. The solitary black-and-white BBC channel usually did not begin service until mid-afternoon and there were frequent shutdowns, or 'interludes', when they killed time with film sequences of a clay pot being thrown on a wheel, or a punt-prow gliding somnambulistically through plantations of river reeds. Unless you lived within a couple of miles of the BBC's London transmitter, reception tended to be poor; on the Isle of Wight, it was atrocious. At regular intervals, the picture would collapse sideways into horizontal black and grey stripes, or flick downward in individual squares like frames of film. The only person we knew who could put it right was a taxi-driver from the Esplanade rank named Mr Stiles. We'd have to wait for hours, or even days, until Mr Stiles had time to drop by, in his peaked chauffeur's cap, and twiddle knobs until the picture stabilized again.

With the television's arrival, I ceased to be totally bedridden and became capable of the few brave steps from my parents' bedroom into the adjacent sitting-room, where I would lie on the big brocade Chesterfield sofa, covered with a rug. In the curtain-drawn twilight considered necessary for TV-viewing in those days, I watched all of what little was on – Test cricket, Russian ballet, the afternoon adventures of puppets like Andy Pandy, Mr Turnip and Bill and Ben the Flowerpot Men. I knew every note of the long drawn-out overture played as a sound track to the test card before transmission began. Beside me in the darkness watched Mrs Kennie, knitting-needles ever in play. 'Verra gude,' was her invariable judgement on everything.

After I had been 'convalescing' two or three further weeks, domestic life at Dunraven changed radically for the better. Grandma Norman and her companion Uncle Wally, that summer, had taken accommodation at a house called The Ferns, across Ryde in West Street. It was a deliberate decision of hers not to put up at the Star Hotel, as she had the previous year, to avoid any suspicion of favouring Uncle Phil. For the mysterious total estrangement of her two 'boys' still continued as unrelentingly as ever.

Uncle Wally had begun the season as her usual, uncomplaining consort, wearing his City gent's suit and grey Homburg hat on the hottest days, amusing himself on the Western and in adjoining bar-parlours while she went on coining it at the Kiosk. But he had now suddenly and uncharacteristically become the centre of attention by falling ill. Not seriously so, it appeared, but ill enough to need better rest and care than rented rooms could provide. So, to my unspeakable joy, it was arranged that Grandma Norman and he should spend what remained of the summer at Dunraven. Uncle Wally would have my bedroom with the green lino and Mickey Mouse washbasin; Grandma Norman and I would share the big back room overlooking the garden where my father had once tried to keep a barn owl.

She arrived with a cloth carrier-bag from which protruded a long white cardboard box. 'This is for you,' she announced, pulling it from among the pint Guinness bottles she intended to share with Uncle Wally and throwing it on to my rug-covered lap. Inside was a toy Winchester repeating rifle, the kind I'd dreamed about for months. 'Your Daddy sent it for you,' she explained. 'He says he's sorry he hasn't been to see you, but he's so busy down on that pier, poor lamb.'

For a blissful time we seemed to have returned to our old life, sharing the same bed again, talking together in the darkness I could stare at with fearlessly wide-open eyes as long as Grandma Norman was beside me. I picture myself lying in half-light and watching her undress after her return from another bonanza day down at the Kiosk. ('Took eighty pounds today, y'know.') She is over by the big, uncurtained left-hand window, with the faint sparkle of the Esplanade pricking the darkness behind her. She has already taken off her nylon overall, grey flannel skirt and blouse and big, lace-up corset, and now pulls down the elasticated waist of her pink bloomers to scratch the small of her back and her bare upper bottom with the pointed handle of her comb. Earlier this evening, I fell in love with a woman named Hélène Cordet as she learned how to paint highlights in a television art programme. Adoration of Hélène Cordet and relief to be with Grandma Norman again fills me to the brim.

*

TO GIVE FURTHER ZEST to this sudden upswing, the government announced the end of sweet-rationing. It was goodbye for ever to dreary ration-books and price tags reading 'Six-pence and only one point'. Grandma Norman brought home a *Daily Mirror* whose front page showed a little girl gnaw-ing at a vast chocolate bar – a prophecy, as I realized, of still greater business for the Kiosk. The Mars company hastily rushed out an advertisement featuring their best-known celebrity fan, the musical comedy star Sally-Anne Howes. In the previous, ration-era one, she used to say, 'I buy Mars every week because Mars are marvellous.' In the new one she said, 'Now I can buy Mars every day. Isn't that marvellous!'

Uncle Wally became my co-convalescent, sitting around the flat all day, as undemandingly as ever, in his collarless shirt and plaid-trimmed dressing-gown. Two or three times a week, Dr Sim came to see him with apparatus for measuring blood-pressure, apparently the cause of the trouble. Mrs Cass, from downstairs, cooked his lunch as well as mine, and he evidently found her pink-centred kidneys and metallic-tasting gravy as unpalatable as I did. When I crept into the kitchenette to scrape my uneaten portion into the bin under the sink, I'd usually find Uncle Wally had been there ahead of me.

Blood pressure seemed as pleasantly vague an old person's malady as rheumatism and arthritis, producing no discernible symptoms in Uncle Wally beyond cheeks that looked slightly ruddier than usual, and the occasional testy sigh of 'Lord LuvaDUCK!' But then, all of a sudden, for no reason I could see, he was said to have got much worse. Grandma Norman's concern was such that she decided to close the Kiosk for the winter several weeks before its appointed time – when she had as yet sold not quite her seasonal rock-quota of sixteen tons – and take him back for treatment by his own doctor in London.

I had the familiar aching hole in my heart after she and Uncle Wally had gone; my single bed had been made up in my own room again, and I lay on the couch in Dunraven's sitting-room with my mother beside me, drinking tea from a green china cup. I suddenly realized she was looking at me in a way that seemed half nervous, half ashamed, and starting to tell me something in the hypothetical manner grown-ups always used whenever the matter was very serious.

'What would you say . . . if you knew Mummy was going to have another little boy or girl . . . if you were going to have a brother or sister . . .?'

So much for my masterly stratagem to win my parents' attention.

*

LIKE THE overwhelming majority of ten-year-old boys in 1953, I had no idea what caused babies. Prior to this stupefying revelation I had asked my mother about it only once and in a spirit of no very serious inquiry; she'd told me it was something that happened 'when two people love each other very much'. Grandma Norman, to whom I had put the same question in her back room at the Kiosk, was even less explicit, resorting to the biblical imagery of her own Victorian childhood. 'The seed of Woman,' she began portentously, 'is in Man . . .' At that point, a query from Maria about the price of half-pounds of Quality Street had terminated the discussion.

Certainly, for as long as I could remember, my parents had shown few signs of loving each other, even a little. But I vaguely knew about something else that happened between them – something to do with bed and late nights after they'd been out to a pub or club, when I'd find them covered by just a sheet with their legs intimately knotted up but their faces antagonistic, even in sleep. I called it 'stale fish' to myself because of the strong accompanying odour. The rows and struggles of recent years seemed more or less to have put an end to stale fish, but I somehow divined that it had materialized again while I was away in hospital – possibly even encouraged by my absence.

I turned the prospect over and over in my mind, not hurt or angry, just numbly incredulous. In ten years of being an only child, I'd often wondered how it would be to have a brother or sister, always deciding that I'd prefer a sister. But in all that time, it had never seemed even remotely possible. Having one child seemed enough, in fact rather more than enough, for my parents to manage. My mother had lately turned forty; an age which in those days, for middle-class women at least, was considered well beyond childbearing. My first coherent thought was how horribly embarrassing it all promised to be.

For all these months, she had never shown any unhappiness in front of me. But suddenly it all burst out. The day after our 'What would you say?' conversation, I went into the room where she now slept alone to find her on the bed, curled around our old black telephone, crying hysterically, 'Come back, Clive! Come back, Clive! Come back!' From the receiver I could hear my father's voice in the same dull, patient tone he used in his pier-head broadcasts. It was the worst crying I'd ever seen, a terrible, deaf, crazy-faced blend of sobbing, laughing and praying: 'Come back, Clive! Come back, Clive! Come back! . . .' I began to cry myself. 'Let me speak to him,' I pleaded, though God only knew what I'd have found to say. But she didn't seem to hear me or even see me. She was wrapped in a cocoon of grief in which no one could touch her.

Later that evening, dry-eyed and composed again, she formally confirmed what I'd so long suspected: that my father had run away with someone, but this time wouldn't be coming back. 'Who is it?' I asked, despite already knowing the answer. I remember the seeming eternity of that moment in our big, cheerless sitting-room in the autumn twilight; the uneven black floorboards, the walnut linen-press, the motionless mass of trees outside that seemed to draw my eyes into them as I waited for the inevitable. 'It's Joan,' my mother said.

To my surprise, she did not seem to blame him at all. 'It

wasn't his fault, Phil,' she told me earnestly. 'That woman kept on at him for months and months to go off with her. She just wouldn't leave him alone ...' Remembering Joan's shy taciturnity and my father's past record in 'running after' other women, I doubted whether things could have happened quite as she described. But there was comfort for both of us in believing he hadn't really wanted to do what he'd done, and had tried his hardest not to.

'What's happened to George?' I asked, thinking of the big blond barman who'd been Joan's husband in all but name.

'George has gone,' my mother replied.

I remembered the other item of news from the past twenty-four hours that had seemed monumental enough on its own.

'What about the baby?' I said.

'He doesn't care about the baby. He's decided he wants to be with Joan and that's all there is to it.'

The way she described it, my father did not seem a culpable or contemptible figure but, rather, a vaguely noble one, struggling against forces beyond his control. 'Of course, it's all had a lot to do with that mother of Joan's, old Mrs Salsbury. Daddy's had Joan on one side going on at him to run off with her and Mrs Salsbury on the other saying "What are you going to about my daughter?" In the end, the poor man couldn't help himself.' I remembered with a surge of hatred the woman with the daffodil-shaped mouth who'd told me off, that long-ago night at our open-air rink. Along with sympathy for my father I felt a touch of admiration for the way he'd faced up to his responsibilities to the Salsburys.

'I once saw something terrible,' I blurted out. And I told her how I'd stumbled on him and the auburn-headed woman together on that remote Pavilion sun-deck, long before Joan had even appeared on the scene. The secret I'd guiltily nurtured all this time seemed to cause my mother little surprise. 'Yes,' she said thoughtfully. 'I think I may have seen that as well.'

We were closer than for a long time, almost cosy together as we discussed our common rejection. Because there was no one else to tell, my mother told me everything she'd been through during these weeks while I was playing the invalid. She told me how my father had at first proposed not to leave home, but to spend weekdays with Joan and weekends with us. She told me of the sympathy he'd expressed to her which, somehow, seemed even worse than his physical violence – how he'd said he felt sorry for her because at her age no other man would even look at her. She told me how he'd accused her of getting pregnant deliberately just to spoil his life, how it had made no difference to his plans to go off with Joan, how he'd initially even tried to claim he wasn't the baby's father.

I can't say I was traumatized by the thought of our home breaking up. It had been coming for so long – and, anyway, little enough remained to be broken. My father had been out of my life for so long, I'd almost forgotten what he looked like. I wondered what would become of me, but in a dull, incurious way, knowing how utterly powerless I was to influence it.

As things turned out, he had not left Dunraven for good – far from it. He returned after a week or so, to pick up some clothes from the maplewood wardrobe he called his 'compactum'. I remember how overjoyed his old gundog was to see him, and how I wished I could have been an uninvolved dog or cat at that moment, rather than myself. He talked to my mother in their bedroom, in an undertone that sounded angry and bored at the same time, but to me uttered not a word of explanation or regret. Later, I entered the sitting-room to find him seated in the armchair, so like a clean-cut film star, so especially like Humphrey Bogart with his pale, soulful face and cupid's-bow mouth and wavy peak of dark hair. His right-hand fingers were tapping on the chintz arm in the way I remembered so well. He seemed to be wrestling with some abstruse moral problem that had nothing to do with these present events and, certainly, nothing to do with me.

I took all my courage and went up to him. 'Won't you come back to us, Dad?' I said, feeling how weak and useless were the words even as they left my mouth.

'Mind your own business, Philip,' he answered tonelessly.

I went into my bedroom and lay down on the green lino floor beside the toy soldiers I always kept set out there. Through my window, the trees over Trinity churchyard hung in showers of gold and green that rustled gently in a feather-light breeze. It was still lovely Coronation weather.

Ten

I THOUGHT IT WAS all over there and then – my parents' marriage, life at Dunraven, perhaps even life on the Isle of Wight. But I was wrong. For almost a year to come, my mother and I were to be left stranded at this apparent breaking-point, each both dreading and yearning for the final blow that would put us out of our misery, or at least unquestionably into it. Until almost the end of the dead-end year 1954, we were a family falling apart in freeze-frame.

If my father suffered any pains of conscience about what he was doing, he never showed them, To be sure, the only restraints holding him back until now seemed to have been purely business ones. With the summer season over, Coronation mania finally dying down and the massed navies of the world gone from Spithead, nothing remained to prevent his running away with Joan literally as well as metaphorically. Soon after his brief reappearance at Dunraven, he locked up the Pavilion and caught a ferry with Joan for the mainland, leaving my mother to face pregnancy as best she could and – so far as I know – without so much as a backward glance at me.

The two of us continued to live at Dunraven, she as utterly mystified as I was about where he had gone, how long he would be away, whether or not he intended to return for the birth of his new baby and what his intentions then might be, assuming that he had any at all. In the newspapers of that time there used to be an advertisement by the Anti-Vivisection League showing a dog, a cat and other defenceless animals huddled together in terror as the cruel vivisectioner's shadow loomed over them. It always made me think of my mother and myself in that gloomy house, with our two dogs and Siamese cat, waiting as unresistingly for our own *coup de grâce*.

We were not left entirely on our own. For we still had Mrs Kennie, the bristly-chinned little Glasgwegian woman who had originally been sent from the Pavilion as a sickroom companion for me. She now came in every day to help my mother around the house and tend to me in my still-ongoing convalescence. The understanding was that when the baby arrived, around next February, if circumstances still remained as at present, Mrs Kennie would become its nursemaid.

I watched my mother's pregnancy advance with a mixture of concern and distaste. Even at the best of times, she had been fiercely discouraged from taking any special care with her clothes and grooming. In her present devastated state, she could hardly have been expected to try to make the best of herself, especially when her main audience was only a ten-year-old boy. Yet I found I desperately minded both the physical changes in her and the little effort she made to minimize them. By an unfortunate coincidence, her friend Mrs Bailey from the Royal Esplanade Hotel, who was six or seven years her junior, had fallen pregnant at almost exactly the same moment she had. Mrs Bailey was seen around town in a range of chic sack dresses, her golden hair perfectly done, glowing with health and happiness. My mother, by contrast, wore the same blue polka-dot smock and grey pleated skirt day in and day out, and seldom bothered to put on any make-up. I felt angry with her for not being slim any more, not being well-dressed, not being pretty, not being pleased.

With her better-off friends, like Mrs Bailey and the Dorley Browns, she affected light-heartedness and flippancy. She had read in some magazine that the film actress Jean Simmons was also expecting a baby and that, whatever its gender, it was to be called Tracy, a name then virtually unknown in Britain. My mother announced that if our new baby was a girl, she would be called Tracey Irene Hanham Norman. Hanham was Grandma Norman's family name – but, my mother made it clear, no tribute to her was intended. 'It's so that when the baby grows up to be a famous novelist, she can call herself Tracey Hanham Norman.' Lucky baby, I thought, to have its future assured as 'a famous novelist' before even being born.

But when the two of us were by ourselves, she never bothered to put on any cheerful front. There were times when I could hardly bear to look at her, with her lump swelling ever more uncontrollably under the polka-dot smock and her face sweaty and exhausted, lighting one Senior Service, stubbing it out barely half-smoked, then lighting another. After those initial moments of confidence, she seldom mentioned the thing that hung over us both. She kept her misery to herself, sleeping and crying alone in the bedroom with the concrete balcony, the mock Louis XIV chair and my father's 'compactum'. I was not the sort of boy who could crawl in there with her, cling to her and find the small comfort of shared grief.

She made intermittent efforts to tell me I shouldn't feel threatened by the baby; that both she and 'Daddy' – so she still rather tenderly referred to him – would still go on loving me 'as much as we always have'. Another moment of closeness came during one of the newly arrived dark evenings as we walked home together arm-in-arm from the Commodore cinema, down Star Street and along Dover Street, past the dimly lit porch of Holy Trinity church. The smell of wet leaves and bonfires was in the air – a smell that for evermore would fill me with dread. 'After the baby's born, we can still go out together, just you and I, can't we?' she said in an almost pleading way, squeezing my arm. I agreed fervently, even though I couldn't imagine in what circumstances or surroundings we might be doing it.

As much as I resented and dreaded the baby, I also worried on its behalf. The one thing I knew about babies was that they cost money. My extensive study of *Woman* and *Woman's Own* magazines and Dreft soap powder advertisements had taught me what a multiplicity of things were needed for their upkeep – prams, carry-cots, rattles, above all piles and piles of miniature garments in downy fresh wool. A fragment of song-lyric kept repeating uneasily in my head – 'as soft and as pink as a nurser-ee'. What hope had our drab brown rooms of metamorphosing into anything like that? I knew that my mother was already running short of money and having to sell bits of furniture to keep us going. One particular week, she had only a single pound note in her purse, which she referred to, with unconvincing gaiety, as '*the* pound'. During one of Dr Sim's visits, I overheard her telling him she had no idea how she would support a little baby all on her own like this. 'The Lord will provide,' was his not very heartening response.

*

ALL THIS TIME, I continued to enjoy the status of poor little invalid. Medical science had failed to detect the slightest trace of polio; my blood corpuscles had resumed their normal balance months since. I was out of bed and leading an ostensibly normal life, ranging freely out of doors and playing on the beach. Yet, with Ryde School now well into a new autumn term, I continued to be marked absent.

Not that I was consciously faking or fantasizing. My original subterfuge to dodge school, nearly four months earlier, had all but faded from my memory. I sincerely believed myself to have passed through a grave illness, even though no symptoms had ever presented themselves and I remained still unsure precisely what the grown-up world believed my malady to have been. Mrs Kennie, and quite a few other people, thought I had been in hospital with rheumatic fever, which sounded even better than rheumatism, so I did not contradict them. To those my own age who asked what ailed me, I confided that I had 'a weak heart' with an air of quiet heroism.

How come neither of my parents ever had the slightest suspicion it was all moonshine? The answer is that, preoccupied with battling each other as they were, I had become the very last thing on their mind. Having me at home as a permanent invalid may even have been less trouble in some ways than having me back at school. Dimly I realized the irony of having started this whole masquerade to get them to love me more. I had succeeded only in making myself more unnoticeable than ever.

The thought of returning to school was now one almost too awful to contemplate. This new term after the long summer holiday had seen the transition of my class from the Junior to the Senior School, a terrifying place where rugby was played instead of soccer, where the curriculum widened to include Latin, algebra and geometry, where you had classes on Saturday morning as well as through the week, and where the slightest misdemeanour could earn you a beating from giant, blue-chinned prefects. I had convinced myself that, with all the work I had missed in the final Junior School term, I'd be held back in its comparative security for another year. Just before term began, a telephone call came from the school. Despite my long, and continuing, absence, they were letting me go up into the Senior School anyway. 'Oh yes, he'll be *thrilled*,' I heard my mother say in her la-di-da voice.

I was not reassured when my classmate and erstwhile friend Bobby Greenham came to tea and graphically described the various horrible initiations which awaited me – things called 'scrum-downs' in mud and freezing cold; the brutal Latin master known as 'Swill'; the new boy from Turkey whose name Bobby pronounced 'Belchie'. As I listened in dismay, he flashed his brilliant, unsympathetic smile. 'I expect you'll have tests galore when you come back,' he said.

I clung to illness as a last vestige of security in a world that seemed to be dissolving under my feet. When I saw TV programmes or read newspaper stories about girls and boys my age in wheelchairs or forced to use crutches or wear calipers, I envied them their unignorable claim on their families' attention and their right to stay away from school for ever if they liked. The wish I wished most often was to be back in hospital with the nurses, the bedpans, the Victorian stuffed animals and the bright, warm security of every day.

Life at Dunraven had suddenly become uncomfortably crowded. With a strangely parallel inopportuneness, my mother's cocker spaniel, Melody, gave birth to a litter of four puppies, sired by my father's old Labrador. Because of Melody's age, and the pelvic injury she'd suffered years earlier, the birth had to be by Caesarian and the puppies died one by one before they'd even had time to open their eyes. I buried each of them in a shoebox in the flats' communal back garden, standing by myself with my eyes also tight shut as I tried to think of suitable prayers.

Because Mrs Kennie worked such long hours for us, my mother gave permission for her youngest son, Robert, to have some of his meals with me. He proved to be a pale, puny twelve-year-old with a busby of black hair slabbed over his forehead, a wide, gummy smile and a voice that, surprisingly, bore no trace of his mother's Glasgwegian accent. He had a measured, portentous way of speaking, as if everything he described should be ranked as an eighth wonder of the world. He told me his eldest sister, Grace, was married to a Pole named Stefan, that the Polish for 'thank you' was something that sounded like 'gin queer', and that at his former school in Glasgow, some girls would invite you to kiss them and then, as you came close, drive their knee into your privates.

Our rented television set also made us a powerful magnet for other members of the Kennie family. In the evening, I would walk into our sitting-room to find it plunged into darkness and not only Mrs Kennie and Robert but also her grown-up sons, Ron and George, and her younger grown-up daughter, pony-tailed Gladys, all with their respective girl- and boyfriend, gathered around the screen in a blue drift of cigarette smoke as dense as a cinema's. Sometimes my mother would clear them out by saying she wanted the freedom to walk around the flat half-dressed, but by the following night they would all be back again.

At one such Kennie clan-gathering I joined, the figure on the screen was that of Lita Roza, a female vocalist then second in popularity only to Ruby Murray, performing her latest record-release, 'Little Things Mean a Lot'. The lyrics brought tears to my eyes, so perfectly did they express the aching lack in my mother's life that I knew myself unable to fill:

> Give her your hand when she's lost the way,
> Give her your shoulder to cry on.

Whether the day be bright or grey,
Give her your heart to rely on.

Through the smoke-wreathed darkness, I saw Mrs Kennie
nod approvingly to George or Ron or possibly Gladys.
'That's the most important thing,' she said. 'Givin' someone
your heart to rely on.'

*

BOTH OF my mother's parents, my Grandma and Grandad
Bassill, were still living; and that autumn, when there was still
no sign of my father and our financial plight worsened, she
had no choice but to turn to them for help. I accompanied her
up to London to spend a week with them, catching the boat
from the now deserted pier-head, taking the fast, hot train
from Portsmouth Harbour to Portsmouth Town, Haslemere,
Guildford, Woking and finally the huge glass hangar of
Waterloo, a journey always previously associated in my mind
with holidays and excitement.

Grandma and Grandad Bassill had always been somewhat
overshadowed by the stardom of Grandma Norman, but still
had plenty of colour and interest of their own. Grandma, tiny
and peppery, was a true London cockney, one of a family
of thirteen whose father, Alfred Skittrell, had been stage-
manager at Gatti's music-hall in Westminster Bridge Road.
Slender, quiet Grandad – full name Frank Augustus Bassill –
had spent forty years as a cameraman with the Pathé newsreel
company. He had been through both world wars as an official
cinematographer, travelled the world on assignment and met
leaders and statesmen from Winston Churchill to Mahatma
Gandhi. Thanks mainly to a munificent expense-account,
often paid in gold, he had raised himself into the aspirant
middle class, educating my mother and her younger brother,

Frank, at private schools, taking Grandma on cruises to Madeira and, once or twice, even to Royal Ascot.

In his mid-seventies, Grandad had developed gangrene in his right leg and had to have it amputated. He was just learning to walk with an artificial limb when the gangrene was found to have infected his left leg, and that had to come off as well. Although Grandma was also well into her seventies, she buckled down uncomplainingly to the task of caring for him, never seeking an iota of help from the state. These were the people of real character in my family.

Coincidentally, Grandma and Grandad also lived in Clapham, just across the Common from Grandma Norman. You caught the Northern Line to the same glass-domed Underground station, Clapham Common, to reach both their houses – walking round into the Old Town to Grandma Norman's in Lydon Road, or along the broad South Side to Grandma and Grandad's in Lynette Avenue. As my mother and I came out of the tube this time, I asked if we'd have time to go over and see Grandma Norman. '*No, we will not,*' she replied, angrily emphasizing every word. I divined that she held Grandma Norman in some way responsible for our present predicament, though I had no idea why, and was – of course – incapable of asking.

Grandma and Grandad's terraced house in Clapham South may not have provided the fun and fascination that Grandma Norman's did. But it gave a sense of security we had never needed more than at this moment. What a blessed relief it felt to be in their bright, warm back kitchen, with the plastic flowers and tea-cosies and napkin-rings, and Grandad seated at the table in his wheelchair (at his age, he was only allowed short artificial legs with rockers in place of feet), and Grandma out in her red-tiled scullery, cooking beans on toast for me and 'an 'erring' for my mother.

Nothing was said about my father, at least not in front of me, but Grandma Bassill's maternal indignation was obvious. On the kitchen mantelpiece she had always kept a wartime photograph of him and my mother, taken at an RAF station on the day 57 Squadron left for service in France. It was an especially good photograph of him, cap on the side of his head, feet apart, hands carelessly in pockets and pipe in mouth, his face split by his widest, dimpliest smile. This Grandma had now obliterated by wedging a small snapshot of Grandad into the upper right-hand corner of the frame.

She was fiercely loyal and supportive, but not always the soul of tact. For instance, she could not understand why my mother was not already furiously knitting jackets and bootees for the new baby – indeed, was almost consciously post-poning it by knitting a scarf for me in the Ryde School colours, blue, gold and red. 'All that stuff you ought to be getting ready and you're knitting Phil a scarf . . . it just doesn't seem to make sense, Renie.' She was also loudly disapproving of my mother's chain-smoking, not because of any harm it might do the baby but simply on grounds of waste. 'Renie's getting through at least forty fags a day,' I heard her tell Grandad. 'She hardly smokes half of one before she stubs it out and lights another.'

Since Grandad's second amputation, they had slept on the ground floor in what had formerly been their dining-room. The first floor was let to lodgers – a huge Irishwoman named Nancy and her emaciated husband, John, who worked as chief cellarman at a big West End hotel. He was always bringing bottles of whisky and gin home to Grandma, who steadfastly refused to believe he acquired them by any means other than totally honest ones.

My mother and I slept on the remote top floor, where a small pink bedroom led through to a larger green one. As always, I was given the pink outer room, whose white chest-of-drawers displayed a yellowing picture of Grandad in a top hat, filming the 1923 Wembley Exhibition. In the corner next to the wardrobe stood a huge metal cabin trunk plastered with labels from all the faraway places he had visited for Pathé News. The beds in this and the adjacent green room were positioned head-to-head. Through the half-open connecting door I could see my mother's bedside table and overflowing ashtray; and through the wall I could hear her crying.

Our predicament had naturally been explained to Grandma Bassill's cleaner, Mrs Coombs, a gaunt, genteel woman straight out of an Ealing film comedy who always kept on her 1920s-style cloche hat while she did the house-work. Mrs Coombs lived in Brixton, in a state of affronted horror at its growing black population; she would often declare that her house was 'the last oasis of respectability in Somerleyton Road'. One day as she was cleaning the stairs, she saw my mother, who had got up late, go along the first-floor corridor to the bathroom. Mistaking her expression of habitual dull misery for one of sudden anguish, Mrs Coombs gasped, 'What's the matter, dear?' threw down the dustpan and brush and tried to follow her into the bathroom just as she was shutting the door behind her. 'I actually trapped her old hatchet face in between the door and the upright,' my mother told me later, laughing despite herself.

The day before we returned to Ryde, Grandma Bassill took me into her 'best' front sitting-room, the one with the 1930s cocktail cabinet, the Magicoal fire and the hand-coloured photographs of cousin Fay and cousin Sylvia. 'When you were born,' she told me, 'I started putting money away for you every year on your birthday. It's built up to twenty-one pounds. But your Mummy's so hard up that she's asked me to give it to her, and I've said I will.' I assented without thinking. Sums of such huge magnitude had little meaning for me.

On the train journey back to Portsmouth, we sat in the dining-car. These used to be rather formal places with scarlet-jacketed stewards and snowy tablecloths: the menus were headed 'Tariff', and they always served Schweppes ginger beer in thick brown bottles with a perforated effect on the glass. My mother wore the only fur coat she'd ever possessed in my lifetime: an almost black one, beaver I think. I sat beside her, staring at our reflection in the brightly lit window, dreading what we were returning to, whatever it might be, and nestling against the glossy, dark fur just a little, so as not to risk annoying her.

*

THRE WAS ONE bright spot on my horizon, a single glowing thought to make it worthwhile getting up each morning and to cuddle to sleep with the shushing churchyard trees at night. Soon, the school term would end, meaning I couldn't be sent back for at least another four weeks. And in the second week of my unearned Christmas holidays, I was to return to London to stay with Grandma Norman. Everything that was so fractured and formless now would magically sort itself out, I felt certain, once I had made it back to her.

So, at last, here I was getting off the train for a second time underneath the Waterloo girders. And there, beyond the ticket-barrier – thank you, God – was the blessedly familiar tall figure in its big-checked coat and squashy green corduroy hat, its arms open wide to receive me. And – thank you, God, thank you, Jesus – here I was, running to be engulfed by her and to breathe again that divine scent of handbag-leather and peppermint and unwashed hair, and hear that voice full of West Country comfort tell me I was still her darling precious little bit of all right. Not until I'd almost reached her did I see that she wasn't alone. Next to her stood my father.

I emerged from the Grandma Norman hug and, reluctantly, turned to face him. But the hazel eyes that had seemed to look through me last time I met them were now full of kindliness. 'Hello, old son,' he said, and kissed me on the forehead with a rasp of his winter-cold face.

It was a moment for many questions, all deserving to be shouted rather than spoken. Where had he been all these weeks? Was he living in London now? Did he intend to come back to Ryde for the birth of his new baby? To divorce my mother? To marry Joan? Why? What? How? Most of all, how could he? It was not simply that I failed to put any of these burningly legitimate queries; I did not even think of asking them. Seeing him here, so strong and manly, in his tweed jacket with the leather elbow-patches, made inconceivable the thought that he could have done or be doing anything but right.

As we crossed the pigeon-fluttering station concourse to the Underground, I became conscious that there was something not quite as usual about Grandma Norman. The smile she smiled at me, while as adoring as ever, seemed to falter, somehow, at its edges. She moved at a pace far slower than her usual confident, slightly pigeon-toed stride; my father walked close beside her with an arm tightly linked in hers as if to stop her from stumbling. And, all too clearly, her mind was not focused on the time-honoured ritual of our Waterloo meetings. High on the wall near the exit was an enormous bas-relief figure of an early-nineteenth-century dandy in top hat and tasselled boots, striding along euphorically with a monocle held to his eye. He was the emblem of Johnnie Walker whisky, 'born 1824,' as the caption said, 'still going strong'. 'There's old Johnnie Walker,' Grandma Norman would always say, as if his smile was part of my welcome to London and her world. But today she passed beneath his dashing boot-heels without giving him a glance. I told myself that her preoccupation must be due to anxiety about Uncle Wally who – according to the last bulletin I'd heard – still suffered from not-very-serious-sounding blood pressure and had been taken into hospital in Wandsworth. One of our first ports of call, presumably, would be to visit him there. I pictured his ruddy complexion and grizzled moustache amid the cheery brightness of a hospital ward; lucky him.

'How's Uncle Wally?' I asked my father casually just after we'd arrived at Grandma Norman's house. His response was to put his arm around my shoulders and draw me out of her earshot. 'I'm very sorry to tell you this, old son,' he said, very softly, 'but Uncle Wally died.'

'Died?' I repeated blankly.

'He seemed to be doing well, he was sitting up and talking to the nurses,' my father said. 'But then he suddenly got worse. Nanny and I were with him at the end. He sent his love to you, and to Dina and Roger.'

In life, Uncle Wally had seemed the least compelling adjunct to Grandma Norman's existence. But his death had completely devastated her. Indeed, it seemed to have killed her, too – or, at least, killed the personality who in my eyes had only ever stood for towering strength. That night, as we sat around the supper table in her upstairs back kitchen, she began to cry. It was something I had never seen her do, and only imagined her doing in the pain of being separated from me. The slanting Queen of Tonga eyes no longer sparkled with humour and mischief, but screwed up tight in anguish; the deep-dimpled, rosy cheeks ran with tears; the rich West Country voice could only murmur brokenly as my father went over and put his arms around her.

I kissed her and said how sorry I was. But in truth, Uncle Wally's presence had always been such a slight one, you hardly noticed he was no longer around. I pictured him seated at this same green-baize-covered table in a shirt without a collar, emptying out shreds of tobacco from his day's cigarette-ends to be rolled into fresh cigarettes tomorrow. And the rare occasions when he would smile and sing that warbly little music-hall song of his, holding Grandma Norman's hands and swaying her arms to and fro: 'I think she likes me . . . I know she likes me . . . because she said so . . .' What concerned me far more, if I'm honest, was the extent to which her mourning for Uncle Wally would spoil my stay with her and dilute her concentration on me.

My father did not stay the night at her house, as I'd feared he might. At about 9.30, he said he had to go – not specifying where or to whom – but promised to return tomorrow. As he stood at the glass-paned kitchen door, Grandma Norman clung to him so tightly that he had gently to disengage her arms from around his neck. Would we still have our trad-itional jaunt up to the West End, I was wondering anxiously? And to the Natural History Museum, and Apsley House and Battersea Pleasure Gardens?

Even the safest place I knew, the enormous brass bed in which we always slept together, had lost its former power to exclude the rest of the world. Bliss had departed from the giant feather mattress that was so heavenly-soft, I could mould it into hills and valleys. For in the next feather valley, I could hear her softly crying for Uncle Wally again.

It seemed hardly right to intrude my problems on to hers. But:

'Gran?'

No answer.

'Gran?'

'What, loved one?'
'Have you heard about Dad and Mum?'
'I have,' her voice replied gravely.
'And about the baby?'
'Yes, I've heard about the baby.'
Another long pause.
'Gran, what's going to happen, do you think?'
'I can't tell you, love. I only hope and pray that everything will sort itself out.'

Then she said a prayer, the first I'd ever heard from her lips. Until that moment, Grandma Norman, for me, had always been at least as strong as Heaven. 'The grace of our Lord Jesus Christ, the love of God and the fellowship of the Holy Ghost be with us all, evermore . . . Amen.'

Over the following days, it seemed to me that the whole house wore a shroud of mourning. On the ground floor lived a couple named Mr and Mrs O'Halloran whose principal *raison d'être* was to care for the four cats that had come into Grandma Norman's possession over the years. Mrs O'Halloran, a little, wiry woman in a turban, shopped for their food in the Brixton arcades, filled the house with a permanent odour of boiling liver and heart, and periodically rent the air with wheedling cries of 'Toby! Toby, Toby, To-bee! Corky! Corky, Corky, Cor-kee! Amber! Amber, Amber, Am-ber! Judy! Judy, Judy, Jud-ee!'

Now Mrs O'Halloran crept around with a handkerchief pressed to her nose and cancelled all cat-cries out of respect for 'Mr Hall'. And Mr O'Halloran, a burly Irish glazier, sat beside their kitchen range and the saucepans of boiling liver and heart, shaking his cropped head in disbelief that things could come to such a pass.

It was as if the vitality had gone out of everything I had once found unique and exciting – the china cabinet full of long-nosed Staffordshire greyhounds, the framed sketches and watercolours by Chelsea artists Grandma Norman had known in the Roaring Twenties, the sea horses, sea cows and scrimshawed whale's tooth which Grandpa Norman had brought back from sea voyages before the Great War. Even my old friend the bear on iron wheels no longer went 'Ur' when I pulled the leather tab on his back, as if he had decided his more fitting role was that of funeral mute.

My father came every day from wherever he was living or staying, usually arriving at around noon and not leaving until early evening. He sat with Grandma Norman for hour after hour in the kitchen or in her seldom-used best sitting-room (next to Uncle Wally's old bedroom), talking quietly to her, stroking her hand with both of his, sometimes pushing a stray lock of grey hair off her forehead, almost as if he were the fond parent and she the distraught child. Several times he cooked lunch for the three of us, arranging Grandma Norman's on a tray with a napkin, some crustless bread and butter and a glass of Guinness, its restorative powers never needed more than now. I remembered the loving little boy she used to talk about, who selflessly cleaned the house and washed up for her when she was prostrated by one of her 'mugrains'. It charmed me to see him, as his gentle and tender side always charmed me. I never thought to wish he could give even a fraction of this same tenderness to his pregnant, demoralized wife.

For the first few days, my only clues to his metropolitan life away from Grandma Norman were his occasional references to television programmes he'd seen in pubs during the later evenings. '*What's My Line?* was very good last night . . . Then that Liberace came on . . . Ugh, he's such a nance . . . Makes you feel almost dirty to watch him . . .' But he never gave the pub's name or its location or mentioned if he'd been alone or accompanied. So far as one could tell, he was alone out there in the teeming city, drinking in pubs and staring up at wall-mounted television sets until duty called him back to his mother.

Then it suddenly emerged that he'd become one of the relief sorters whom the Post Office hired each December to deal with the huge extra volume of pre-Christmas mail. He was doing it, he said, 'to earn some extra money for Christmas'. I knew there was a tradition of people like students working for the Post Office at Christmas time. But it still struck me as a peculiar occupation for a former wing-commander, himself accustomed to employing dozens of people. I pictured him sorting letters, cards and parcels into pigeon-holes with his usual inimitable degree of care and precision, and the Post Office's management gradually real-izing what an exceptional find the season had brought them.

That explained, if only in abstract terms, why his nights seemed to be so crowded and full of incident while his days were left free for coming to Clapham Old Town and minis-tering to Grandma Norman. Wherever Joan was – if she really was there and if it really was Joan – she could not be accused of monopolizing him.

He was even at liberty to spend two separate whole days with Grandma Norman and me, accompanying us on our bus-trips up to the West End. Having what Grandma Norman called 'a mooch-round' the capital's major monuments and department stores, visiting news theatres, having Welsh rare-bits at Lyons' Corner Houses and eating ice-creams in the street, was the traditional high point of my stays with her. But this time, instead of enjoying it all as much as I did, she looked bleak and abstracted; a couple of times, she even burst out crying for Uncle Wally in public. It happened once in Picca-dilly Circus, as we waited to cross in a throng of shoppers opposite the giant neon signs for Wrigley's chewing-gum and Schweppes tonic water. I heard my father remonstrate with her almost in exasperation, his words swept away by the icy wind: 'You can't *do* it . . . Life's too *short*, Mother . . .'

As always happened, Grandma Norman's presence defused the terror and mystery of him for me. And being out in London with him, of course, meant presents. In Hamleys toy soldier department, my most unmissable port of call, he bought me a box of five Napoleonic lancers on stationary horses, with frothing black-and-white helmet plumes. When we emerged from Hamleys, my father pointed across Regent Street to the outsize letters FST and asked what I thought they stood for.

'First, second and third, Dad?' I suggested.

He shook his head – but I could tell he thought my guess not a bad one.

'No. It stands for Fifty Shilling Tailors.'

When at last Grandma Norman and I were alone in the big bed, I tried asking her where he went each night. Her reply was always the same: 'Your guess is as good as mine, love.' Of course she must have known; she was the one person on earth to whom he confided everything. I could only suppose that, with the trauma of Uncle Wally's loss, all these new political complexities were simply too much for her to think about.

She seemed positively to enjoy the illusion that my father had somehow become a bachelor again and that, for all the present sadness, they were re-recreating their relationship in his fancy-free years back in in the early thirties. She made a point of laying in all his favourite foods, like belly of pork, Gorgonzola cheese and pickled onions, in case he arrived before lunch or had time to stay to supper. She was always buying one-ounce tins of his pipe-tobacco, Log Cabin, and slipping them into my pocket for me to give to him. She spoke of him, not as an errant husband with a girlfriend shamefully concealed somewhere out there in London's mighty roar, but as a storm-tossed traveller, a Ulysses returning to the first and safest of all his harbours. Indeed, she told me that, a few nights before my arrival, he had spent the night beside her in her brass bed, as if he were still a baby rather than a man recently turned forty. 'He had such a nasty, fluey cold,' she said. 'I couldn't let him go off by himself on that draughty Underground, so I made him come in the big bed with me. He loved it, bless him.' I wonder if Joan had any idea of the competition she faced.

*

WHATEVER extra money for Christmas he had earned from the Post Office did not find its way back to Ryde. That year, my mother could afford to buy me only one present – a 'Captain Cutlass' cap-pistol, which I already had anyway. The two of us ate a gloomy Christmas lunch in the bay window of Dunraven's sitting-room, looking out at leafless trees and the redbrick air-raid shelter.

I tried to cheer her up by repeating 'A *lovely* Christmas dinner!' as George had said to his wife, Gaye, in *The Gambols* comic strip. But her misery was impenetrable.

Eleven

THE MODERN WORLD has probably never seen a more tranquil year than 1954. For a time, the fighting in Korea had looked horribly like a prelude to World War Three. But, thank goodness, it had all been sorted out, the way everything in the early fifties always seemed to be. With nothing left to worry about but a few barely audible terrorists in Kenya and Algeria, the whole globe seemed to sigh and settle back into slumberous peace. The just-perfected hydrogen-bomb was seen less as a threat to humanity than an exciting toy – a new, improved atom-bomb – in whose development Britain was of course an important partner. Cinema newsreels used to show its test explosions in the spirit of some giant firework display, stressing how selflessly the development teams had worked to bring it to fruition, rather than its horrific power to cause death. One's heart glowed for the teams as they proudly watched their gracefully-billowing mushroom cloud from exposed positions a mile or so off, happily unaware that there was any such thing as radiation poisoning.

The excitement of the Coronation had died down, leaving the country, if possible, even quieter and greyer than before. For Prime Minister we still had the great Winston Churchill – now very old but still wielding his outsize cigars and giving wartime V-for-victory signs – which meant that as a nation we remained impervious to any outside enemy. Both the cinema and early TV news reflected national life on a relentlessly upbeat note: new housing, new cars, new labour-saving devices, everybody working as hard and selflessly as the H-bomb teams did to make life measurably a little better every day. Our new young Queen toured the friendly-sounding Commonwealth that had replaced the old Empire, greeted at every stop by Maoris and Zulus performing war dances that now were intended only for her entertainment. That, above all, seemed to symbolize how hatred and violence had disappeared from the world, leaving only smiles, handshakes and sweet reason.

Even today, I find it hard to watch film-footage of events in 1954 – the Queen receiving a rapturous welcome in Australia; Roger Bannister running the first four-minute mile; Lester Piggott winning the Derby, aged only eighteen, on Never Say Die. The same chill always grips my heart to see that orderly, untroubled black-and-white world and realize that I'm in it too, somewhere.

*

THE START OF the new school term in January found me still at home and clinging to convalescence like a drowning man to a spar. I managed to keep it going for almost three further weeks, at which point I was examined again by Dr Sim during one of his prenatal visits to my mother. Afterwards, out of my earshot, he told her bluntly that she had two choices. She could return me to the existence of a normal boy, with or without leg-pains, or resign herself to having a hypochondriacal weakling on her hands indefinitely. When he'd gone, she came and told me I was going back to school the following day. I wept and pleaded ('Just another few days! *Please!* For my sake!'), but she stood firm.

The terrible moment, when it came, proved nowhere near as bad as I had expected. My first morning back happened to coincide with a heavy fall of snow, highly unusual for the Island, which always had the effect of turning school routine upside-down and cancelling its more unpleasant features like games and cross-country running. My classmates in what had become Form One, Senior School, received me with some awe and respect, for my absence of almost six months had shattered all known records – and I was quick to make it clear that my 'weak' heart was still very much in play. The white-blanketed playing-fields meant that my induction into the dreaded rugby was postponed for the foreseeable future. The new Turkish boy, on whom I had for some reason focused most of my fear, turned out to be as fat as a Levantine Billy Bunter. His name was not 'Belchie', as Bobby Greenham had said, but Balci, aptly pronounced 'Bulgy'.

Not that I myself was anyone to talk. Months of lying in bed and on couches had left me pallid and seriously over-weight for my slight stature. I had no inkling of this until my first PT class, conducted by the same bald little ex-navy sadist who used to take us in Junior School. Our first exercise, as ever, was to rush in a body to one end of the Assembly Hall, then back to the other end. The last boy each way received Mr Savage's traditional reward, 'a piece of Cadbury's whole nut chocolate', meaning a cut across the bare buttocks with the whistle he wore on a cord around his neck. With a malevolent ear-to-ear grin, he had already welcomed me back to his class as 'Porky'. Now as I ran, I realized he was capering beside me, panting exaggeratedly, with one hand clutched to his white singlet in the region of his heart.

By contrast, the ordeal of starting to learn Latin, which

had been giving me nightmares since Bobby's visit, proved relatively painless. Our new Latin master, Mr Wheeler – nick-named 'Swill' – was certainly an intimidating figure with his receding sandy hair, protruding front teeth and habit of hurling chalk fragments, or their own exercise books, at class malefactors. But he took me patiently through all the intro-ductory work I had missed, which turned out mostly to be straightforward memorizing – 'amo amas amat', 'mensa mensa mensam'. Determined though I was to hang back and be 'no good', I soon found I could put together the elementary sentences about Caesar laying waste to Gaul or Cotta over-coming the Belgians 'by, with or from arrows'.

There was positive pleasure in Senior School history and English, both taught by our form-master, Mr Chesterton – nicknamed 'Charlie' – a tall, rosy-faced, elegant man with the pious look and soothing voice of some minor archdeacon. Even the most cloddish members of the class loved Charlie's history lessons, which would start out on some conventional topic like William Rufus or Richard the Lionheart, but quickly digress into a dozen different avenues, from the wounds inflicted by a broadsword to Second World War battles like Cassino and El Alamein, and great moments in his numerous favourite films. When I joined his form, he had just reached the Age of Chivalry and, to my delight, encouraged us to fill our exercise books with drawings of knights, castles and siege-catapults.

Even better were his English literature periods, where the term's set book was Kenneth Grahame's *The Wind in the Willows*. In early afternoon dusk, with snow glimmering on the quadrangle outside, it was pleasant to read about Ratty and Mole finding shelter from the stormy Wild Wood in Mr Badger's cosy underground home. 'The ruddy brick floor smiled up at the smoky ceiling,' Charlie read out in his soft, churchy tones. 'The oaken settles, shiny with long wear, exchanged cheerful glances with each other; plates on the dresser grinned at pots on the shelf, and the merry firelight flickered and played over everything without distinction . . .' One afternoon, when I was first to answer a question, he gave me a prize of a chocolate toffee. To my surprise, I realized I was almost liking this.

The baby destined to grow up into a famous novelist was due some time in mid-February. To my relief, some serious preparations to receive it were finally getting under way. Piles of little garments began to collect at the Dunraven flat, and both my mother and Mrs Kennie had begun knitting as frantically as if to supply a frozen regiment at the Russian front. On my third day back at school, I returned home to find a pram standing in the front porch. I had fantasized about a super-deluxe Silver Cross in midnight blue, with mudguards and coachwork like an expensive limousine. This was an obviously second-hand model in cream and maroon, handed on by some friend who had no further use for it. But better any pram than no pram at all.

The ever-swifter passage of my last weeks as an only child brought yet another worry into focus. When my mother went into hospital to have the baby – an ordeal she was resigned to facing all on her own – what was to be done with me? In former times I might have stayed with Uncle Phil, Auntie Lorna and my two cousins at the Star Hotel. But the unconcluded war between Uncle Phil and my father made that impossible. We had no other family on the Island with whom I could be billeted for three to four weeks, nor any friends intimate enough for us to beg such a favour.

The solution was imparted to me, like all the worst news, in Dunraven's big sitting-room at tea time. 'I'm afraid,' my mother said, then paused in the way she had. 'I'm afraid you're going to have to be a boarder at Ryde School. Just for a month,' she added hastily. 'While I'm in hospital and getting myself sorted out afterwards.'

I gazed at her, numb with dismay. It was not only that Ryde School's boarding-house, with its ferocious Matron, was a byword for savage severity and hardship. I felt hardly less appalled by the incongruity of my position. The boarding-house was for boys from far away on the mainland or from foreign lands like Sweden and Persia. How could one conceivably go to boarding school in the same town as one's own home?

As always, my mother won by throwing herself on my mercy. 'It'll only be for a month, Phil . . . I wouldn't ask you if there was anything else we could do. It's the one way you can help me and be a really good boy . . . And it's only for a month. Only a month, I *promise*.'

Again, the ordeal wasn't as bad as I expected – at least, not quite as bad. In the continuing Arctic weather, the boarders had made a slide between the upper and lower playing-fields, which made staying behind after school seem almost attractive. For my first evening meal in the boarders' house we had perfectly-cooked boiled eggs – a once-in-a-lifetime rarity, but I was hardly to know that. Later, as I undressed for my first night in big, freezing cold Dormitory One, boys kept coming along to have a look at me and ask with sympathetic smiles what I thought of it all so far. A few minutes after lights-out (at the amazingly early time of 8.30), the door from the corridor burst open and a prefect bounded in and announced he'd overheard someone talking. No one being disposed to own up, he ordered all twenty-odd boys out of bed to be slippered – i.e. beaten on the behind three times with a gym shoe. Everyone had to bend low over the iron foot-rail of his bed and the prefect took a run-up like a fast bowler, using the gym shoe over-arm.

When my turn came the prefect looked keenly at me. 'How long have you been here?' he demanded.

'About three hours,' I told him.

'All right . . . get back into bed.'

It was certainly a harsh and cruel place, run on the old English public school principle that keeping small boys starving, frozen and terrified was somehow character-building. Bullying was rife and largely unchecked, especi-ally from the foreign boys whose parents clearly had found the Isle of Wight on a map and mistaken Ryde School for a second Eton or Harrow. The fat Turkish boy Balci (Bulgy) in particular suffered agonies of persecution from his older compatriots, who had names like Ghobadian, Koyuncu and Sarper. They would steal his food, hold him down and fart in his face or open his letters from home and tell him his mother had died. The altercations between them were so violent that 'Swill' Wheeler, one of the two housemasters, had learned to quel them in Turkish. '*Soos behr!*' he would bellow, meaning 'Shut up, idiot!'

On the plus side, the other housemaster was elegant, soft-spoken 'Charlie' Chesterton whose history and English lessons I now so adored. He seemed to like me, too, one afternoon choosing me to help him carry his entire collection of shoes from the Basement, where they had been cleaned, up to his bedroom in a tiny, sea-facing attic. As we wound our way up the narrow stairs with our armfuls of slip-ons and brogues, Charlie softly sang the 'Inchworm Song' from yet another of his favourite films, Danny Kaye's *Hans Christian Andersen*.

Matron was a nightmare, it's true – but a nightmare impartially visited on all forty-four boarders, even the very youngest (who could be as young as four). She was a short, stocky woman, dressed in the dark blue blouse and starched apron of a hospital sister. Her eyes were small and beady, and her teeth stuck up from her lower jaw like the tusks of a warthog. When we arose each morning, Blase (pronounced 'Blarz-er'), our Dutch dormitory prefect, gave us two minutes exactly to straighten our beds army-style with the bottom sheet straight and the blankets folded into squares and piled at the end. While we were at breakfast, Matron would go round the dormitories and strip any bed she considered unsatisfactory, earning its occupant an automatic prefectorial slippering. When we sat at meals, she would stalk between the tables with a creak of her starched apron, occasionally jabbing two fingers into the small of someone's back as a reminder to sit up straight.

Matron had been apprised of my recent medical history, but any hope of maternal care and attention vanished as I looked into her tusky, never-smiling face. 'Tell me something, Narman,' she said, giving even my surname a kind of built-in snarl. 'Are you sure all this weak heart and leg-pain stuff isn't just a lot of imagination?'

I made no particular friends except a boy named Millard R. (to distinguish him from his older brother, Millard J.), who gave me some of his Sandwich Spread at my first teatime. He had a comforting, Queen-of-Tonga kind of look, which led me to tell him a terrible secret: that among my clothes my mother had packed a white woollen bed-jacket, given to me by Grandma Norman for the nights when I slept with her as an honorary old lady. Knowing what ridicule it would call down on my head, I'd hidden it at the bottom of my dormitory locker. Millard listened sympathetically and agreed not to tell anyone else. But every now and then he would smile at me and pensively murmur, 'Poor old woolly bed-jacket.'

Nor did I talk to anyone about my family situation, even though I knew there were others around me whose parents were divorced or separated, or who had packed them off to the Island, Dotheboys Hall-style, just to get rid of them. Small boys in those days were bound by a code of stiff upper lip as rigid as in any nineteenth-century Guards regiment. You gave away nothing that would draw the instant, delightedly mocking crowd, pointing at you and chanting, 'Whoo-hoo-*hoo*!' The only person who seemed to know about my circumstances was the headmaster's widowed mother, whose husband had founded the school in 1921 and who still worked there as a kind of honorary housekeeper. I could only conclude she must have belonged to the same morning-coffee network as friends of my mother like Mrs Bailey and Mrs Dorley Brown. 'How's Mum?' she always asked me sympathetically when I saw her in her purple-flowered smock, arranging flowers in the front hall.

It was a question I had no means of answering. After my mother dropped me at the school with a single small suitcase and a carrier-bag full of oranges (now designated as 'tuck'), I did not see her again until after the baby was born. I didn't even know the baby *had* been born, on the snowy night of 24 February. I didn't know that on the evening she went into labour, she'd been to see the film *From Here to Eternity* with her friends the Dorley Browns, and that it was they who took her in their two-tone Ford Zephyr to the nearest maternity hospital, St Mary's on the far side of Newport.

I didn't know either that my father, belatedly smitten by conscience, had travelled back to Ryde from wherever he was with Joan, gained admittance to our empty flat by climbing through a window, then found his way to St Mary's and walked into my mother's room just as she was first holding the newborn baby girl in her arms. I did not hear until years later how all his dark insinuations that she might not be his child melted away at the first moment he set eyes on her.

The first I knew of my sister's existence was a letter from him, about a week afterwards, written from Grandma Norman's home in London. I remember precisely where I was as I unfolded the single blue sheet and saw his familiar, large-looped hand. It was on the gravelled slope outside the assembly hall – the same place where, a year before, Michael Rooke had publicly announced, 'Your father's been to prison, Norman.'

He wrote that 'little Irene' would make no difference to his feelings towards me. I felt confused because I'd thought the baby was to be named Tracey. My father's preference for my mother's name Irene, in my ever hopeful mind, suggested some lingering tenderness towards her.

*

AFTER FOUR WEEKS exactly, as promised, I regained my freedom. The longed-for day, however, saw no celebrations to welcome me back to normal life. No one even troubled to come to the school to collect me. As a too-well-authenticated 'good boy', I was left to pack my own case, say my farewells to Dormitory One, Millard R., Charlie and Matron, and walk home alone. On my way, I stopped at Fred P. Mellish the High Street stationers and bought a small soft toy for the new baby. I remember my first sight of her: a tiny head, turned away and fast asleep under a white knitted blanket. My mother – and everyone else – referred to her as 'Tracey' which I myself preferred, 'Irene' to my ears being a name too redolent of 'suffering and suffering'. I laid the toy I'd brought on the pillow beside her.

Now the baby was here, I found to my surprise that I didn't feel in the least resentful or threatened. I was more relieved that my mother's ordeal was over and that, presumably, she would now return to her former shape, throw away her polka-dot smock and start using make-up again. I was thankful that, after all, we seemed to have enough baby clothes and nappies and Johnson's Baby Powder and 'gripe water' and a pram. Above all, I thanked God (several times each day) that I wasn't a boarder any more. It was wonderful to use an inside lavatory rather than a freezing and squalid outside one, to eat thin bread and butter rather than doorsteps meanly smeared with margarine, to go to bed at whatever hour I liked, then spend further unlimited time reading or drawing, snuggled with a hot-water-bottle and my resurrected bed-jacket.

I didn't mind even when people clustered around my baby sister and exclaimed how beautiful she was. I myself could discern nothing especially attractive in the tiny, white-swaddled shape I saw periodically displayed, with its blank blue eyes and crab-like waving limbs. I saw only a hairless skull, a face like a little old granny's, a mindlessly amiable mouth on which bubbles of spit eternally formed and dissolved as though from some geyser deep within. But it was a relief to me to know she was thought beautiful – that after all the muddle and misgivings of the past months, we had a baby that could hold its head high, or would do eventually.

As if in apology for all the disruption she had caused, the baby was a model of considerateness, sleeping soundly through each night, accepting breast and bottle with equal willingness, crying only on the rarest occasions. Mrs Kennie, that over-experienced mother, took her over almost completely, bathing and changing her, hand-washing her relays of nappies – we had no washing-machine, nor did anyone we knew, not even the pace-setting Dorley Browns – and taking her out in the second-hand pram. My duties were limited to jiggling the pram occasionally and watching to see that Lou, our errant Siamese cat, did not creep into her cot and go to sleep on her face. Far from disrupting my life, baby-care brought a new orderliness that I positively welcomed. If nowhere else, I found reassurance in the sight of nappies drying on the line and the all-pervading odour of iron-warmed woollens and milk.

In no time at all, it seemed, spring was here again, and the town stirring and making ready for another season. Coronation spirit lingered, with red, white and blue pennants still fluttering along the Esplanade, the confectioners and gift shops still full of 'E.R.' merchandise. Teddy Hoare, the swash-buckling owner of the Hotel Ryde Castle, had decided to let his giant papier-mâché Guardsmen stand guard on his battlements a second summer. There they still were, presenting arms rather forlornly at the sea where the world's navies had so recently congregated.

At Easter (thank you again, God) Grandma Norman arrived from London to reopen the Kiosk. I had wondered uneasily whether, in her grief for Uncle Wally, she might have lost interest in selling sweets and rock. I can see now that it must have been the best possible form of therapy to get back at the first opportunity to her customers, her travellers and her beloved 'men on the gate'. With her, to help her and also lend comfort in non-retailing hours, she brought her friend Mrs Dunwoody – 'Auntie Geordie' – accompanied, as ever, by Sue-Sue, the caramel-coloured Pekinese. They took rooms in a block of flats named Crofton House at the top of George Street, behind the Commodore cinema.

Grandma Norman's return to the Island seemed my mother's best chance of bringing matters with my father to some resolution. She was, after all, *de facto* head of the family, not only its most charismatic member but the one who had always most passionately preached the necessity of family love and cohesion. She was also the only person in the world to whom my father listened and whose bad opinion he feared. Her acquiescence in his behaviour thus far – my mother reasoned – must have stemmed from incomplete knowledge of the facts. So at the first opportunity she went to Grandma Norman at the Kiosk and told her the whole story.

Grandma Norman listened with an expression of heartfelt sympathy, now and again shaking her head in sheer disbelief, never forgetting to call my mother 'love' and 'my duck' according to her wont. But she refused to utter a single word in condemnation of my father. Ever since her young widowhood in 1918 had left the three of them pitted against the world together, her abiding first principle had been to side with her two 'boys'. The catalogue of cruelty and irresponsibility which my mother described to her made no difference. She would support my father, she said, 'even if he did a murder'.

I knew what was coming, but was still mortified beyond words to see what instant, utter rapture transfigured Grandma Norman's face when Tracey was first brought to see her at the Kiosk. I could only stand there with an insincere, sickly grin on my face, but shrivelling inside, as the baby was gathered into the wonderful, leathery embrace that had always been my private refuge and the endearments that had always belonged to me alone – 'My little love, my little duck, my little bit o' fat, my little bit o' fluff' – rained down on its uncomprehending, hairless head. Yes, I *was* jealous now: jealous in the way that makes one feel grubby all over. At the same time, to do myself justice, I felt glad that life had given her something to make up for losing Uncle Wally.

The Kiosk was a neutral state in the feud between my father and Uncle Phil, which continued, or at least remained unrevoked, beside the larger family crisis. With pig-headed loyalty, I continued to obey the law of dissociation, not only from Uncle Phil but from kind, put-upon Auntie Lorna, my godmother, and my cousins Dina and Roger. When I approached the Kiosk, I always took a roundabout route through the crowds of taxi and charabanc men, in case Uncle Phil might be serving at one of its windows or Roger might be in the back room having bread and cheese and Branston pickle.

Dina I couldn't help seeing as she was working there this year, along with her friend Ann Feltham. Revivifyingly humorous as well as beautiful, Dina paid no attention to the feud, treating me, like always, as a kindred spirit and confidant. I would find her alone in the back room, mutinously watching a saucepan boil on Grandma Norman's single gas-ring. 'It's *three* boiled eggs,' she'd whisper. 'For Mrs Dunwoody. Honestly, that woman is *such* a pig . . .' Or she'd describe in graphic detail the latest time my grandmother's famously flatulent companion had blown off in front of a window crowded with customers. 'Suddenly there's this terrible cracking noise . . . She tried to blame Sue-Sue the dog as usual, but everyone knew it was her. It must have blown a hole through her bloomers as wide as the Simplon Pass.'

Back in her pink nylon overall and blue canvas 'bumpers', in the place she loved best, Grandma Norman seemed almost her old self again. Everyone around the Kiosk knew of her loss and treated her with sweetness and consideration – not only the taxi-drivers and 'men on the gate' but Esplanade station porters and booking-clerks, Southern Vectis bus-drivers and conductors, the staff from adjacent W.H. Smith, Arthur the newspaper-seller and tiny, wizened Johnny who ran her daily horse-racing bets. Outwardly, she seemed the same as ever, dominating the main window, serving out 'dears' and 'loves' and 'my ducks' with each chocolate bar or twenty Weights or half-ounce of St Bruno or handful of change. It was only in her back room, as she took her one-eye-open afternoon 'rest', that she sometimes, distressingly, let the mask fall.

Seated beside her deckchair, amid the ceiling-high rock-boxes, I'd sometimes raise the question of what was happening, or not happening, between my mother and father. But I still did not like to burden her aching heart with extra heartache of mine. And, of course, nothing could be said about my father, apart from how good and kind he was and what a sweet little boy he used to be. Grandma Norman spoke of the present situation as of some natural catastrophe which, given time and patience, would dissipate of its own accord. 'I shouldn't worry about it too much, love,' she would tell me. 'These things generally all come out in the wash, y'know . . .' Then a shouted query from one of her staff would divert her attention to more immediate problems: 'Mrs Norman – how much are the Cadbury's Vogue, please?'

'Three and a penny the quarter-pound boxes, six and six the halves.'

*

BY THE TIME she was two months old, my sister had developed a mass of springy white-gold curls and the beam of a contented angel. Even I could see she was the type of baby who belonged in advertisements for Johnson's powder or Farley's Rusks. When Mrs Kennie took her out, passers-by would go into spontaneous raptures over her. 'And she's got a smile for everyone,' Mrs Kennie said. Rather than an old lady full of rheumatics, I now wished I were a baby, swaddled in soft wool, sheltered in my pram from wind and bad weather, absolved from all worry or blame. I tried to recall the sensations of my own babyhood, but could get back no further than about the age of two. How I wished I had made more of every heavenly cot-borne, bubble-blowing moment.

Tracey's mint-fresh perfection heightened the feeling I'd had for some time that my own life was virtually over or, at least, hardly worth going on with from here. April 13 brought my eleventh birthday, two days before Grandma Norman's sixty-fifth and Uncle Phil's God knew what. My mother ordered me a cake from Harvey's bakery on the Esplanade, but when we unpacked it some of the icing was damaged and she made me take it back again. The baker came from the rear of the shop to inspect it with no very good grace, his white chef's hat tipped back on his head. Outside there were already crowds of holidaymakers outside Abell's Gift Shop. I felt a sudden sense that nothing I could see was quite real, that everything was flimsy and temporary, that even the brilliant New Elizabethan sunshine had somehow turned rancid. I had got into the habit of saying lengthy prayers before I went to sleep each night (it having been the only activity at boarding-school in which one was completely immune from bullying or slippering). I remember praying that my little sister would grow up to be as great a success as her brother was a failure.

My mother by now had given up any lingering hope that my father might come back, and had decided – unbeknownst to me, of course – to start proceedings for divorce. As long as he continued to keep his whereabouts secret, however, she could not provide the necessary evidence of adultery with Joan. She had even hired a private detective to track the two of them down. But after London and the Christmas post their trail had gone cold.

My father's only communication to her since Tracey's birth had arrived early in April: a letter with a Portsmouth post-mark but no other clue as to its origin. The letter gave her detailed instructions for the reopening of the Pier Pavilion at Easter and the running of its arcade and restaurant in his absence. She was further ordered to pay all its takings into his account at the National Provincial Bank's Union Street branch. If she carried out his orders, my father wrote, she would again start to receive a regular housekeeping allowance. If not, she would get nothing.

I knew nothing about the letter either, but I remember what a change came over her at about this time. Its nonchalant cruelty must have acted like a dash of cold water in the face, changing her long timidity and submissiveness at last into anger and a determination to fight back. My first inkling of this was her sudden announcement that she intended to learn to drive. It was something my father had never let her do, for all his own brilliance as a driver and his record as a wartime flying instructor, supposedly with bottomless reserves of calm and patience. For her to take the initiative now was a clear act of rebellion, albeit of a purely theoretical kind since we didn't have a car and never went anywhere. I remember her euphoria when she came home from her first lesson with the Island School of Motoring. '*What* do you think they're teaching me to drive in?' she said. 'The *only* Ford Popular on the whole Isle of Wight!' It was in this transformed state of mind that she managed a retaliatory coup one can only describe as brilliant.

Gifts for the baby were also now coming from my father, using the Kiosk as a kind of secret agent's mail drop. (Grandma Norman, needless to say, professed total ignorance as to his whereabouts.) One day, some little dresses and bootees arrived in a carrier-bag bearing the name of a draper's shop in Portsmouth. As my mother studied this name, some powerful instinct whispered to her that it was just the sort of not-very-high-class place where Joan might seek temporary employment.

Next day, she took a ferry to Portsmouth and found her way to the shop. The female staff serving there did not include Joan, but my mother still felt powerfully that she was on the right scent. She sought out the shop's manager and asked whether it employed anyone called – here she could only guess – 'Joan Salsbury'. Yes, the manager replied, but today was her day off. My mother pretended to be a friend of Joan's who needed to contact her urgently but had lost her address. The manager directed her to a house a few streets away. She then summoned her private detective to go to the house and confront the fugitives. As a divorce judge would later hear, the detective's first knock produced all the evidence that was needed:

Q. 'What was Mr Norman doing when Miss Salsbury opened the door?'

A. 'Putting on his trousers.'

My mother followed up this triumph by passing her driving-test at the first attempt, then immediately going out and spending her entire savings – £5 – on buying a car of her own. It was a 1929 Austin Seven, a humble little saloon, not much more than a black box on wheels, that made people openly laugh and point as it chugged past them. It was incapable of more than about 30 mph and had great difficulty in climbing Ryde's hilly streets. But as a symbol of new-won independence and enterprise, its value was incalculable.

With her Austin 'buzzbox' to open up the most distant of Ryde's suburbs, my mother's spirits rose higher than I'd seen them since the pre-Joan skating days. She seemed to take more interest in our fragments of home and, especially, in me, buying me my first pair of school long trousers, helping me with my long-division homework, agreeing that the 'Neptune Man', who delivered fizzy drinks in swirly-necked bottles, could leave one of cherryade and one of cream soda every Thursday. She made an effort to be nice to Mrs Kennie's son, Robert, once even planting a brave kiss on top of his black busby hair as she left the two of us having supper in the kitchenette.

Since my father's departure, she had continued his practice of filling out a weekly coupon for Littlewood's football pools, whose top prize of £75,000 was the largest gambling windfall then available in Britain. (The very name Littlewood's reminded me of him, especially since their main rival in the pools business was called Vernon's.) My mother and I would often discuss in detail how gloriously our lives would be changed, not *if* but *when* she 'won the pools'. 'I'll do you a beautiful new bedroom,' she promised, 'full of this new modern G-Plan furniture . . .' I would go to bed as excitedly as if she had already won, picturing my bare little bedroom transformed by shiny, interlocking wooden units. (You can understand, perhaps, why nowadays I want no part of that wistful national catchphrase, 'When we win the Lottery . . .')

On yet another of the almost monotonously beautiful days early in my Easter holidays, she suggested a family outing to the beach. It was something she could never have done with my father around, and innumerable duties calling to her from the pier-head. I could sense the rebellion in the idea: that we should pretend to be just normal people at the seaside.

With the baby and my cousin Dina, we went in her Austin Seven to Seaview, the pretty little cove a mile or so to the east of Ryde where the beach is littered with flat-topped rocks and brightly-coloured skiffs bob on almost translucent water. In the five years we'd lived on the Island, I'd been there only two or three times, never with either of my parents.

I wore a plaid shirt, a white cricket cap and sunglasses, and foraged around the rock-pools with a bucket and shrimping-net. Dina sat on the rocks nearby, lifting up each of the baby's chubby legs in turn as if she were a slow-motion can-can dancer. It should have been a carefree afternoon but, remember, I was not that kind of boy. I couldn't repress a thought that I shouldn't really be here and that I was doing something I oughtn't. The westerly headland of Puckpool Park blotted out the pier's whole length, but the sound of the trams rattling along it still carried accusingly over the summer air. I knew we were truants and that, some day, there would be a price to be paid.

The next afternoon, I came into the flat to hear my mother talking on the telephone in their – her – bedroom. And also an unfamiliar sound: her laughter. I peeped around the half-open door to see her lying full-length on their – her – bed, with the receiver at her ear. She was talking to a friend (Mrs Bailey? Mrs Dorley Brown?) about my father and how she'd bested him, and laughing in the strained, snuffly way she always did in front of other people. 'Yes . . . he did. *Giggle*. Yes. Yes. *Giggle*. The papers were served on him on Wednesday. No, not really . . . *Giggle*. Only that he's been a bit more polite . . .'

As I stood there, unseen, I was overcome by helpless rage. Whatever he'd done, I hated hearing my father talked about and mocked in this way and this put-on voice. I hated even more the idea of strangers being let into our private pain. I waited until she had hung up, then confronted her as she came out into the twilit hallway. 'You bloody fucker,' I said in what came out as a low, disbelieving voice. I had only recently heard the word 'fucker' for the first time; it had never passed my lips before. It sounded almost onomatopoeic, like the noise my cousin Roger could make with a hand stuck inside his armpit.

My mother stared at me, not understanding for a moment. I noticed how tired she looked, her face bereft of make-up and shining greasily in the gloom. 'I heard what you said about

Dad,' I continued lamely, ' . . . you bloody fucker!' Furious that I'd eavesdropped on her, she grabbed my arm and pushed me backwards into my bedroom, shouting how dare I, how *dare* I? I picked up a wire coat-hanger, whether to defend myself or attack her I'm not sure. But I could feel my indignation already ebbing away, my words tailing off. What was the point? It was all hopeless. I dropped the hanger on to my chilly green bed quilt and just let her anger rain down on me. How dare I? How *dare* I? . . .

*

A WEEK LATER, she sold her Austin Seven. Three days after that, she left the Island, taking the baby and her cocker spaniel, Melody. I remained behind. Alone.

Twelve

It was not like being abandoned – or, at least, didn't feel like it at the time. My mother could pay the legal expenses of divorcing my father only if she found herself a job. This had to be away from the Island, far, far away, to forestall any attempt by him to sabotage it. The baby and Melody were to be left in London, in the care of Grandma and Grandad Bassill. But asking Grandma Bassill to look after me as well as a baby and a dog, all on top of caring for Grandad, was clearly out of the question. Besides, I was just back at school for the summer term; I could hardly go absent again after all the work I'd recently missed. At Dunraven, I'd have Mrs Kennie to see to my meals, and Nigger and Louis the Siamese for company. I'd be all right, wouldn't I? Stupid, self-effacing, over-considerate child that I was, I said I'd be quite all right.

What puzzles me now is why Grandma Norman, hitherto always my shield in everything, didn't scoop me up and carry me off to stay with her and Mrs Dunwoody at Crofton House. I can only record that she didn't, and that at the time it never crossed my mind to wonder why. I had given up wondering why about anything. If a team of white-coated scientists had turned up and announced that the next H-bomb test would not take place on Christmas Island in the far

Pacific, but in Dunraven's back garden, I'd have accepted it with the same numb resignation.

So it came about that I was left by myself in the gloomy flat in the gloomy house at the end of the gloomy cobbled lane, opposite the gloomy, shadowy churchyard. Maintaining my reputation as a 'good boy' and – stupidly, *stupidly!* – being no trouble to anyone.

*

IN SOME WAYS, it meant wonderful freedom and free will. I could get up each morning without the bother of washing or cleaning my teeth. I didn't have to wait around for my mother to give me breakfast – which she often did in a less than good mood – but could skip it altogether, as I preferred, and set off for school at 7.45, even though it was only fifteen minutes walk away and morning assembly didn't take place until 8.50. Such was (and still is) my pathological fear of being late.

In my scuffed sandals, with the early sun in my eyes, I would trudge up Ryde's gentle lateral hills – Wood Street, then Star Street – smelling the keen scent of breakfast bacon wafted from normal family homes, listening to the mutter of unworrying 1954 news on distant radio sets. Lodged in my right cheek would be the sherbet lemon that generally served me in lieu of breakfast. I would feel its lemony shell grow smaller and more brittle with sucking until it dissolved in a cool, fizzy cloud on my tongue.

At the top of Star Street, I always lingered a few minutes outside the Commodore, studying the framed stills of films currently showing or soon to come. That summer, they included *Mogambo* with Clark Gable and Ava Gardner, and *Dial M for Murder* with Grace Kelly and Ray Milland. There was also a revival of *Gone with the Wind*, which I'd never heard of but was curious to see because of its American Civil

War background. I remember looking at the colour still of Confederate wounded in Atlanta town square and thinking that, losing side or not, wounded or not, I'd happily change places with any of them.

I always crossed the street then, so as to avoid passing the side door of the adjacent Star Hotel and thereby preclude any accidental encounter with Uncle Phil or Auntie Lorna. In there it was all enemy territory now – the ground-floor bar 'parlour', the long staircase lined with pictures of French dogs using kerbside pissoirs, the big upstairs sitting-room where Mr Ross had told me I looked like Prince Philip. I never saw anyone leaving or entering, but once, when I thought I was safely past, I met my cousin Roger. He was sitting precariously in the front basket of a delivery-boy's bicycle being pedalled by one of his tough Green Street friends. 'Take it easy, Jeff,' he was laughing in a quasi-American accent. 'Take it *easy* . . .' As they passed, he added a mocking 'Howdy, cousin', but I ignored him and walked on with my nose in the air.

Despite all my firm intentions, I couldn't help betraying my father in the end. On my way up Star Street a few mornings later, I was smitten by an attack of diarrhoea. It was impossible to wait until I got to school – and, in any case, the school lavatories were disgusting. I had no choice but to go to the Star's side door and guiltily yank at its rusty old bell-lever. Luckily, the jangling peal was answered by Auntie Lorna, who welcomed me in and allowed me to use the first-floor lavatory as if there were no hostilities at all between us. Her wooden plaque still hung high on the wall with its air of cheeriness against all odds: 'Don't worry. Stick a geranium in yer 'at and be 'appy.'

When school ended at five past four, I walked home through the bustling town to the wide, quiet streets that were once supposed to have given us better quality of life as a family. A faint smell of rotten eggs from the Rink Road gasworks hung permanently in the air. Sometimes, the Fire Station's siren would go off: a laboriously cranked-up 'Wheee-eee-EEE!' that never seemed to worry anyone or produce the answering clang of a fire-engine. A slave to habit, then as now, I always took the same short cut to Trinity Street through Holy Trinity's churchyard, which involved walking along the garden-wall of a mock-Cotswold stone guesthouse named the Tredegar. Guests strolling or playing croquet on the manicured lawn would stare up at me as I passed.

At Dunraven, Mrs Kennie would have tidied the flat and be waiting to give me my tea – usually a boiled egg over-cooked until its yolk was nearly as pale as its white. To begin with, she'd ask me if I wanted her to sleep the night there. I always said, 'No, that's all right,' (*Good boy!*) so she gave up asking and went home to her Monkton Street lodgings and her son, Robert.

*

I HAD SOMETHING like 200 toy soldiers permanently set out on my bedroom floor in a landscape of twig barricades and blockhouses made from upturned cardboard boxes. Most were the traditional lead sort manufactured by the firm of W. Britain, drenched in paint that no one yet had learned to call toxic and equipped with needle-sharp swords, bayonets and lances that no one yet considered lethally dangerous. Lighter-weight plastic figures were starting to appear and, because they were so much cheaper, I had accumulated a good few. But I never took them as seriously as the lead ones, using them mainly as cannon-fodder in my battle tableaux.

Over the years, I'd had crazes for various historical periods: Napoleonic, the Crimean War, the Indian Mutiny, knights in armour, cowboys and Indians, Canadian Mounties, French Foreign Legion. Lately, I had concentrated on the American Civil War, turned on to the subject by films like *Springfield Rifle*, starring Gary Cooper (which I'd seen in London with Grandad Bassill in the days when he still had his own legs) and, especially, *The Red Badge of Courage*, starring Audie Murphy. Britain's as yet manufactured only a very limited Civil War range; however, I could co-opt other nineteenth-century uniforms with perfect historical accuracy as foreign mercenaries as well as using my store of cowboys as civilians caught up in the conflict.

I always rooted for the beaten South over the victorious North, even though I knew they had stood for preserving slavery and their opponents for abolishing it. What counted more with me was the aesthetic appeal of their grey and gold uniforms and their air of gallant, chivalrous underdog. I maintained my allegiance even to the point of being glad that in 1954's just-ended war South Korea had beaten the North. A child psychologist doubtless would have found it significant that in the battles I staged, defenders came off better than attackers. For me it was always preferable to be inside a fort or behind a wall or barricade – safe, snug, covered.

Each figure in the collection had its own recognizable personality for me, each tiny rudimentary face its own individual voice. I had two special favourites, to whom I always gave the best cover and whom I never allowed to be killed. One was a Confederate officer down on one knee, whose movable arms raised a set of field-glasses to his eyes. The other was a cowboy, also kneeling, on whom an unusual wealth of decorative detail had been lavished. His hat was a pure white Stetson; his bright red shirt was piped in white; spots of silver gleamed on his cartridge-belt and spurs and levelled Winchester rifle. He was a tiny figment of the style and elegance for which I hungered without yet even knowing it.

Each evening after Mrs Kennie had gone, I'd lie down beside my army, resting my cheek on the ragged green lino so as to be not that much taller than they were. I played with them, I now realize, not from any love of battles or killing but because they were the one department of my life where I had control and could impose order. Amid an incessant *pshaow! pshaow!* of ricocheting rifle-fire, I'd talk aloud my favourite battle-narrative. A brave Confederate force, helped by their heroic scout with his white Stetson and Winchester rifle, fought off wave after wave of attacks by drab blue-clad Union troops from behind defences that could never be breached. Meanwhile, from the high bluff of my bedspread, a lone grey-coated officer surveyed the scene through binoculars with unfaltering coolness despite the bullets (*pshaow! pshaow!*) that whistled around him.

After an hour or so the rifle-fire would die away, and Dunraven would fall quieter than any house I'd ever know or ever would again. No sound came from the flat above ours or from either of the two flats beneath. No sound could be heard from the three old stone cottages to our right or from the Tredegar guesthouse along at the junction with Wood Street. For hour after hour would endure the thick, grey 1954 silence that one could actually hear, broken only by a breeze springing from nowhere and hissing gently among the churchyard trees that filled my bedroom window.

Out in the dusky hallway, old Nigger the Labrador was barely visible, lying where you were most likely to trip over him. At any footfall, his tail would thump on the bare boards in the hope that it would be my father, and that the two of them could go out shooting as of old. Sometimes a plaintive cry – almost like that of the departed baby – would herald a visit by Louis, the Siamese cat. Mrs Cass downstairs had by now virtually adopted him but he still occasionally returned to us for a brief look around, though seldom finding anything to detain him long. I'd call him and stroke his chocolate-milk fur, for I'd always loved him. But his odorous breath delivered a rebuff even more eloquent than did his squinty blue eyes. How could anything I might offer compete with the family circle of a fishmonger?

At some point during the early evening, our upstairs neighbours, Mr and Mrs Allen, would let themselves in through the front door and cross our hall to reach the boarded-off staircase to their flat. Despite this horribly inconvenient intimacy, we had never got to know the Allens or anything about them, let alone visited the first-floor rooms they inhabited. They were a retired couple of tweedy respectability, Mrs Allen the slightly friendlier of the two. They must have known I was by myself, but never made any acknowledgement of it, greeting me with the same formal 'Good evening' that they used to my mother, then vanishing up their staircase, at whose summit I caught an occasional glimpse of potted ferns. From now until school tomorrow morning, I was on my own.

Our rented Ferguson TV set had been sent back to the shop in one of the earliest of my mother's economy measures. Without it, there was no snug place in the flat to settle for the evening, not even a friendly lamp into whose bright circle I could retire to read or draw. I spent my solitary evenings mainly in transit, searching through the formerly private cupboards and drawers that were now all open to me, as the big, bare rooms dwindled into twilight first, then darkness.

Reminders of my father were everywhere. Or, rather, I conjured them everywhere, from the fascination that had always equalled my fear. On the sitting-room bookcase, for instance, stood a bronze head of pharaoh Rameses II, dull grey in colour, with eyes as blank as a death mask's and a flat, sloping top to his skull. I had always recognized this as a personal possession of my father's rather than a general household ornament, though where he had acquired it, and from what passing interest in Egyptology, I had no idea. Uncle Phil possessed a companion head – that of the pharaoh's wife, Queen Nefertiti – which for me had always symbolized the elemental bond between the brothers as well as subtly saying something about their respective characters. Now, the bronze face that looked back at me was a reminder of bonds shattered on every side. With its sightless almond eyes and sensitive mouth, it might have been a cast of my father's own features. The very name Rameses seemed to have been coined especially for his over-emphatic lips to shape.

On the wall above hung his Peter Scott painting – or so I'd always taken it to be – of wild geese flying in a three-layer skein over yellow marshland. From my earliest childhood, the design of their wings had seemed to form my father's face in semi-profile, his eyes and sensitive mouth and the line of his brow impressed like God's on the cloudy, cold-blue sky. Wherever I went in the room, that geese-wing face seemed to follow me with a look of brooding sadness, perhaps comparing the son it had wanted with the boy I had turned out to be.

The main repository of my family's papers was a tall chest-of-drawers with brass handles which stood just inside the sitting-room door. It was here that I'd usually round off the evening, searching through each drawer as if for clues to the mystery of who I was and what had brought me to this endless, twilight moment. The two small upper drawers contained miscellaneous rubble: orange and gold gun cartridges, the empty box from a Yard-O-Led propelling pencil, a weightless gold ball from some years-ago Christmas tree, a robin on a spike that looked like sugar but wasn't – for I once tried gnawing at it – from some years-ago Christmas cake. Had we really once been a family that decorated a Christmas tree and shared cake or chocolate log for Christmas tea?

In the stiff-to-open wide bottom drawer were the few family photographs we possessed – tiny black-and-white snapshots mostly, taken with a Box Brownie camera, some now curling over with age. My mother as a young girl in the thirties, still sheltered and happy, wearing a white tennis skirt and swinging a racket in a press. My father in bathing-trunks, lying on a shingle beach long before we came to the Island. They had the air of strangers never destined to meet, let alone produce me. The idea even occurred to me that perhaps I didn't belong to them at all. It was a train of thought I had no way of continuing – but it came back time and again. Perhaps I didn't belong to them at all.

There also were some glossy aerial photographs, taken by my father during his time on RAF reconnaissance operations. One showed, etched into a grass hillside, the huge figure of a naked prehistoric man with an upward-straining penis and testicles baldly dangling. The figure glared with close-set eyes, bared its teeth and waved a cudgel over its head as if to discourage prying eyes from above. There were also some low-flying shots of London residential streets which, with a thrill, I recognized as Grandma Norman's neighbourhood in Clapham. There was the northerly edge of the Common, and Orlando Road with the bombsite on the corner that still hadn't been cleared. And there was Lydon Road and her house, number 26. Even on active service, I reflected, my father could never stray very far from her.

At the bottom of the drawer lay some thick documents with red wax seals, tied together with pink string, which,

I realized, must be connected with my parents' divorce. Though their legal language was almost incomprehensible, my skimming eye alighted on one sentence, in what was evidently a statement from Joan: '... and I admit that I shared a bed with him at the Oxford Hotel, Portsmouth...' Mulling the admission over – without, of course, really understanding it – I remembered I'd once had lunch at that very hotel with my cousin Roger and Mr Ross during one of the old Dutchman's antique-scouting trips to the mainland. Was it possible that my father and Joan had been upstairs, 'sharing a bed' in that so innocent-seeming phrase, even as the three of us sat downstairs eating chicken-pot pie with white sauce?

*

I MISSED and longed for my mother all the time, but with a dull, hopeless ache that never found relief in tears. I had no idea where she was or whether she had in fact found the job she'd gone away to seek. She did not write or telephone. Grandma Bassill, looking after the baby up in London, must have known her whereabouts: yes, of course I could easily have rung up Grandma Bassill, asked where she was, then got in touch with her and begged her to come back, or let me come and be with her. But in my catalepsy of numb acceptance (*Good boy!*) the idea never even occurred to me.

As much as I pined for my mother, I worried about her. I was always thinking about the refinement, even glamour, her life had once held and how it had been eroded by our years on the Island. Just inside the ever-open side door was still hanging her Jaeger camelhair coat – the one she'd worn that evening at the Western skating-rink when she mysteriously volunteered to be swung around by the trick-skater Jimmy Webster. For me, it symbolized the better existence that she'd once had, and that I longed with all my heart for her to have again. Every evening, in the thickening twilight, I'd go and look at it and stroke its hand-stitched lapels and the brown silk lining that was now faded and torn. I wanted her to be back in the world where Jaeger camel coats were brand-new, and she could drink dry Martinis and see West End shows and be taken to supper at the Savoy again by Ivor Novello.

The words of Novello's wartime song, 'We'll Gather Lilacs', had always reminded me so much of her and the kind of love I wished she could have. I remembered once lying in bed, listening to her sing it half under her breath as she got ready to go out – lying as still as I could, so as not to disturb the place where she'd tucked me in:

> And in the evening by the firelight's glow
> You'll hold me close and never let me go.
> Your eyes will tell me all I want to know
> When you come home once more . . .

I thought, too, of our happiest time as a family, when she and my father had managed the Cross Keys Hotel in St Neots, when life had seemed to consist of cosy log fires and twinkling horse-brasses and we *had* had chocolate log with a robin decoration for Christmas tea. In another drawer I found a booklet about the hotel with its emblem of two crossed golden keys stamped on the cover. Inside were black-and-white photographs of its long Georgian façade, its much older inner courtyard, its beam-and-brick bar, its dining-room of tables and wheelback chairs, with copper warming-pans hanging on the walls. Why, oh why had we ever let Uncle Phil lure us away from such a heavenly place?

The Cross Keys is an old posting house of great charm. It stands on the banks of the River Ouse and overlooks the spacious Market Square. Its site was once the gateway of the original St Neots Priory. Parts of the building date back to the twelfth century, and its interesting Courtyard is fourteenth century. It has, of course, been renovated and adapted from time to time, and was re-fronted in the eighteenth century. Great care has, however, been taken to preserve the character and traditions of the House, as can be seen from the present charming Bars and Lounges . . .

In present days, special attention is given to the cuisine and choice of wines. All the beds give ease and comfort, and the service both upstairs and below is prompt and courteous.

To live in an hotel again, the Cross Keys or any one, was my idea of Heaven. In the formless chaos of my existence, nothing seemed more alluring than the order and certainty of hotel life – the routines and rituals that went on unvaryingly day after day: the cleaning, food preparation and bar opening; the menu for dinner typewritten and slipped into its polished brass frame outside the front entrance at exactly the same time each evening. I could relive it a little in Grand Hotel, a weekly radio programme of light classical music such as one still heard played in high-class hotels by full orchestras. It came on the BBC's Light Programme long after the official 9 p.m. bedtime to which I still adhered (*Good boy!*), so I'd turn up the volume of the big cabinet radio in the sitting-room and leave the door open so that I could hear it while I lay in bed.

'We are now taking you into the Palm Court of Grand Hotel . . .' the announcer's voice would intone amid a buzz of background talk and the convivial clink of glasses as the imaginary guests waited for the recital to begin. I'd drift to sleep with that pleasant vision of bright lights . . . luxury . . . companionability . . . security.

*

I CARRIED ON in this way through the hot high summer of 1954: plodding to and fro along the narrow channel my life had become; weaving the cloak of aloneness I would wear for decades to come; not even conscious of being unhappy, so normal had become the feeling – or, rather, lack of it – inside me.

Then something happened that was even worse than my father going away. He came back again.

Thirteen

HE DID SO without any advance warning, turning up late one night after I'd gone to bed – not needing to ring or knock, since the flat's side door still stood permanently open. I remember opening my eyes to the usual sunshine and green-gold trees, and instantly knowing something was different. I can feel now the heart-stopped trepidation with which I got out of bed, peeped into the hallway and saw the door of 'their' bedroom closed instead of wide open, the way I always left it. As I listened, still praying I was wrong, I smelt stale pipe tobacco and heard the early-morning sound he always made that was half-way between a sneeze and a cough. *'Buffalo!'* it seemed to go, over and over again in a kind of fit, *'Buffalo! Buffalo! Buffalo!'*

What would you expect to be the normal reaction of a boy who hadn't seen his father for something like six months and now suddenly found him at home again? To go straight in and awaken him, of course, whether with an ecstatic welcome or withering anger and reproach. But – do I have to go on saying this? – I was not that sort of boy. The sort of boy I was put on his school uniform in a sweating trance of horror, then went and sat in the kitchenette with his usual dumb passivity, waiting to discover what appalling new turn his life was about to take.

At about a quarter to eight, almost my normal departure time, I heard a door open and the familiar rapid, soft footsteps come along the uncarpeted corridor, as always like a surprise attack on covert wrongdoing. I wondered whether his almost psychic knowledge of me and my ways had already led him to the sitting-room chest-of-drawers and the rifled private papers and photographs. Or whether, perhaps, he had discovered I'd taken a few covert sips from a bottle of sticky liqueur in the linen-press cocktail cabinet, or that I'd looked at a board-game called Totopoly that had been 'put away' for me until I was older, or that, in moments, of extreme boredom, I'd used our heavy silver dinner-knives to carve bits of hard skin off my feet. Before the crime even had a name, culprit phrases trembled on my lips: 'I didn't know . . . It wasn't my fault . . . I'm sorry.'

In the months – years – since he had been a permanent fixture at home, I'd forgotten his sheer, overwhelming physicality, especially on first getting up in the mornings. Never for him the prissy formality of pyjamas and dressing-gown. He was half-dressed in a loose white singlet and grey trousers, his bare feet thrust into red leather slippers that he'd left behind all this time in his 'compactum'. Bluish stubble coated his lower face like a mask, and curly black hair spilled over the arc of his singlet. I saw again the manly gold ring on the second finger of his left hand . . . the yellow-brown streaks inside the two fingers which held his cigarettes . . . the gouge of a prehistoric vaccination mark in the pale skin of his left shoulder. His masculinity was like an onslaught, making me, in my glasses and short trousers, feel somehow wispy and girlish, and reminding me how I dreaded ever having to sleep in a bed with him and what I'd awoken to find his fingers doing in that long-ago early morning at the other flat. Physical dread of him, and self-disgust at feeling such a thing, almost paralysed me.

He greeted me with no Grandma Norman-style bear hug, just a wan smile and a rather bleary 'Hello, old son,' suggesting his previous night's journey had been from somewhere much further away than Portsmouth – if that, indeed, was where he'd come from. Then, without another word, he picked up the electric kettle and began filling it at the sink. I realized there was to be no explanation as to why he had returned. For there was to be no acknowledgement that he'd ever been away. He bustled around, opening drawers and cupboards as Louis the Siamese waved a kinky tail between his legs and old Nigger's tail thumped against the bare floor-boards in incredulous delight.

It was as if none of the past year had happened; as if there had never been a Joan or a mysterious flight to London or a Christmas job with the Post Office or a baby or a 'shared' bed at the Oxford Hotel, Portsmouth; as if he were simply a conscientious father, forcing himself out of bed at a less than civilized hour to get his son off to school. I remember thinking – as I sometimes had before – that he derived some obscure pleasure from keeping me utterly in the dark and how, with this studied nonchalance, he seemed to be almost daring me to ask the questions I knew were impermissible.

By far the most immediate horror was his destruction of the morning routine I'd followed for all these solitary weeks. He boiled me an egg, made a slice of toast under the oven-grill and put them in front of me just as the high-level electric clock showed five to eight, the time I usually would have reached the Commodore's portico and be looking at the stills for *Mogambo* or *Dial M for Murder* or the enviable Confederate wounded in Atlanta's town square. It was a perfectly nice boiled egg, as firm as a nun's white wimple on the outside, sticky gold in the middle. But I could force down only a couple of mouthfuls. Panic surging inside me gave the white an oddly metallic taste. The toast rasped like cinders at the back of my throat.

Time had not dulled his ability to read my thoughts, especially the more demeaning ones. Calmly – at first – he told me it was far too early to set off for school and that I should start the day with a proper breakfast inside me, as if that were an ongoing daily concern of his. 'It's ridiculous, setting off for school at only just after eight,' he said. 'How long does it take you to get there? Only about ten minutes . . .' As of old, his vehemence made some words seem almost tiring for him to articulate. 'You could leave here at quarter to nine – at quarter to nine, Philip – and be in ample time. Still be in *ampoo* time.'

Sweating and breathless, with the taste of metallic egg-white in my mouth, I did the thing most calculated to enrage him most. I began to whimper. The hazel eyes looked at me with familiar disgust, quickly shading to suspicion. 'Well, if you have to be there so early, Philip, you won't mind telling me why. Just tell me – if you really have to be there so early, what do you have to be there *for*?' He kept me until almost 8.20, when the egg had gone cold and sweat was pouring down my face. Then, with a half-despairing 'Grrr!' he indicated that he washed his hands of me. I grabbed my satchel and bolted out into the drearily perfect sunshine.

*

I CAME BACK from school that afternoon, hoping he might have gone as abruptly as he'd reappeared. But his so-familiar alien smell was still there. His pipe and tin of Log Cabin tobacco were still there. Oh God, *he* was still there.

Nothing further was said about that morning's scene over

the boiled egg. For now, a more serious offence had to be answered. During the day, my father had needed to get into the Second World War air-raid shelter that was part of our flat's domain. This, as I have explained – or should have – was not the traditional semi-underground arrangement but a one-storey red-brick structure, a few yards to the east of the house, which once must have presented an inviting target to any German bombers passing over it. The shelter was now kept locked and, when my father had searched for the key, he had not found it in its usual drawer. The only possible conclusion was that I'd taken it for some reason, then forgotten to put it back. Unable to find it anywhere in the flat, he'd had to break the glass in the shelter's single high-level window and get in that way. Climbing out again, he'd torn his trousers on the broken glass.

I had no idea whether or not I'd taken the key. Probably I had. But to begin with, he seemed less annoyed than pleased with his own agility in shinning up to the window, forcing entry, then leaping down again. Thinking I discerned a half-smile on his face, I was unguarded enough to ask, 'Why did you want to get into the shelter, Dad?'

The half-smile abruptly vanished. 'Never mind why I wanted to get into the shelter, Philip. The point is that, if you hadn't been mucking around with the key and lost it, I wouldn't have done this' – he showed me the rip near his left pocket – 'to a nice pair of Daks trousers.'

'But it wasn't my fault you tore your trousers, Dad,' I protested.

'Fundamentally you were to blame, Philip.'

'It wasn't, Dad . . .'

'*Fundamentally*, Philip, you were to blame.'

To my dismay, there was no sign of Mrs Kennie, though she clearly had been in to clean the flat as usual. I found myself listening desperately for the voice of Mrs Cass through her open kitchen window below the front steps, or the Allens' key scraping in the lock. Anyone – *anyone* – to lighten the ordeal of being alone with him.

He cooked me some crumpets he must have got from the baker's in Monkton Street and made tea in our absurdly over-formal silver pot. Afterwards, I did my homework at the big sitting-room table – pretended to do it, rather, for all the time I could hear him moving around the flat, continuing the process of re-acquaintance and investigation. Each opening or shutting door, each creak of a loose floorboard, made me stiffen in fear that some further fault or neglect in my care of the flat was about to be revealed. My eyes bored into the purple-covered exercise-book lying beside me – '*Name: P. Norman. Form: One. Subject: History. Manufactured by the Educational Supply Association.* School and Charlie and Simon de Monfort seemed to belong to a different universe.

My homework completed, after a fashion, I sat on at the table. I knew without having to ask that there was no question of my going out or lying down beside my soldiers or drawing or reading or pursuing any other of my usual evening activities. As of old, his presence automatically suspended all choice and free will on my part. The two hours or so until darkness seemed to stretch in front of me like a desert. And then (Oh, *God*!) there would be bedtime.

After a few minutes, no longer hearing any sounds inside the flat, I got up and crept to the left-hand of the two rear-facing windows. I saw that he had begun gardening.

In addition to the central lawn with its unfruitful walnut tree, our portion of the garden included the flower and vege-table beds abutting its westerly boundary. At the start of our tenancy, these had borne a few straggly roses and primroses and aubretia (a name that always reminded me of my mother) and even the occasional potato and parsnip for the pot. But for months past they had been bare and untended. Now, to my bafflement, I saw my father digging in one of them with a fork. He worked with his familiar total concentration, making each plunge of the fork seem to be at a scientifically exact angle, shaking loose dirt through the prongs with the finesse of some prospector seeking gold. He did not plant anything, just turned and churned the lumpy earth as though it, at least, merited some recompense for his months of neglect. By the time darkness fell, all the beds were as perfectly-contoured and sprinkly-topped as chocolate cakes fresh from the oven.

At ten o'clock, I went to bed – thank God – in my own bed. He came in to say goodnight, only that, and planted a rough-chinned kiss on my forehead. When I awoke ('*Buffalo! Buffalo!*') he was still there. In the afternoon when I returned from school, despite all my entreaties to God on the way down Star Street and along the garden-wall of the Tredegar guesthouse, he was *still* there.

The grass around the walnut tree had not been cut since the previous summer and was now so long that it grew sideways rather than upright. That second evening, my father decided he would cut it – or, rather, that we should cut it together.

Our household did not include a lawnmower nor any kind of mechanical grass-cutter. All we had was a small hand sickle, such as used to feature, crossed with a hammer, on old Communist Russian flags. With this medieval-looking implement, my father did the cutting; I followed him with a rake, collecting the loose grass into heaps to be parcelled up in newspaper (no plastic sacks then) and disposed of in the dustbin. The lawn cannot have measured more than about forty feet by thirty, and cutting it, even by such primitively laborious means, can't have needed more than three or four evenings. But to me, it seemed to go on for ever.

We worked, for the most part, in silence and completely by ourselves. Although three other flats shared the garden, no one ever appeared but Mr Cass, a huge, bald man who kept chickens behind a wire fence on its eastern side. I was bored out of my mind and, after the first half-hour or so, tired enough to drop. My shoulders and legs ached, and the slide of the rake's wooden handle through my left palm made it red and sore. But I never uttered so much as a word of complaint. I knew there could be no stopping until my father decided we had finished and that if he sensed me to be in any way mutinous, that moment was likely to recede even further into the future. So I dumbly followed him, raking and heaping, heaping and raking as one after another noiseless 1954 twilight thickened around us.

I can see him now, bent down low in his open-necked lovat shirt, sweeping the sickle blade through flattened grass with the tireless regularity of a metronome. His hazel eyes are blank with mechanical absorption, his tongue peeps out and presses against his upper lip. Looking down on the dark-peaked forehead, I wrestle once again with the utter mystery of his motives and intentions. Why has he come back like this when he must know that my mother and the baby aren't here? (The idea he might have wanted to see me never enters my head.) Does it mean a rift with Joan, possibly brought on by her complaining mother? Above all, if we are still breaking up as a family – as I have no doubt we still are – what need can we possibly have of dug-over flowerbeds and a neatly cut lawn?

While my arms automatically worked the rake, I went into a kind of trance, half-shutting my eyes and pretending the grass, three feet below, was the jungle of wartime Burma where I was just coming in to land on a commando mission by glider. As I passed one after another point of seeming total exhaustion, and still he showed no sign of stopping, I would murmur the same phrase about myself in a kind of rhythm: 'He worked like a Trojan . . . he worked like a *Trojan* . . .'

One evening, I picked up a stone which, to my eyes, bore an uncanny resemblance to a solidified roast potato. It became the basis of another private fantasy to relieve the boredom of raking. A Victorian boy who used to spend summers at Dunraven had been unable to finish everything on his plate one lunch-time, so he had covertly slipped a potato into a pocket of his knickerbockers. Later, he'd flung it from an upstairs window onto the lawn where it had lain, atrophying into rock-like hardness, until I found it.

I was thinking about the Victorian boy when my father suddenly appeared beside me, holding up his bared left forearm. 'See?' he said softly. 'There's a mosquito just about to sting me.' I could just make it out in the gathering gloom, poised almost elegantly on its long back legs, its upraised barb like a tiny scarlet sword. He made no attempt to brush it off, but kept his arm still and watched it closely as though fascinated by this vignette of Nature in action. 'See it?' he whispered like some wildlife expert on television. 'It's getting ready to have a real go at me . . .'

Not until well after Holy Trinity's bell had struck eight would he decide that we'd done enough for tonight and could go in to supper. We always ate in the kitchen – or, as he pronounced it, 'kitching'. After his essay into egg-boiling, he did not attempt to cook, but each night set out a cold picnic on the plastic tablecloth – bread, cold meat, cheese and an earthenware jar of pickled onions which had stood in the larder so long that their skins had turned black. He did not put out plates, but simply ripped open the greaseproof paper bags the food came in, and we helped ourselves with knives or our fingers. I yearned for my mother's finesse; the napkins and cruet she would have produced for even this scratch meal; her wafer-thin bread and butter with the crusts cut off.

He had always relished the kind of cold delicacies I could hardly bear to look at, let alone eat – belly of pork in strips of white, blubbery fat; Gorgonzola cheese so rank it sometimes had live maggots crawling in it. But one night as we sat there, something made me try one of the blackened pickled onions. I found I liked the way my teeth crunched through its tight-woven layers and the sour vinegar seemed to run into my very eardrums. 'I've cultivated a taste for pickled onions, Dad,' I said, proud to have found this affinity with him – and slightly amazed at myself for coming out with a word like 'cultivated'.

In answer, he put his arm around my shoulders and drew me close to him. 'I hear . . .' he said softly into my ear. 'I *hear* . . . that you want a portable radio.' How had he discovered that was what I wanted most in the world? I could only guess Grandma Norman must have told him. Rigid with excitement, I turned and looked at him. 'We shall have to see what we can do,' he went on – then started smiling, and I realized it was a joke. While my attention was distracted, he'd filched the other two pickled onions from my plate.

After we finished eating, he would sit back in his chair, take out his Dunhill pipe (with the white dot on its stem) and start to fill it from his oilskin tobacco-pouch. I remembered how watching him coax out the brown-gold strands with his thumbs and tamp them firmly down had always had a soothing, reassuring effect, like seeing a cat wash itself. When he lit his pipe, holding a match to its well-seasoned bowl as he blew out sidelong clouds of fragrant blue smoke, he seemed the most rock-solid, reliable person on earth. I wondered how I ever could have believed him anything else.

We would sit on at the table, not turning on the overhead

light, until I could see only the glimmer of his shirt and the red sparkle of his pipe as he drew on it. At these times, he would be in a mellow, reflective mood, telling me about life in the RAF when he'd first joined in the 1930s – the servants, the made-to-measure uniforms, the wonderful food that used to be served in the officers' mess. 'One evening, the buffet would be all game, the next it'd be all fish. And anything you wanted to drink. I'd sometimes have five Pimm's Number Ones before I even went in to dinner . . .'

This would lead on to the general wonderfulness of life in the 1930s, in particular the astounding cheapness of every-thing compared to nowadays. 'You could go into Montague Burton or the Fifty Shilling Tailor . . . get a beautiful ready-made suit for about two pounds ten. A nice car, you needed just a few quid. My first Bullnose Morris I got for six pounds, I think.'

'And were the pubs nice?' I'd ask, deliberately spinning out the conversation – for after it came the horrible recurring uncertainty of bedtime.

'Ooh, *beautiful*!' he said with feeling. 'You'd sit out in a lovely garden . . . Get beer or shandy in a quart pot . . . Beautiful crusty bread and cheese, as much as you could eat for about sixpence.'

I thought with envy of that mythic time 'before the war', which stretched back to the hilarious twenties and the Victorian and Edwardian times, and thence into the colour and clash of 'history'. I'd missed it all – the Bullnose Morrises, the beautiful food, the five Pimm's Number Ones before dinner. For me, there was only the grey, inert world of 1954, where everything seemed to have been settled and squared away long before I could play any part in it, and all colour, drama and promise were over for ever. History had reached a dead end. Time itself seemed to be winding down to a full stop.

Once, in the pipe-glowing dusk, I asked a daring thing that made my voice resonate weirdly inside my own head. 'Have you ever killed a man, Dad?' He admitted that he had. 'It was when I was with the Blenheim squadrons in Alsace-Lorraine. He was a Frenchman – a fifth-columnist. I shot him with the Smith and Wesson I had to wear as orderly officer. He died in the ambulance. But I don't really want to talk about it, Philip . . .' I didn't press him further and he puffed at his failing pipe with a solemn look on his face that, for once, I could understand. Somehow in that moment we seemed closer than we had ever been.

We finished cutting the lawn one sweltering Monday evening. The next day when I returned from school, he'd gone again. Mrs Kennie was waiting for me with an over-boiled egg I could eat and another story about losing half her stomach.

*

THIS TIME, however, he had gone no further than the end of the pier. In the daytime he was there, running the slot-machine arcade and restaurants. At night, he was back with Joan – or so I supposed – either at their hideaway in Portsmouth or some other hideaway on this side of the water.

For all his return to that more pressing other world, he seemed anxious to preserve the links that had been formed by our grass-cutting and twilit suppers at Dunraven. A new order was established under which I no longer returned to Dunraven and Mrs Kennie after school, but, instead, walked down to the front and caught a tram to the Pier Pavilion. I did my homework on the unfrequented promenade balcony, then had my tea out on the sun-roof. He had also evidently been seized with concern for our two animals, Nigger and Louis. When

I returned home each evening, I took with me a parcel of kitchen-scraps to feed to them.

I realized a kind of privilege was implied in his making himself available to me and me alone in this way. Yet I hated having to go to the Pavilion again and having to spend time there. The dusky yellow dome with its rows of slot-machines seemed to embody the unending still-life my life had become. The glassed-in faces of Sweeney Todd and the Automatic Palmist stared forth at me with the blankness of dull eternity. Under its giant down-pointing arrow, the jukebox endlessly played that summer's hit record, 'Wheel of Fortune' by Kay Starr, whose cheesey Deep Southern voice could have been writing a thought-bubble above my own head:

> The-her whee-heel of For-*chun*
> Goes spi-hinning arou-hound.
> Will the arrow point my way?
> Will this be my-hy da-hay?

Everybody I saw in the summer crowds seemed to have a happier, safer and more pointful existence than I did. Everywhere I looked, I saw a life that struck me as infinitely preferable to mine. My recurring fantasy was to find myself magically transformed into an elderly man named Fred Wellspring – 'Mister Fred' to me – whom we employed to run the rifle range and tend its adjacent cash-desk. He was like some idealized old man in an Enid Blyton story with his bald head, kindly eyes and little blob of sandy moustache. He lived in a pretty cottage in George Street with his red-haired wife, their grown-up daughter, Josie, and Josie's Alsatian, Leo. I thought enviously of the idyllic life he must lead outside the Pavilion; at times I even tried questioning him about it, though his replies were always evasive. When, for instance, I asked,

'What did you have for breakfast this morning?' Mr Fred would twitch his little moustache and answer, 'Filleted egg.'

At about 6.30, I'd go to the kitchen and collect the cat-and-dog food, usually cold scraps of fried fish wrapped in a newspaper parcel so loose that I had to carry it in my arms. Then I would make my way down the non-public main stair-case and across the arcade to the Amplifier Room, as I always had to, for formal permission to depart. My father would be standing in the doorway at the top of the short staircase from where he could watch both the machines and the pier-head outside. There was never an evening when my heart didn't jump into my mouth with the question, 'Can I go now, Dad?'

On many nights, he would treat it as a perfectly reasonable request, twitching aside a fold of the parcel to see what I was taking home for Nigger and Louis and then waving me off with one of his dimpling, irresistible smiles. He might adopt the manner of a genial sergeant-major, eyeing me up and down, then offering some friendly advice on how the overall picture might be improved: 'That hair could do with a bit of a comb,' or (glancing down at my brown Birthday sandals, discoloured and rotted by sea-salt), 'Those shoes could do with a little bit of a polish.'

But at other times, his eyes would bore into me mistrust-fully. 'You are going straight home, aren't you, Philip?' he'd say, as if he thought I might be planning to run around Ryde with a gang of delinquents until the small hours of the fol-lowing morning. I was going straight home – having nowhere else to go – yet his piercing, knowing gaze still made my protestations sound somehow hollow and shifty. 'Well, make sure you do,' he'd say, still far from convinced. 'And you're not to spend too long hanging round the Kiosk while Nanny's busy.'

Sometimes, the look that greeted me was hurt but resigned,

as though he'd cherished some special hopes for these after-school visits of mine, but had known all along that I'd disappoint him. 'All right, Philip,' he would say in a flat voice. 'I know how much you hate being down here with me.'

One evening, he fixed me with a look so severe that I felt sure I must have done something even more heinous than losing the air-raid shelter key. 'A little while ago,' he said, 'you called your mummy a very terrible name.' He could only have meant the time when – coming to his defence – I'd called her a bloody fucker, though how he could possibly have known about it mystified me: as far as I knew, the two of them had not been in contact since. Still more baffling was the reverential tone in which he said 'your mummy'.

'It was a terrible name to have called your mummy,' he continued, 'and I was very upset about it. But yesterday someone came up to me and said what a very nice and well-mannered little boy you were. And I was proud of you, Philip.' He did not tell me the well-wisher's name; I did not enquire or even speculate to myself who it might have been. In my present state of mind, a compliment was barely distinguishable from a blow.

Another evening, he didn't wait for me to speak, but grimly beckoned me into the Amplifier Room, motioned me to sit down beside his big roll-top desk, and shut the door. 'Have I ever done anything to make you fear me, Philip?' he asked. Before I could answer, he took a sheet of dark blue notepaper from the top of his Trix amplifier and held it out to me. 'Your mummy's written to me,' he said. 'I want you to read what she says.'

The sight of my mother's writing, like regular sea-waves, brought a sudden lump to my throat. The letter was about me, I could tell, but in my confusion only odd sentences registered on my brain. 'He is neglected ... his hair and shoes are filthy . . . he hates and fears you . . .' How could she know such things, I wondered, when she hadn't seen me for all these weeks? The only possible explanation was that some friend of hers had seen me around town and got in touch with her.

I looked up from the letter and met hazel eyes full of wounded amazement.

'*Have* I ever done anything to make you fear me?' he repeated.

Another kind of boy, in another era, might have seized this matchless opening. But I wasn't . . . and it wasn't. Instead, gathering all the horrified vehemence I could into my voice, I answered, '*No*, Dad.'

'I've never hit you, have I?' He paused, reviewing our far from abundant time together over the years. 'Well, only once . . . across the legs up at Nanny's when you made such a silly fuss about having your fingernails cut.'

'*No*, Dad,' I repeated fervently.

'Then what does she mean by it, old son?'

'I don't know, Dad,' I said.

He stared sadly through the net-curtained window, across the Triangle with its bobbing ghosts of Mr Vernon's ice-cream tins, to the berth where an almost empty Portsmouth ferry was making ready to cast. 'I've tried so hard to win your confidence, Philip,' he said dully. 'But none of it's been any good, has it?' With a thump of blue-black foam behind it, the ferry sidled away from its berth. I wanted to say he could have my confidence and keep it for ever but, instead, just sat there dumbly, guiltily. He gave me another long, regretful look, then shrugged and sighed. 'All right, old son. Get off home now, if you want to.'

Blind loyalty to him possessed me once again. The next day, I wrote to my mother, care of Grandma Bassill in London. Indignantly I denied that I 'feared' him and was neglected. 'Dad has been very good,' I ended, adding with a literary flourish that came all too easily, 'and Mrs Kennie has been like a mother to me.'

A few afternoons later, as I sat having tea on the sun-roof, my father sent for me. I found him standing by his desk with the telephone receiver in his hand. 'I hear you've written your mummy a nasty letter,' he said. 'Here she is on the phone to speak to you.'

I grabbed the receiver from him, realizing that the bit about Mrs Kennie must be the trouble. 'Mum,' I said in desperation, 'I'm sorry I wrote you that letter. I didn't mean it.'

'Then why did you do it?' her voice demanded in a flat, hurt tone. Outside in the arcade, the jukebox was starting up again:

The-her whee-heel of For-*chun* Goes spin-hinning arou-hound . . .

*

WALK WITH ME, if you like, down the pier back to shore at this, the nadir of my life. A still, sunless evening with the tide out almost to its full half-mile extent. To my left and right, glistening deserts of wet sand, here and there forked into inky heaps by fishermen gathering ragworm for bait. The smell of sea and seaweed, mixed with cold batter from the newspaper parcel in my arms. On the beach below, a pony galloping at full-tilt, ridden by a girl in hacking jacket and jodhpurs. Could it be Jean Black or her dark, disdainful twin sister, Janet? Over there, the Western, where our summer skating-rink used to be. A peak-capped man stacking deckchairs. The patiently hanging heads of Eade's donkeys. A group of boys spreading out wide to play catch. Among them, Bobby Greenham's white shirt, bulged by the wind like a sail.

The Kiosk. Never not busy. Grandma Norman in her grey tailored costume and open pink overall. 'Ten Seniors, duck? . . . Half an ounce of Old Holborn, love? . . . One and six, and six is two shillings. Thank you – and what's yours, dear? . . .' The thump of the rubber fridge-lid, the tinny whirr of spinning candyfloss. Her usual advice, with one eye on the windows: 'Don't worry too much . . . These things usually all come out in the wash . . .' 'Cheerio, then,' I say, hoping she'll ask me to stay a bit longer. But she answers promptly, 'Cheer-o.' An ice-lolly to suck on the remainder of my journey. The green side door shuts, locking itself, behind me. On its glass pane, the faded smile of Sally-Anne Howes from sweet-rationed days long ago. 'I buy Mars every week because Mars are marvellous.'

The Esplanade. Southern Vectis bus-shelters with their unchanging adverts. 'It's a man's life in the Army', 'Coughs and sneezes spread diseases', 'Fight VD'. Read's luxury coaches. Paul's luxury coaches. 'Mystery Tour this evening' written on a blackboard in many-coloured chalks. My parcel-carrying shadow thrown ahead of me on the reddish pavement, absurdly long-legged, a semi-fastened sandal strap curling out on either side. Holidaymaking crowds I hardly notice, and who don't seem to see me. I've always been afraid of ghosts, but not any longer. Isn't this just how a ghost must feel, looking in at life as through a pane of thick, deadening glass?

Cross over and turn right at the ivy-covered Hotel Ryde Castle. No more giant papier-mâché Guardsmen up on the ramparts. But bright ideas still pouring from its owner, Teddy Hoare. A bar called the Hunter's Den, hung with African spears and shields. In the conservatory side-entrance, a glass case containing the head and shoulders of a honey-coloured lion, peering out from a clump of bleached jungle grass.

Nearby, an easel-mounted signboard for a children's room now renamed the Children's Den. Photographs of boys and girls from normal families jubilantly flourishing soft drinks and packets of crisps. Lucky them. Lucky the participants in that Mystery Tour, riding round the Island in pleasant evening sun to their unscary denouement.

Then up Dover Street, leaving behind the noisy front and the quiet sea. People relaxing before dinner in rockeried guest-house gardens. Lucky them. The boy with the Mongoloid face I always see, walking between his mother and father in his black school cap. Lucky even him. Left into Belvedere Street, past the cottage hospital, then right into Trinity Street. At its cobbled far end, the churchyard wall, the feathery trees, the vermilion brick and dark chimneys of Dunraven. The ghost returns to its haunted house.

*

I WAS READING in bed late one night when my father walked in unexpectedly and dropped a large brown cardboard box on to my counterpane. Inside was a Vidor portable radio in a rose-pink and beige attaché case with tuning knobs of iridescent pale green. While I was still goggling, he went out to the kitchenette and discovered another crime. 'You've drunk up all the baby's orange juice,' he told me as I sat with the unbelievable present on my lap. 'There isn't a single bottle left. I'm cross about that, Philip . . .' It was my only warning that my mother and the baby were about to return.

And here we were, my newly augmented family together in a home for the first and only time, for an hour or so. The year-long freeze frame had jerked back into action. My world really was breaking up at last.

Only at this moment did I ever find the courage to reproach my father – for something I thought buried in the past, which now made me burst into tears and almost shout at him:

'I heard something terrible at school. A boy named Rooke said you'd been put in prison.'

He looked at my mother in mystification, then remembered the incident on the Duver toll-road, when he'd pushed the toll-collector into the nettles and the *Portsmouth Evening News* said 'Ex-Wing-Commander's Expensive Night Out'.

'Oh ... that was *nothing*, old son,' he said in a laughing-off voice. 'All that happened was that the police thought I shouldn't drive any more that night, so they said I might as well spend the night at the police station. That's all it was ...' Indeed, that was just how I had interpreted it at the time: the police being concerned only to offer him an interesting experience. But I still cried and shouted, making the most of my single moment of power.

Everything was settled. The flat was to be given up and our furniture – including everything of mine, even my soldiers – would go into storage. He was to return to Joan. My mother was leaving the Island again with the baby (lucky, uninvolved baby!) and Melody, her spaniel. Louis the Siamese was to be given to Mrs Cass downstairs, who had already as good as adopted him. Nigger the Labrador was too old and infirm to cope with all these changes, and so had to be put down. My father did the job himself with one of his sporting guns, in Whitefield Woods, just outside Ryde. I watched the huge old dog shamble trustfully away at his heels: an RAF accessory that had outlived its usefulness.

That left only one further chattel to be disposed of: me. I wanted to go with my mother – wanted to more than I can say – but knew it was impossible before anyone even told me. I would clearly be an intolerable burden on her on top of having to work and look after my sister. There was nowhere for me to go, I knew, but the floor still seemed to drop away beneath me as she broke the inevitable news.

'I'm afraid . . . I'm afraid it's back to boarding-school.'

Though I protested, pleaded, even cried some more, I knew in my heart it would have no effect. They knew they could depend on me to be a good boy yet again.

I remember, in those final hours, going out to fetch my mother some cigarettes and walking back up Winton Street, past Dunraven's southerly garden wall. On the other side, I could hear Mr Cass clucking to his chickens. The cobbled path was strewn with branches erupting into creamy sticky buds. The weather was still beautiful. Into the future as far as I could see, week after week, weekend after weekend, there was not a single thing to look forward to. Then, amid the engulfing despair, I remembered a solitary gleam of comfort. It was two-tone rose-pink and beige in design, with tuning knobs of iridescent pale green.

'At least,' I thought, 'I'll have my radio.'

Part Three

The Rest Room

Fourteen

I DIDN'T HAVE MY RADIO. When my mother brought it to the boarding-house along with my clothes, it was instantly confiscated by Matron on the grounds that I was too junior to enjoy such a luxury. For several weeks afterwards, I had no idea what had become of it; then one day, passing the open door of the Sick Bay, I saw its beige and pink mini-suitcase shape just inside, standing against the wall. The Sick Bay happened to stay empty that whole term and my radio was never moved from its place there. I would pay it surreptitious visits, but never dared even open its lid, let alone switch it on. An older boy named Steele who was a radio-nut warned me that if it went on being unused in this way, its two batteries – each larger than many modern transistor sets – would eventually corrode and leak into its mechanism with disastrous results. So that was something else to worry about.

I became a boarder again in September of 1954. But unlike the earlier incarceration while Tracey was being born, I had no promise or prospect of release. This time, it felt like a life sentence. Previously, I had been treated as a visitor, sometimes even called 'a guest', and had been allowed to remain in my day-boy house, Seaford. Now I had to change over to Westmont, the boarders-only house whose captive members were indoctrinated with ferocious competitiveness in the pursuit of school cups and trophies. The news was broken to me during prep on my third night by Blase the Dutch prefect – the only unpleasant Dutch person I would ever meet. 'Norman, I have the pleasure to valcome you to Vastmont,' he informed me with little sign of pleasure on his gaunt, jug-eared face.

The school was in Queen's Road, on the way out of Ryde to Binstead and Newport, just a few minutes' walk from the town centre and seafront. But as far as I was concerned, it could have been the outer reaches of Siberia. From this high eminence, the sea was no more than a grey glimmer beyond the encircling box hedge of the sports field. Away to the east, a fraction of the pier-head obtruded from the screening foliage of elm and wind-sculpted macrocarpa trees. Many times was I to stand at the Senior Reading Room's French windows, gazing out at that view with the hopelessness of a convict on Alcatraz.

I knew that my father and mother were now divorced, although when they had reached that final, irrevocable moment, and before what authority, I had, as usual, not the faintest idea. My father had once again totally disappeared. My mother had found some kind of hotel job on the mainland; she hadn't told me exactly where. I wrote to her care of Grandma and Grandad Bassill in London, who were again – so I presumed – looking after my baby sister, Tracey. With my mother's new status as a divorcee I realized it was now incorrect to address her letters to 'Mrs C.T. Norman', as formerly. But I felt that to write to 'Mrs Irene Norman' might be too painful a reminder that she no longer had a husband. So I put just 'Mrs Norman' on the envelope, hoping she would realize and appreciate my care for her feelings.

For weeks, the only substantial news to reach me was that

the other side of our family, too, had now crumbled into ruin. Auntie Lorna had left Uncle Phil and the Star Hotel and taken my cousins, Dina and Roger, back to London to seek refuge among her numerous brothers and sisters. The situation differed from my mother's and mine in that Uncle Phil had not run away with someone else; he had simply gone on being Uncle Phil to a point where his fragile wife had feared for her physical as well as mental survival. The breaking-point had come one day at the Star when a drunken Uncle Phil – enraged perhaps by another chair sticking into his back – had begun knocking Auntie Lorna about yet again. In a doughty attempt to protect her mother, sixteen-year-old Dina had picked up a glass cookie-jar and whacked her father across the mouth with it, knocking out two of his front teeth. She and Auntie Lorna and Roger had then fled the Island, in such terror of reprisals from Uncle Phil that they had to have a police escort to see them down the pier and off on the ferry.

I felt no sorrow or pity that my cousins had suffered my own fate; just my usual numb acceptance that I wouldn't see them and Auntie Lorna – and, for that matter, Uncle Phil – ever again. They'd been out of my life too long already for it to matter.

The Billy Bunter books I read and re-read so many times had given me an impossibly romantic concept of boarding-school life. Those mythical schools like Greyfriars and St Jim's were huge, rambling places with ivy-covered clock towers and monastic cloisters, peopled by so many hundreds of boys that the headmasters recognized only the most senior. Ryde School, by contrast, had just forty-four boarders, accommodated in a single grey-brick Victorian house in conditions of claustrophobic intimacy. At Greyfriars, even junior boys had their own studies and, outside school hours, seemed to enjoy unlimited free time for their study feasts and 'rags'.

But at Ryde School, at least for juniors like me, the concept of privacy was unknown, and to seek it instantly marked one down as peculiar and suspect. Between classes, there was never a moment when we were not watched over, spied on, hounded and harassed. The only solitude one could find – and that by no means inviolable – was in bed at night.

We lived mainly in what was known as 'the Basement', a subterranean network of whitewashed rooms where the day-boys also changed for games and used the primitive showers afterwards. It was a place almost triumphantly devoid of any cheer or comfort, its main amenity the hot water pipes on which we would huddle for warmth or attempt to dry our permanently sodden games gear. The Basement came as a special shock, I remember, to an American boy named Martinet (pronounced 'Martin-ay'), who had previously known only the luxury of secondary education in California. He would often describe how, when he first came with his parents to see the school, they had been received in the headmaster's comfortable ground-floor drawing-room, which Martinet had naively assumed to be part of the boys' domain. 'I thought to myself, "This looks great," ' he'd say with an expressive roll of his eyes. ' "This is gonna be *just* like home." '

The public-school tradition of younger boys 'fagging' – i.e. acting as domestic slaves – for older ones did not exist. Instead, each junior was burdened with menial duties for the general community in such number as to ensure he enjoyed the barest minimum of free time or peace of mind. At meals, one might be a server or clearer, either way having to bolt one's own food down at ulcer-generating speed. When classes ended at 4.05 p.m., one might be 'on counterpanes', the finale to each morning's bedmaking ritual when we left the sides of our white cotton coverlets folded up to the middle to give space for the maids to sweep under the beds. Being 'on counterpanes' meant going around the dormitories unfolding the coverlets so their sides hung down again. Or one might be 'on flannels', which meant tidying the facecloths on their lines in the (single) communal bathroom. Each cloth had to be wrung out, then folded into a square of identical dimensions to its neighbour. Matron kept an unceasing vigil over the counterpanes and flannels and had no qualms about reporting any defaulter for an instant prefectorial slippering.

Peak time both for chastisement and the fermentation of ulcers came after the 6 p.m. evening meal, when a prefect would ask who had been awarded plus and minus points for work or behaviour in class that day. The house accumulating the most plus points received an end-of-term trophy called the Citizenship Cup, which Westmont was obsessed with winning above all others. Those who put up their hands as plus-point-winners were rewarded with a curt 'Well done.' Those who put up their hands for minus points underwent public interrogation as to the nature of their crime by the presiding prefect, invariably followed by a command to 'see me afterwards', meaning three with the slipper. Anyone so unlucky as to raise both hands, for two minus points on the same day, could expect treatment like an informer discovered in some wartime French Resistance unit.

The other standard punishment, for crimes of lesser moment than failing to fold face-flannels, was being sent to bed an hour or half-hour before one's appointed time. For me, that was never a punishment; indeed, most evenings found me heading for Dormitory One twenty minutes or so before my time of 8.30. The one thing I looked forward to every day was getting into bed, pulling the covers over my head so that no one could hear, and then settling down to a good cry.

In an all-male society whose contact with females was limited to Matron and the kitchen staff, it was inevitable that homosexuality should run riot. The worst offenders were the boys from Turkey and Iran, who seemed to mature twice as fast as the rest of us, and competed for the prettier small boys as if they were so many *Arabian Nights* houris. If the boarding-house gave little scope for such activity, its extensive grounds offered plenty. I briefly belonged to an organization known as 'the Pioneers', a ruse by the school to get us to do outdoor maintenance work that otherwise would have needed paid groundsmen. One Saturday afternoon, as a gang of us cleared undergrowth in the ravine beyond the playing field, we came upon an Iranian prefect kissing a diminutive third-former. Not only kissing him but embracing him and bending him backward with melodramatic passion reminiscent of Clark Gable and Vivien Leigh on the poster for *Gone with the Wind*.

I became friendly with a boy named Miln who was at the school on a scholarship from the old London County Council. A brown-skinned, dignified individual a few months my junior, he lived in Soho, where his Belgian-born mother worked as a cashier at various well-known restaurants. Knowing Miln meant also knowing Wilds, a younger boy with a melon-shaped head and protruding ears who accompanied him everywhere, playing Sancho Panza to his Don Quixote. Despite being clever in class as well as a model of neatness and decorum, Miln was not popular with the Westmont regime personified by Matron and the prefects. He was considered too clever, insolent, subversive – the usual fate of individualists under tyranny.

Even for those heartless, boy-toughening times, we were appallingly underfed. At breakfast, each minuscule portion of baked beans would be ladled out beside its small, hard triangle of fried bread so as to take up the maximum space on the plate. It was a tradition to count your beans before the master or prefect had finished saying Grace. The average portion of beans per boy, I suppose, would have been about thirty. At other meals, our diet was fifties school food at its worst – grey meat full of fat and gristle and lengths of white windpipe; waterlogged cabbage, horny-skinned fish, puddings of prunes, dried figs or 'frogspawn' tapioca. We bought our own butter, sugar and jam to eke out the school's paltry allotment. If ever there chanced to be enough of a half-way palatable dish for second helpings, the biggest boys were always called up first; by the time the smallest ones' turn came around, there would seldom be anything left for them.

I have never known such raging, ravening hunger as I did in those months. I remember one day, in the chilly Senior Reading Room, opening a magazine at an advertisement for Payne's Poppets ('Stop at the shop that has Poppets!') and feeling my whole body scream for the taste of chocolate-covered hazelnuts. The few things on the school menu that I did like – cottage pie, for instance – came in such tiny servings that one received barely more than a taste. Some evenings, waiting to do serving duty in a still-empty dining-room, I would watch Mrs Eadie, the cook, wheel in her wooden trolley bearing the large enamel dish of cottage pie intended to serve all forty-four boarders, plus the staff. Some nights, she would gaze pensively through the window at the half-obscured Solent and remark that her husband was serving on the merchant ship just then sailing past . As she dug her spoon into the cottage pie's browned potato crust to dole out the first niggardly portion, I knew I could have eaten the forty-four servings by myself.

When I reached class each morning, I sought vicarious comfort by quizzing day boys about what they'd had for breakfast in the enviable comfort of their homes. A boy named Fletcher used to reply, 'Porridge and toast.' One named Squire used to reply, 'Fishcakes.' Bobby Greenham, my former friend, used to grin facetiously and reply, 'Something to eat.' In the long, empty day, with nothing but disgusting school lunch to look forward to, it was sheer torment to read the bubble-and-squeak scene in *The Wind in the Willows*, or about Mr Trabb and his 'feather-bed' hot rolls with 'butter between the blankets' in *Great Expectations*, or even the bits about unleavened bread and the Lord smelling 'a sweet savour' in the Old Testament. Among the daytime teaching staff, the one who disliked me most was our geography master, Mr Symonds, a heavy-jowled man with shaggy eyebrows whom we nicknamed 'Sinbad'. When Sinbad recited the agricultural products of the Scottish Central Lowlands, I suspected he gave extra emphasis to each word just to torment me: 'Bacon ... eggs ... butter ... cheese ...' On cross-country runs, Miln would masochistically shout out the names of everything we most longed for as we trampled through freezing mud: 'Tea ... toast ... crumpets ... *Marmite!*'

Like many of my fellow boarders, my main solace came from reading about those even worse off than we were. There was at this time a craze for stories about the Second World War, mostly published in the new-fangled Pan paperback editions. It was a curious fad, since the war had ended only nine years earlier; indeed, its world seemed very close to ours, especially the tales about German prison camps like Colditz Castle and Stalag Luft III. I also discovered C. S. Forester's Hornblower stories, set in the harsh British navy of Napoleonic times and starting out – many of them – in nearby 'Pompey'. At least, I thought, I wasn't being tied to a grating and lashed with a cat o' nine tails, or forced to eat weevily ship's biscuit and drink water 'six months in cask and almost solid with green living things'. Not quite, anyway.

I was not a conspicuous member of the house, though I received my share of slipperings for getting minus points, folding face-flannels asymmetrically and consorting with the subversive Miln. The homo community did not lay a finger on me – doubtless because I wasn't pretty enough. At any rate, I was never in anything like the same sexual dread of Iranian prefects as I'd once been of my own father. The only faintly homoerotic glimmer I ever felt myself was towards a day boy named Kenney (no kin, of course, to our former retainer Mrs Kennie), who had lately appeared in the form above mine. He was a tiny, impeccably neat boy, a reputed brainbox at maths and science, who seemed to pass through school life without suffering any of the physical and verbal abuse the rest of us did. I hardly knew him, speaking to him only casually in the playground or if we were on the same table at lunch. Miniature and flawless as he was, he made me feel ungainly and tongue-tied, like some old cobbler in a fairytale with a perfect little elf or sprite dancing on the palm of his hand. Just the same, every Sunday night brought me the glowing thought, 'Another week of Kenney.'

My worst problems came from having been sent into captivity with only a fraction of what was specified by the school's equipment-list. I didn't have a 'best' grey flannel suit or a white cricket cap or a hockey stick or a separate pair of indoor and outdoor shoes. Indoors and out, I wore the same pair of scruffy Birthday sandals I'd had at Dunraven. The school outfitter was not in Ryde nor, indeed, on the Island, but a shop called Knight & Lee in Portsmouth. Getting there involved not just the ferry-trip but also a complicated bus-journey afterwards. Even when my parents were ostensibly together, there had been far too much pressure on my mother to allow any but the rarest trips to Knight & Lee. Now, as I accepted (*Good boy!*), there was no hope at all. I must make do with the uniform I'd mostly had in Junior School prior to my 'illness', eked out by the few palpably non-regulation things she had scraped to buy me since. There was no sympathy from Matron as she surveyed my meagre wardrobe with the tusky frown that seemed reserved for me. 'You *know* you're meant to have two pair of these, Narman . . . and why isn't this marked?' Respectable boys had all their things marked with Cash's woven nametapes whereas mine, at best, bore an amateurish smudge of black ink. You'll understand what satisfaction it gives me today to look over my daughter's school uniform and see a perfectly sewn Cash's tape inside every garment.

I became mildly celebrated for both talking and walking in my sleep, sometimes simultaneously. Late one night, a prefect found me wandering the corridors far from my own dormitory and asked me what I was doing. 'Looking for the composition I wrote this evening,' I answered – or so I was told later. Another night, I sleep-walked down the main staircase, which juniors were forbidden to use, and had to be led back to bed by the headmaster himself. At times when nocturnal wanderlust did not seize me, I'd lie in bed with my eyes open, holding apparently sensible conversations while fast asleep. It became a favourite sport among the dormitory prefects, as they undressed for bed, to question me in intimate detail about my family and background. I told them all about the pier and our various businesses and how my father had run away with Joan – and, next morning, remembered not a word of what I'd said.

A modern school might have shown some curiosity as to my psychological condition. But to Westmont in 1954, I was just 'old Norman who walks and talks in his sleep'. One of the housemasters did voice some concern after a boarders' group photograph showed me looking at the camera pale and unsmiling, with my head at a myopically sidelong angle. (I had lost my glasses months before, but hadn't liked to bother anyone for a new pair.) In – for him – an unusually sympathetic manner, the housemaster pointed out my haunted look and the odd cast of my head in the photograph and asked me whether I was worried about anything. But he quickly lost interest, and took to addressing me in class and on the playing-field as 'Parrot Face'.

*

I HAVE SAID that three times in my childhood I knew the sensation of a dream coming true. The first was when I wished Grandma Norman would run a sweetshop; the second came out of the blue in this winter of never-ending 1954, just at the moment when life seemed to have settled at rock-bottom. I stood at the boarders' letter-rack with its white tape lattice-work, reading my mother's words over and over: 'What do you think! I'm going back to *the Cross Keys*!'

The news took my breath away – so much so that an older boy (Harris E., his name was, to distinguish him from Harris C.) glanced at me in concern and asked if I was all right. *All right?* I couldn't count how many times during my family's drawn-out death throes I'd wished we could return to the Cross Keys Hotel in St Neots and the idyllic country life we'd enjoyed before Uncle Phil lured my father down to the Island. Turning the clock back to those fire-glowing late forties had always seemed the most utter impossibility. Now, after I'd long since ceased pining, it had happened.

The full story followed in slightly disjointed form – for she clearly was almost as excited and incredulous as I was. Her first post-Island job as a hotel housekeeper had been a temporary one lasting only a few months. When it ended, acting on pure impulse, she had written to the Cross Keys' owners, a brewery called Paine and Co., reminding them that she'd helped run the place six years earlier and asking if by any chance it needed a manager. Paine & Co. remembered her well, possibly remembering, too, that she had done most of the work while my father was out country-squiring. And by an extraordinary coincidence the Cross Keys *did* need a manager. It was as simple as that.

In a miraculously short time, another letter from her arrived in a white envelope with the unchanged design of two medieval crossed keys etched in black on its flap. I could have kissed – probably did – the sheet of small-size notepaper bearing the letterhead of Paradise Regained (Office: St Neots 368. Residents: St Neots 11). 'Everything is just the same,' she assured me in the smudgy print of what could only be a hotel office typewriter. Glorious it felt to write back to her there, taking care to let Miln and the others see that I'd acquired a proper address at last – 'Mrs Norman [How she must appreciate my tact!], The Cross Keys Hotel, Market Square, St Neots, Huntingdonshire'.

With end of term and Christmas holidays only a few weeks off, the miracle could not have been better timed. Until that point, I still had no idea where or with whom I'd be for Christmas. Now I could look forward to spending the whole four weeks with her at – I could still hardly believe it – at *the Cross Keys*. 'I'm sure we shall have a lovely time,' she wrote me in another letter. I spent the term's final weeks lost in a glowing daydream of open log fires and horse-brasses, with myself stretched almost horizontal in an easy chair and gorging Christmas tuck. The robin cake-ornament in that hopeless drawer at Dunraven would come alive and sing again.

Inevitably, going back to the Cross Keys in real life could not possibly measure up to so stupendous a vision. Everything was 'just the same', as my mother had said: the red-brick eighteenth-century façade and its Elizabethan courtyard had not been altered one jot since we'd left it for Ryde in 1949. The last major renovation had, in fact, been carried out during my father's tenure. I remembered him personally supervising the construction of the oak-beamed bar to the left of the archway, and a new passageway connecting the kitchen and dining-room. There, just as before, were the worn red Turkey carpets, the framed prints of 'Cries of Old London', the big open fireplaces, the horse-brasses – yet all of it smaller and somehow duller than in the gorgeous brochure of my memory.

I had pictured myself rushing thankfully into my mother's arms and the two of us being together, happily – triumphantly – for the first time since I couldn't remember when. But that daydream didn't come to pass either. She was only on trial as the Cross Keys' manageress and had to prove she could do the job – the more so since Paine & Co. had their head office on the other side of the Market Square and could keep her under continual observation. She was too preoccupied with administrative detail for us to spend much time together, though work was not the only thing that claimed her attention. She had acquired an instant circle of friends among the local farming community who remembered her from our previous tenure. I was always being introduced to a Mrs this or 'Uncle' that who claimed to have known me then. As a single woman, only just past forty, she also – despite my father's cruel prediction – began to receive attention from men, albeit mainly married ones. From the Island's dull servitude, her life had changed to one of hectic social gaiety. Between tasting the day's soup in the kitchen or drinking champagne with red-faced men in Prince-of-Wales-checked suits in the hotel office, she seemed to have little time for me.

Helping her as receptionist and deputy manageress she had a young woman called Julia Roberts who'd previously worked for her friend Mrs Bailey at Ryde's Royal Esplanade Hotel. She and Julia had become close confederates, even sharing a twin-bedded room (the very same one she and my father once occupied) overlooking the crossed-keys sign and the Market Square. I could not take up a room that might be let for money, so had to be put in the staff annexe, across the courtyard from the main building. My sister Tracey, now ten months old, spent almost all of her time with her nursemaid, a plump, elderly woman named Mrs Basson, who lived in the lane behind the hotel garage. Occasionally, Mrs Basson would wheel her into the hotel in her pushchair for a ceremonial visit. In my entire stay, I saw her only about twice.

I was disappointed and angry about my mother's seeming lack of interest in me. Yet a part of me breathed a sigh of heartfelt relief that she had found this immeasurably better existence and this circle of prosperous and convivial new friends. On the few occasions I went into her bedroom, I would look around hopefully for signs of improvement in her quality of life. On the twin bed nearest the window lay a circular red satin nightdress-case. I hoped that the bed was my mother's and the nightdress-case was a sign that she could at last afford to buy nice things for herself. But, to my disappointment, it turned out to be Julia's.

On the few occasions when my mother and I talked intimately, it was always about my father and the misdeeds on his part that had not ceased even after they were no longer married. She told me that when he found out she was returning to the Cross Keys, he'd done his best to stop her, telephoning Paine & Co. and warning them she was not reliable. I realized the full depth of her bitterness when I glimpsed a half-finished letter she was typing to him, care of

Grandma Norman in London – for she had no more idea of his current whereabouts than I did. 'Dear Mr Norman . . .' the letter began.

Since I was legally in her custody, I had assumed her return to the Cross Keys meant that I'd now be leaving Ryde School and the Island to live with her and Tracey in St Neots. But this could not be, as she explained to me very gently and regretfully soon after my arrival. Her job at the hotel might end within months, even weeks, and there was no telling where the quest for work might take her next. Rather than disrupt my education, it was better I stayed where I was.

Besides, as she further explained, there was a matter of principle at stake. At the divorce hearing – which only she had attended – the judge had made an order for my father to pay her £5 per week in maintenance. With her new-found robustness, she had stood up and said that any such order was a waste of time, since she doubted that she'd ever see a penny of it. How could he help her, then? the judge had asked. My mother answered she was afraid that directly her back was turned, my father would adopt the Uncle Phil approach to education, taking me away from Ryde School and sending me to the town secondary modern. She therefore requested, and was granted, an order, that he must continue paying fees for me at the school of her choice. That was why I must be a good boy and go on putting up with it.

Within a very few days of arriving at the Cross Keys, I was actively aware of not enjoying myself. The feature of hotel life I had totally forgotten was that there were guests everywhere, ringing bells to sub-divide my mother's attention even more minutely, entering to form murmurous groups in lounges where I'd hoped to enjoy the open fire alone. To recompense Paine & Co. for having me there, I was expected to make myself useful by running errands for Julia the receptionist (at least a hundred per hour, it seemed) and helping sort empty bottles from the bar into their proper crates, light and brown ales, Britvic fruit juices, 'splits' and Babycham.

Just as I used to at the Pier Pavilion, I took to hanging around the staff, finding them a more ready source of interest and companionship. I grew especially fond of the house-keeper, a genteely spoken woman named Mrs O'Connor, also a recent divorcee who had a son of about my own age named Patrick living with her parents in nearby Bedford. I was also charmed by the chef, Bernard, a man with bulging, humorous eyes and a manner which no one outside theatrical circles had yet learned to call camp. He had the room next to mine in the annexe and, when he finished work each evening, would look in to say goodnight to me, still in his apron, chequered trousers and tall, starched hat. For ten minutes or more, he'd stand in the doorway, telling me about his home at Market Deeping, near Peterborough, his daughter Bernice and his wartime service as a medical orderly in the Libyan desert, all with the eloquent eye-rolls and twitches of the mouth that made me sometimes almost cry with laughter as I lay there in bed. When at last he pulled the latched door shut, he jumped backward with a scandalized squeak, as if he'd only just avoided trapping his own genitals in it.

My fondness for Bernard and Mrs O'Connor led to ten-sions with my mother, who, I felt, adopted too curt and impersonal a manner towards such warm and wonderful people. There was finally a bitter row in the hotel office, when she accused me of 'siding with the staff' against her. At the holiday's end, when she saw me off for my two-stage (solitary) train journey back to Portsmouth, I could sense a certain relief in her cheerful wave.

About two weeks into the new term, I was doing prep between Miln and Wilds in the Senior Reading Room when a prefect came and told me I was wanted on the telephone. I followed him in trepidation, with every eye in the room fixed on me, for we were allowed to receive phone-calls only in dire emergencies.

The school telephone was an ancient, dial-less instrument in the dark corridor outside the headmaster's study. I picked up the receiver and, for the first time in more than six months, heard my father's voice.

He was speaking from Ryde, though he didn't say where. He asked me a few questions about how I was and my school work, which I answered in tongue-tied monosyllables. Then, with an air of cutting to the chase, he said, 'I want you to meet me.' His tone was low and ominous. I assumed he must have some further bad news to impart to me, or that I'd done something else wrong in the Dunraven era which he'd only just found out about.

Fifteen

THE NEXT SATURDAY afternoon, I got permission from Charlie to go downtown and set off with my heart in my indoor/outdoor shoes. I reached our agreed rendezvous, the Theatre Royal cinema, a quarter of an hour too early, and hung around, looking into shop windows and envying every passer-by for not being a Ryde School boarder. As the Town Hall clock struck four, I saw him on his way up Union Street with his unmistakable, round-shouldered, head-thrusting, checking-on-everything gait. I remember how, in that moment of wild panic, my attention fixed on his overcoat, which was of brown herringbone tweed. Had he owned it in the days when he kept his clothes in a 'compactum'? I thought so, yet couldn't be completely certain.

The afternoon's ordeal turned out not to be such a terrible one after all. He took me to the Theatre Royal to see *The Battle of the River Plate*, starring Anthony Quayle and John Gregson. On the way in, he bought me a Mars and a Bounty bar and one of each for himself as well. Just as the lights dimmed, he turned to me with a smile – his same old irresistible, dimply smile – and asked, 'Which are you going to eat first? Your Mars or your Bounty?' as if he, too, were just a schoolboy at heart.

Afterwards we went to a café called the Maypole, one of the few remaining open during winter. I had beans on toast which, I remember, was toasted only on its top side. As we discussed the film, a fictionalized account of the sinking of the German battleship *Graf Spee*, it felt as if we'd last seen each other only yesterday. My father did not mention any part of the previous year – not the divorce or my mother or the new baby or what had happened to our flat at Dunraven and its furniture, or Uncle Phil or my departed aunt and cousins. He did not tell me where he'd been or what he'd been doing all these months, or whether the state of 'running away' with Joan still existed or why he was now back in Ryde or where he was living. And, of course, I could not bring myself to ask. Instead, I asked why a vessel of the *Graf Spee*'s size had been called a 'pocket' battleship. He replied that it was just a name.

After tea, he walked me back to school as far as the John Street turning, where he drew me against the roughness of his brown tweed coat and kissed me on the side of my head. 'Here's some pocket money,' he said, putting his hand into his coat and giving me two half-crowns. The way he said 'pocket money' told me that he was back in my life.

It became a regular thing for the rest of that term. We met on Saturday afternoons and saw a film at the Theatre Royal, the Commodore or the Scala. Afterwards, we had tea at a café, then my father walked me half-way back to school, hugging me goodbye and giving me five shillings.

I remained baffled as to why, after all this time, he had suddenly remembered me and decided he wanted my company. He continued to explain nothing, confide nothing, say nothing about where all this was leading, if anywhere. He treated me with a kindliness and gentleness that, even in his best moments, I had never known before. Yet I felt no sense that he was trying to make amends or express tacit apology or remorse. Rather, it was as if I was receiving a second chance to win his affection and approval, to make myself the kind of son he had always wanted and deserved. The past, with all its uneasy transactions between us, had been cancelled at a stroke. In the winter-empty streets, the cinema darkness, the steamy-windowed cafés, we were beginning anew.

By the second or third of these Saturday outings, all my fears and doubts where he was concerned had melted away. I rediscovered how gently his rough beard scraped against my cheek when he kissed me, how rock-steady and dependable his tweedy clothes and, especially, the lighting of his pipe always made him appear. He was unfailingly good-humoured and attentive, listening sympathetically to my horror stories of life in the boarding-house and of Matron. Towards masters and prefects who made my life difficult he counselled almost Quaker-like mildness. 'Remember,' he told me, 'a soft word turneth away wrath.' Hard to believe this was the same man who had wrenched Alfie Vernon's shirt off his back and pushed the Duver tollgate-keeper into the stinging nettles.

One afternoon, he showed me the gold ring which he'd always worn on the second finger of his left hand, but which, I now realized for the first time, bore a tiny heraldic device. 'It's the emblem of the Norman family which I hope you'll wear, too, one day,' he told me. 'And there's a family motto as well, which I hope you'll always live by. It's "Press Forward".'

There was only one feature of our shared history that I remember us ever discussing. Despite the changes in all other departments of my father's life, I knew he still controlled the Pier Pavilion and, apparently, intended to reopen it next summer. One Saturday over tea, in my new mood of confidence, I asked him what he'd do with the Pavilion if he had unlimited money at his disposal.

He found the question more interesting than I could ever

have expected. 'Shall I tell you what I'd do with it?' he said. 'I'd repaint it all in a modern colour scheme – something like red and grey. I'd run a tea dance in the afternoons, and up on the stage I'd put a Hammond electric organ.'

'Not a band?' I queried.

'No-o. You can get all the sounds a band would make from a nice Hammond or Compton organ.'

I could visualize everything precisely as he spoke. With hope in such desperately short supply elsewhere, it seemed the most wonderful of pipe dreams.

*

SO HERE I WAS on the pier tram again as its two green cars slid out of the Esplanade station. Here again was the familiar regular 'bang-bang-bang' noise as it traversed the naked girders over boiling grey winter sea. Here again were the varnished wooden seats, the leather hand-straps, the advertisement cards for Barry O'Brien's summer shows on rival piers in Sandown and Shanklin. Here was the boy conductor, in his black serge trousers and waistcoat, clattering from the rear to the front car via a wind-blown open platform. I wondered if he might no longer recognize me as my father's son and try to make me pay for my ride. But he walked past me without a word, went into his sealed-off forward compartment and slammed the door shut behind him.

Approaching it by tram always showed the Pavilion at its most dramatic. It stood at the head of a V-shaped estuary between the tramway and a curved wooden wall that screened off the pier-head railway station. Big as it was, it did not come fully into view until well over half-way through the tram's outward journey. As it came into my view, that winter day in 1955, I almost shouted with astonishment. I'd seen it last with the colour scheme it had had since my father took it over: the dull yellow and green livery of British Railways Southern Region. Now its whole slatted-wood immensity was a soft designer grey, its terraced windows outlined in pinkish red. All that remained as before was the paler grey fish-scale pattern of its dome. My father had not been voicing an impossible dream but a *fait accompli*.

The porticoed entrance, off the tram station, was likewise newly grey and red. I went to the wide glass-paned door and squinted into what used to be the vestibule to our roller-skating rink. After some minutes of thumping on the glass with the flat of my hand and rapping it with a sixpenny piece, a small figure in an apron materialized on the other side. As it drew back the bolt to let me in, I saw a familiar shock of grey hair, a creased cardigan and whiskery chin. It was Mrs Kennie, that almost-forgotten companion of my bogus sickbed. 'Hello, son,' she greeted me nonchalantly in her Glaswegian brogue.

I followed Mrs Kennie up the unlit main staircase, whose panelled walls were now grey and red but whose stairs remained murky with long-accumulated grease from the nearby kitchens. 'Strictly no admittance,' it still said in my father's voice on the kitchen door. 'Except to staff.' As we reached the top, I saw that the promenade balcony also had been repainted grey and red, though the iron-riveted hollow of the dome above it remained its former shade of dusty yellow.

About a third of the way around the balcony, a table full of people were having lunch. I spotted Joan among them, and also a small girl sitting up with exaggerated straightness and giggling shrilly. With a sinking heart, I recognized Lynette, Joan's so-called 'little sister'. Seeing me at the door, my father rose and came towards me rather hurriedly as if to head me off. Over his jacket he wore the sleeveless, buttonless

brown leather jerkin I remembered so well from shooting
and skating days long ago. As he hugged me with his new
fondness, I caught the summery whiff of spring onions on hs
breath.

While we stood there, Joan picked up some plates from the
table and brought them to the kitchen service-door, which lay
on the other side of us. The act made me instantly conscious
of her changed status: she behaved like a diffident employee
no longer but as though the Pavilion belonged to her, too.
She looked rather smart in a camel-coloured sweater and
brown-and-cream plaid skirt; her hair was cut shorter than I
remembered. Her face wore its old unsmiling, tight-lipped
look, with what I interpreted as an extra dimension of embarrassment and contrition at the sight of me. I presumed it
was understood that, out of loyalty to my mother, I couldn't
possibly speak to her. I was wrong in so presuming. 'Say
good afternoon to *Miss Salsbury*,' my father instructed me
pointedly.

I had known her surname was Salsbury, of course, even in
the living-with-George era when she preferred to be known
as Goldring. Yet this sudden formal renaming took me completely aback. It was as if one's home had lately been broken
up, not by a leggy, importunate siren but by a teacher at one's
own junior school. Either of us might well have protested
that, little as I might know her, she had been 'Joan' to me since
I was seven. But neither of us did.

'Good afternoon,' I mumbled.

'Good afternoon,' she responded in her faint little
Brummie voice. I got the feeling that her elevation in title
discomfited her almost as much as it did me.

The sight of Lynette sitting there, brazenly having lunch
with them, filled me with dismay. Back in the roller-skating
days, when she and I had been thrown together, I'd always

convinced myself that my father found her giggliness and silliness as tiresome as I did, but had tolerated her simply from politeness. One small consolation of these past two years had been that, at least, I didn't have to see Lynette any more. Now, here she was again, as small and brown-skinned and nerve-racking as ever, and seemingly an integral part of whatever new household my father had established. To add to my disquiet, the pretence that she was Joan's – Miss Salsbury's – little sister seemed to have disappeared in the general identity-reshuffle. She now addressed her as 'Mummy' or, rather, 'Moomy', repeatedly and emphatically, as if the habit was still new and wonderful to her. 'Moomy, I do loove you, Moomy . . . you're my Moomy . . .'

To my relief, however, I found I had misread the situation. As Joan's – Miss Salsbury's – daughter, Lynette's domestic arrangements were no different from when she was mas-querading as her little sister. She continued to live with her ex-big-sister's parents, Mr and Mrs Salsbury, the grandfather and grandmother who had until recently been portrayed as her father and mother. Like me, she was here today purely as a visitor. When she left (which, to my hidden joy, she did quite soon after my arrival), her new Moomy packed up several things in a parcel for her to take with her as if she, too, was returning to a kind of boarding-school.

I soon forgot about Lynette, in any case, as my father took me on a tour of the Pavilion in its stunning new incarnation. Repainting it grey and pinky-red proved only the first step in an ambitious plan to drag it out of the Victorian age, where it had slumbered for so long, and plant it in the gleaming contemporary world of two-tone cars, sack dresses and G-Plan furniture. The slot-machines had disappeared, as had the rifle range, the jukebox with its suspended, downward-pointing arrow, and the wooden change-desk. There were no more pinball games showing Hawaiian or space-age scenes as imagined in the 1930s; no more Mutoscopes, no more punchballs, no more crane-grabs, no more hockey machines, no more 'Sweeney Todd', no more 'Copper Mine', no more 'Allwyne de Luxe', no more 'Automatic Palmist'. In a few years from now, the most insignificant of the vanished machines would be worth hundreds of pounds as designer accessories, but in nostalgia-free 1955 they were considered virtually worthless; my father almost had to pay someone to take them away for scrap.

The wide octagonal space that had served alternately as skating-rink and penny arcade was now filled with grey metal tables and matching sling-shaped chairs, arranged as around a circular dance floor. The boarded walls had been covered over with paper in various contemporary designs. On either side of the stage it had vertical red and yellow stripes. Behind the stage it was aquamarine. ('That's the one we had specially designed,' my father said.) The walls nearest the entrance-hall were pale grey with a dense black and white pattern which, on closer inspection, proved to be recipes for cocktails like Crème-de-menthe frappé and Crème de Curaçao, embellished with tilted champagne glasses, cocktail-shakers and Picasso-like faces with both their eyes on the same side of their noses. Evidently my father expected his next summer's clientele to be drawn largely from the Parisian Left Bank.

The changes also included one major territorial acquisition. He had taken over the First and Last, the single-bar pub on the Pavilion's pier-head frontage which hitherto had always been separately operated by Burt's Ventnor brewery. Its old Victorian decor of smoked mirrors and veined marble counter had been ripped out without a moment's regret. In their place was an angled modern bar with a sky-blue Formica counter and a canopy of suspended grey panels with curved ends. Around the wall were benches upholstered in red and black patterned plastic, blue Formica tables and stools with squashy red plastic seats. My father was as delighted with this transformation as a child with a new toy. 'Though I say so myself,' he kept repeating, 'that's a *veddy* nice-looking bar.'

Included in the takeover was the back room where Marje the barmaid used to squat over her trapdoor, weeing directly into the sea. Accessible from the Pavilion's main hall, this room had been provided with a red Formica-topped counter and renamed the Porpoise Bar. Exactly why was made clear by an illustrated wall-panel, which depicted the whiting from Lewis Carroll's poem, and the porpoise close behind it that was treading on its tail. A matching panel, in the same soft pastel colours, showed the Walrus and the Carpenter seated on a rock with oysters ranged on little legs in front of them. Beside each scene, the relevant verse was written in red italic script:

> The Walrus and the Carpenter
> Walked on a mile or so
> And then they rested on a rock
> Conveniently low
> And all the little oysters stood
> And waited in a row.

I was dimly aware that the murals alone must have cost a fortune, never mind the new blue Formica bar, the variegated new wallpapers and the oceans of exterior paint. It fleetingly crossed my mind to wonder how he could possibly have afforded it all, especially after having so recently been unable to afford my mother's court-awarded £5 per week maintenance. I could only guess that Grandma Norman must have stepped in at some point, with some of the accumulated treasure of her seasonal rock sales.

Equally fascinating to me were the relics of the Pavilion's Victorian past that had come to light during its redecoration. Behind the smoked glass mirrors of the old First and Last bar, for example, had been found a cavity containing a newspaper dated 1882 – the year it was built – and some wood shavings from a carpenter's plane, still as pristine as furls from a freshly-sharpened pencil. His quixotic nature stirred, my father had created a time capsule jointly marking the Pavilion's renaissance and the imminent eightieth birthday of our great wartime leader – and still Prime Minister – Sir Winston Churchill. Behind the new bar's contemporary mirrors he had sealed the 1882 newspaper, a modern *Daily Express*, and a message to posterity whose loyal Tory spirit was after Grandma Norman's own heart. 'This newspaper was found in 1955, the year of Sir Winston Churchill's eightieth birthday – bless him!'

I listened to all this with rapt admiration and excitement, for my father seemed on a creative high that nothing could check. His master stroke, I thought, was in choosing a new name for the whole edifice to replace the outmoded and fusty old 'Pier Pavilion'. He told me how he had cudgelled his brain for weeks, then had found the answer in the screaming white flocks that haunted the sky and sea out here, as sleeplessly in winter as in summer. What else could he call his new creation but the Seagull?

*

BEING A BOARDER wasn't nearly so bad after this. I now had a source of refuge and comfort outside the prison walls, which none of my fellow inmates did. And if I didn't have the image of a happy family, like other boys, to console me in my bleak bed at night, at least I had the Pavilion in its thrilling new guise; its red and grey livery, its cocktail-recipe wallpaper and sky-blue Formica, its murals of the chuckling porpoise and the Walrus and the Carpenter.

On Saturdays from here on, my father and I no longer met on the neutral ground of cinema entrances around town. Instead, I would make my way straight to the end of the pier and, usually, spend the whole afternoon there with him and the newly gazetted Miss Salsbury. On perhaps one Sunday in three, rather than joining the junior boarders' spiritless crocodile walk along the seafront to Puckpool, I would be granted a similar exeat.

If my father was completely and overwhelmingly back in my life, I quickly realized I was but partially so in his. For I saw him and Miss Salsbury together only at the Pavilion – the Seagull, as I had to keep reminding myself to call it. I had no idea where they had set up home together; whether they had some lodging in Ryde, or commuted by ferry back to Portsmouth and the hideaway where my mother's private detective had confronted them. When the two of us were alone together, however warm his mood, he continued to say not a word to me about the whole running-away episode – why it had happened, where it had taken him, whether he felt happier or more fulfilled now than he had before. For all his new benignity, I could still see that shadowy realm which bore the signpost, 'Mind your own business, Philip.'

What was immediately clear was that Miss Salsbury had stepped straight into my mother's shoes as his helpmeet in running the Pavilion in its new form. Invariably, when I arrived, I would find her helping him in one of the many small jobs of renovation that lay outside its grand professional redesign. She had a stronger practical bent than my mother ever did, and could use a paintbrush, even a screwdriver, with dexterity. One Saturday, I came in to find her in the entrance-hall, wearing a white kitchen overall and talking to a supplier of something or other for the restaurant when it reopened at Easter. 'Yes, we'd better have a doozen of those,' she told him, and I realized what power had been ceded to her.

No explanation was forthcoming, either, about when and why Mrs Kennie had changed allegiance from my mother's flag to my father's. She was as yet the only employee visible at the Pavilion, where she acted as my father's and Miss Salsbury's personal maid-of-all-work, making tea, washing up and doing ironing on a board set up in the new Porpoise Bar. She was still, as at Dunraven, racked by memories of nameless gastric ordeals yet indefatigably hard-working, capable and cheerful. Miss Salsbury she treated with admiring reverence, and my father – who called her 'Ken' – with a down-to-earthness that obviously amused him. 'Do youse want a drink o' tea?' she would demand unceremoniously. 'Yes, we's do,' he'd answer with a grin.

The huge wooden structure had no central heating and, during those February and March months, was bitterly cold. As dusk fell, we would retreat into the former dressing-room, to the right of the stage, which in my mother's time had been used as the company office. In the intervening months, it had been domesticated by a couple of wooden-armed easy chairs, a one-bar electric fire and – I was excited to discover – a Cossor television set. Half a mile out to sea, the reception was noticeably better than on land, though the picture was intermittently broken up by Morse code wireless messages from ships passing through the Solent.

Consorting on these terms with the person who'd broken up our home made me feel unclean with disloyalty to my mother. But it was hard to resist that television set, especially with all the American comedy shows which the single BBC channel had lately begun showing – *Amos 'n' Andy*, *I Love Lucy*, *The George Burns and Gracie Allen Show*. To add to my unease, four o'clock on Sunday afternoons brought us 'America's Queen of Comedy', Joan Davis, in a show entitled – I prayed, not prophetically – *I Married Joan*. Its star even had a passing look of Joan-that-was with her blowsy blonde hair, thin, lipsticky lips and look of rueful resignation at the domestic mayhem she created.

As at our first reunion, my father insisted that I treat Miss Salsbury with as much formality as if she, and not just her name, were a stranger to me. 'Say "Good afternoon," Philip,' he would always prompt me when I arrived to find her helping repaint the upstairs restaurant or sorting out piles of faded dishtowels in the linen store. 'Good afternoon,' she'd reply with equal formality in that diffident, half-embarrassed little voice, thereafter not speaking to me unless I spoke to her. When we withdrew to the dressing-room, she sat silently in one of the armchairs, usually knitting something in mauve or orange wool, her thin face showing no reaction – as I hoped mine didn't either – when American voices on the TV screen warbled the theme-song 'I mar-ried *Joan* . . .' After a time, she would disappear off to the distant, freezing kitchens and return with a tray of tea and toast or buttered crumpets. I felt I betrayed my mother by eating and drinking things she had prepared – but to a Ryde School boarder, tea and toast from any quarter were not to be gainsaid. Besides, she had a way of making simple things look appetizing rather like my mother's own. This feminine touch was almost as irresistible to me as the food itself.

Lynette was likely to be there, too, for lunch or tea or both. I realized that, as Miss Salsbury's openly acknowledged daughter rather than fictional little sister, she could now claim some familial connection with my father – with me, too, come to that. To my relief, however, he did not demand the same recognition for her as for her mother. I was free to ignore her with all the lofty dignity of my eleven years while covertly watching with eagle eyes to gauge to what extent he now treated her as an unofficial daughter.

Thankfully, it seemed that nothing much in his attitude to her had changed: he was friendly and teasingly jovial – calling her 'Linnit' rather than Lynette – but showed her no physical affection whatever. She, for her part, seemed to make no effort to charm him, greeting his every remark to her with the same witless giggle; concentrating all her attention on the 'Moomy' she could now address as such. Miss Salsbury, I noticed, showed faint embarrassment when Lynette cuddled and clung to her, almost as if she regretted the loss of their old sisterly status. Yet, in her wary, tight-lipped way, she seemed to be an attentive mother. The bright-coloured wool on her knitting-needles invariably metamorphosed into a jumper for Lynette. When the little girl departed (hooray!), it was always with a collection of parcels and carrier-bags, painstakingly packed up for her by her mother. 'There you are, loov,' Miss Salsbury would say, tying the final bow – the most passionate endearment I ever heard from her.

I knew, too, that under these new arrangements my father would be duty-bound to associate with Miss Salsbury's parents, who presumably still dwelt at their impossibly grand private hotel, Wellington Lodge. More even than I dreaded the sight of Lynette, I dreaded renewing acquaintanceship with old Mr and Mrs Salsbury. But thankfully the couple never visited the pier-head, at least not when I was there. Whatever he had to do with them happened in other places, at other times. That was one area where I was quite content to be kept in the dark.

Despite his new obligations to people with Birmingham accents, he made me feel that our relationship was a special and inviolable one. We continued to go regularly to the cinema, just we two, the pursuit we'd always most enjoyed together. 'Quite like old times, isn't it?' he said one afternoon as the Theatre Royal's lights dimmed. 'Us being at the flickers together . . .' Another Saturday, we went to the Commodore to see *The Robe* in brand-new CinemaScope. As the Twentieth Century Fox music segued into a trumpet fanfare and the curtains drew back from their hugely widened screen, I thought of the Pavilion's new decorations and my father's new benevolence, and seemed to feel my world, too, opening out into grandeur and excitement.

Despite all that he must have spent lately on paint, wallpaper, Formica and bar murals, his munificence to me passed all previous bounds. He was always buying me some major thing or other to make my school-life more comfortable, usually without any solicitation from me – a navy-and-red tartan rug for my bed; a mottled scarlet Conway-Stewart fountain pen with an italic nib; a metal studded wooden tuckbox to keep my biscuits and Sandwich Spread secure from our well-known boarding-house thief. On the tuckbox lid he printed my initials, P.F.W.N., with the plastic stencil he'd always used for basic signwriting jobs around the Pavilion; I added a hand-drawn pencil skull and crossbones.

When Westmont achieved its obsessive goal of winning the inter-house championship – its prize a wooden statuette of a rooster and the unwittingly appropriate title 'Cock House' – my father provided crates of soft drinks and tins of crisps for the celebration party. He made an equally generous contribution when Miln and I and our frowned-upon coterie planned an end-of-term feast in wishful imitation of Billy Bunter's Greyfriars. Unluckily, the housemaster who called me 'Parrot Face' got wind of our plan and set out to wreck it. Instead of the post-lights-out debauch we had planned, he told us we could have it only after the regular evening meal, which we must first consume in full. Then, as we belatedly caroused over bottles of cherryade and packets of Clublet cheese biscuits in the Junior Dining Room, he went up to our dormitory and managed to discover a fault in the way the counterpanes had been folded. All of us were ordered upstairs to receive three each with the slipper. Crimson-faced and biting back tears, we then resumed our places at the feast.

One Sunday, I took a schoolfriend with me to the pier-head – a small, bespectacled but famously tough boy named Mick Hale. I'd worried that he might find the visit boring, but all such misgivings vanished when my father asked our help in throwing a grand piano into the sea. This had stood on the Pavilion's stage for years, dust-sheeted and forgotten; now, to make space for the electronic organ that was to play in his new Seagull Ballroom, he'd decided to get rid of it in the way we disposed of most unwanted items. Mick Hale and I joined the gang of volunteers – railway porters, tram conductors and the like – who carried the piano out of the Pavilion to the pier-head's western promontory and heaved it over the rail. Amazingly, it floated and for hours afterwards could be seen, half-submerged but still unmistakable, bobbing slowly out on the tide towards the deep-sea shipping lanes. 'I'd like to be on the *Queen Mary* or the *Mauretania* when she comes in this evening,' my father said, grinning. 'Someone on board is going to look out of a porthole and not be able to believe their eyes.'

'I like your Dad a lot,' Mick Hale said as we walked back to shore together. 'He's very human, isn't he?'

I nodded proudly.

'And who's that Miss Salsbury? Your stepmother?'

'No,' I replied.

'I didn't like her,' Mick Hale said, though, in all honesty, Miss Salsbury had done nothing to earn his dislike. I think he was just saying what he thought I wanted to hear. 'So if she's not your stepmother,' he persisted, 'who is she?'

I cast around for something suitably neutral and menial and finally came up with, 'The barmaid.'

For as long as I could remember, my father had never worn a watch. But that spring, one suddenly appeared on his wrist – bought, so he told me, at a knock-down price from a bar customer who worked on the transatlantic liners. It had gilt Roman numerals on a dark grey face decorated with the moon and a scatter of stars, and a movement warranted to contain '15 rubis'. Its back was transparent, allowing one to view a ticking gold mechanism set with scarlet pinpoints – presumably its 'rubis'. I thought I had never seen such a beautiful thing in my life.

When I departed to join my mother for Easter at the Cross Keys – a journey now holding no allure – my father walked with me to the ferry and enfolded me in a long, tobacco-fragrant hug. As I stepped on to the gangplank, he suddenly asked, 'Have you got a watch? Would you like this one?' Before I could answer, he slipped his moon-and-stars watch off his wrist and strapped it on to mine. 'There,' he said. 'It's yours.'

*

I SAW NOTHING of that first season when the Pavilion became the Seagull and people danced there to electronic organ music as good as a full band. Each night while it was happening, I would be in Dormitory One, between Shipway (D.) and Chard, the boy who still wet his bed. The pier-head was too far away for even a faint scrap of the music to be audible. Strain my ears though I might, all I could hear was the seniors playing volleyball outside, harshly urged on by the house-master who called me Parrot Face.

At Easter, Grandma Norman returned to her summer-time pitch, refreshed by a long journey back into her West Country homeland and visits to Aunt May Chapman and Auntie Annie Collins, her area representatives, as it were, in the old-lady profession. This meant I now had the best of all possible refuges on Saturday and Sunday afternoons. The Westmont regime did not like me going out so much, but could stop it only by 'gating' me for dereliction in counterpane-straightening or flannel-folding, which I was always careful to avoid. The worst that Matron could do was impose a time-limit just too short for most things one might plan for an afternoon out. 'Remember, Narman,' she'd call to me as I passed the open door of her sitting-room, for some reason making her voice tinkly and refined. 'Only *two* ahrs.'

The whole of those two hours I would spend at the Kiosk, holed up with the rock-boxes, the gas-ring and the deckchair in Grandma Norman's back room. While she and her staff dealt with the unending Alamo siege of customers, the rubber fridge-lid stamped and the candyfloss machine whirred, I'd crouch behind the partition, reading her *Daily Express* (racing selections underlined) or *Woman's Own* magazine, or my own current Pan war paperback, *Albert RN*, *The Wooden Horse*, or *The Colditz Story*. Sometimes my fellow boarders on their afternoon walk would come to the windows to buy sweets and be doled out their share of 'loves' and 'my ducks' from Grandma Norman. But I never showed myself, not even to boys I knew. 'All your little friends love these new Barker & Dobson Candy Kisses,' she told me. 'But none of 'em likes saying the name "Candy Kisses".'

Summertime had, of course, cancelled all those cosy cinema-visiting Saturday afternoons with my father. Our meetings now were almost always at the Kiosk, when he called in to do some other maintenance job for Grandma Norman or deliver fresh stock from her storeroom in George Street. Though she never alluded to it in words, she was obviously delighted by the rapprochement that had taken place between us. Sometimes she would pull the two of us into the same bear-hug, as though trying to cement us physically together, murmuring her special endearments first into my father's ear, then into mine, never mind that we were in full view of her staff and three windows crowded with customers. 'Ooh, *that* don't matter,' she'd chuckle in broadest West Country if either of us showed embarrassment. 'I don't care *who* sees me give my boys a bit o' love.'

But the mystery of his domestic arrangements remained, both while he was there and, even more so, after he had gone. I deduced that, while giving him unconditional support, Grandma Norman had said she could never meet or publicly acknowledge the woman for whom he had left my mother. For Miss Salsbury never came anywhere near the Kiosk or was even alluded to inside its walls. So far as Grandma Norman was concerned, each time my father went out through the green side door with the faded Mars Bar poster, it was to vanish into thin air. All my attempts to pump her for information were met by the same head-shake and almost pious closure of her eyes. 'I always make it a practice, love,' she'd say, 'never to ask Any Questions.' You could hear the initial capital letters as plainly as in the radio programme of the same name.

Sometimes I would find Uncle Phil at the Kiosk – for since Auntie Lorna's and my cousins' flight to London, he had remained in Ryde, still running the Star Hotel and apparently living alone there. His estrangement from my father still continued although, as senior partner in their pier-head business, he must presumably have been consulted over the installation of electronic organs, cocktail-recipe wallpaper and murals of the Walrus and the Carpenter. The past year's domestic drama seemed to have had no effect on Uncle Phil: he was still portly and slow-moving, with an air of being preoccupied by weighty intellectual considerations, especially when saying hello to me. When he spoke – or, more rarely, smiled – you could see the still-unrepaired gaps in his front teeth made by Dina with the glass cookie-jar. Grandma Norman remained outraged by this attack on her first-born, quite disregarding the fact that he had been assaulting his wife at the time. 'All his poor mouth was cut and bruised,' she told me. 'Wasn't that a terrible thing for a gurr-ul to do to her father?'

At 4.30, obedient to Matron's edict, I'd walk back up the long hills to prison, invariably with a carrier-bag of sweets and provisions in each hand. 'Here comes that beast Parrot Face, loaded up with tuck,' the housemaster once remarked loudly to a group of seniors as I made my way towards the Basement. Later, in the twilit dormitory, I'd comfort myself by staring at the watch my father had given me – so unbelievably exquisite with its moon-and-stars dial and warranty of '15 rubis'. Inside its transparent back, the noiselessly ticking works and pin-points of ruby-red were a tangible reminder of the wonderful new person my father had become and the promise life now held for me.

*

THE PROMISE was not to be fulfilled, however, until the end of that summer of 1955, after Grandma Norman had shut the Kiosk and returned to London again, and he and I resumed our routine of Saturday and Sunday meetings. One after-noon at the pier-head, he took me through the Porpoise Bar into the closed and empty Seagull Bar and carefully shut the connecting doors behind us. There, amid the sky-blue Formica and red plastic, for the third – and last – time in my childhood, I knew the sensation of a wish coming true.

He began by telling me how, since losing Uncle Wally, Grandma Norman had felt increasingly lonely during the winter months up in London, 'away from all of us'. She was also passing up much valuable trade, since even in winter there were always people around the pier-gates to buy cigarettes and sweets. I realized where all this was leading, but didn't yet dare to believe it . . . So, after weighing up all the pros and cons, he continued, she had decided to move down to Ryde permanently and keep the Kiosk open all year round. And she had said that, once she found a suitable home down here, I could live with her.

As my heart did a joyous back-flip, my father began filling his pipe in a serious way and reminded me of the inevitable stumbling-block to this glorious prospect. My mother would have to be persuaded to let me leave boarding-school and become a day boy again. He would do his best to talk her into it, he promised, if it was what I really wanted. I forgot that his continuing obligation to pay my fees as a boarder represented my mother's one small victory in their divorce. Yes, please, please try to persuade her, I begged him. Please, *please*.

He lit his pipe in clouds of fragrant blue smoke – that moment when being with him always seemed the safest place on earth. On the nearby bar counter stood a placard for Schweppes tonic water. A woman in a black negligée lay on her stomach, above the baffling caption 'Are you a Schweppicure?'

'What neither your Mummy or I want,' he continued, very gently, 'is for you to grow up the kind of boy who spends his time hanging around street-corners.'

'I won't, Dad,' I assured him.

'You've got to give us both your solemn promise about that.'

'I will, Dad.'

He put his arm around my shoulders, drawing me close to him and lowering his voice to a confidential murmur that even the woman on the Schweppes advert couldn't possibly have heard.

'And it's got to be understood that, if ever I find you've broken your promise – that you *are* hanging around street-corners – then it's straight back to boarding-school. Is that agreed?'

We were as close as we could be. Nothing could ever come between us.

'Yes, Dad,' I whispered adoringly.

Sixteen

CASTLE STREET has never ranked high among Ryde's beauty spots. It lies a short distance uphill from the Esplanade and runs roughly parallel with it; an anonymous back lane which few summer visitors see other than by accident. It is mainly a street of rear entrances and delivery bays to cafés and hotels on the seafront. A few pre-Victorian cottages recall a time when its inhabitants were mainly fishermen, putting out from a shore which had no pier as yet, to reap the rich harvest of the Solent.

The new home into which Grandma Norman moved early in 1956 was Number 5 Castle Street. Although she would always refer to it as 'the flat', it was a whole house – to be exact a former pub, situated about fifty yards from the junction with Union Street. Ryde had, and still has, an over-abundance of pubs, and the demise of this particular one had left no scar on the communal memory. As long as I lived there, I never found out what it had been called or anything of its history. Even for these parts, it had been a hostelry of no exceptional charm, tall, narrow and flat-roofed with a frontage of sour yellow brick. The old street façade had been blocked in by a thick glass window and a brown front door, already blistered by a combination of sea air and neglect. On one side of it stood a tumbledown builder's loft, on the other the goods entrance of Grandma Norman's great Esplanade rival, Dinelli's Café.

The former pub's conversion to private dwelling-house had been minimal. Its ground floor comprised a front and a back room, both evidently bars in former times, with floors of naked boards and unpapered walls oozing with damp. Between them lay a cramped hallway ending in stone steps to a cellar that was too structurally unstable to be used any more. Narrow, winding stairs ascended to a kitchen and bedroom on the first floor and two further bedrooms on the second. There was no bathroom and no hot water. The only lavatory was in an open recess on the ground floor at the rear of the old back bar.

These many shortcomings did not bother Grandma Norman nor prevent her from moving in with minimal delay. Even at her conventionally appointed London house, she maintained the Victorian habit of cold water washes from a basin and jug in her bedroom, seldom visiting the black-and-white tiled bathroom two floors down, whose bath was used mainly to set the blancmanges and junkets she made for me and my cousins. (Indeed, she often declared with firm conviction that having too many baths was 'bad' for you.) The only major cosmetic change was to the first-floor front room she had selected as her bedroom, which my father redecorated for her and papered in anachronistically subtle grey-blue stripes. 'It's all Regency striped,' she kept saying, as proudly as if it was the Brighton Pavilion.

Her enormous brass bed, the sea horse, the sea cow, the stuffed bear on wheels and all the other myriad contents of her London home had gone into storage, destined to remain there until she left the Island in the last few years of her life. Moving down to Ryde for her represented a complete break with the past, which now held too many painful memories of Uncle Wally. She did not even bring with her any of the four cats that had lived in Clapham Old Town, cared for by her ground-floor tenants, Mr and Mrs O'Halloran, but suffusing all four storeys with the reek of their urine and the smell of liver being boiled for their meals. The cats had somehow been lost in the move – as, indeed, had the O'Hallorans.

Reinforcements were not long in appearing, however. Grandma Norman had no sooner acquired 5 Castle Street than a cat appeared from its derelict cellar, having found a way in from some neighbouring loading-bay or backyard. It was a female tabby, barely more than a kitten, with oversized ears and wide, entreating eyes. The little thing clearly had no home and was of a friendly, gentle nature, so Grandma Norman adopted her, christening her 'Tibby'. With Tibby in residence, the place soon became a haunt of the neighbourhood toms, making use of the same cellar-access, which sprayed urine everywhere and emitted nocturnal shrieks to wake the dead. Tibby quickly fell pregnant and in time produced a single kitten, also female and with markings identical to hers, which we named Tibby's Daughter.

Furnishing 5 Castle Street was something for which Grandma Norman had neither the time nor the inclination. So it was with relief that she turned to her friend Miss Ball, the frizzy-haired little barrel of a woman who was among her most favoured visitors in the Kiosk's back room. Among manifold business interests in Portsmouth and Ryde, Miss Ball dealt in what she was pleased to call 'antiques'. Fortuitously, she had lately opened a shop in Castle Street, a few doors away from Number 5 and offering the unusual combination of antiques and fruit and vegetables. You'd go in to buy a cabbage and Miss Ball would try to sell you a Victorian trouser-press. If ever I called there with some message from

Grandma Norman, she would pause in her weighing-out of potatoes or carrots, seize one of my hands in both her grimy ones and thrust it under the nose of her customer. 'Look at this boy's hands,' she'd say in her fluting voice. 'Don't you think he's got the hands of a concert pianist?'

To set off Grandma Norman's new Regency-striped bedroom Miss Ball supplied a heavy walnut chest-of-drawers, a 1930s-looking wardrobe with an oval mirror, a marble-topped wash-stand, a flowered jug and basin set and a commode (a wooden armchair with a built-in chamberpot) to save the trouble of going all the way downstairs and out the back to the lavatory. For the kitchen she supplied a cream-coloured wooden cabinet, a quantity of chipped crockery and sepia-handled cutlery, a meat-safe to be fixed outside the window (there was, of course, no refrigerator) and a low steel table with thick legs, the precise function of which was never explained. Grandma Norman would buy anything Miss Ball offered her, however useless or repellent-looking, which was why the new flat also acquired an ostrich egg in a glass case, a do-it-yourself nasal irrigation kit dating from the 1914–18 war and a quite extraordinary number of half-rotted wooden flower-tubs.

As well as providing a year-round home for Grandma Norman, 5 Castle Street housed reserve stock for the Kiosk. The ground-floor front room was a dense plantation of boxed chocolate bars and bottled boiled sweets. Cartons of Woodbine and Senior Service cigarettes were stacked up the staircase wall to the first-floor landing. In the big, damp-oozing back room, brown cardboard boxes of the Kiosk's most triumphantly successful line were piled almost to the ceiling. You made your way to the lavatory through a corridor of rock – sixpenny limes, two-shilling peppermints, five-shilling candystriped 'Husband beaters'; rock shaped like fruit, fried eggs, giant shrimps, kippers and false teeth. Tibby and Tibby's Daughter leapt among the stacks, impregnating them with a mouldy reek of she-cat urine.

The truth was that after losing Uncle Wally Grandma Norman's only interest, other than being as near as possible to her two 'boys', was running the Kiosk. Her new home in Castle Street would never be more to her than a place to sleep. Seven days a week, she got up at 7.15, washed perfunctorily, dressed and left the house without so much as a cup of tea. By eight, the Kiosk would be open and the area around the pier-gates filled with the odour of the bacon and fried bread she was cooking on the gas-ring in her back room.

Even in winter, when her daily clientele numbered only dozens, she stayed open until 9 p.m., taunting her unwitting rival, Dinelli's Café, across the road. Then she would reluctantly take off her pink nylon overall and put on a Burberry raincoat which had been among the last purchases of Grandpa Norman before he sailed to his appointment with that German submarine in 1918. Pushing a basket on wheels, she would walk across the Esplanade and the short way up Union Street, past the Ash Tree Restaurant and the Greyhound pub, to the left turning into Castle Street. The wheeled basket contained bottles of Guinness and tonic water, a large bag of salted crackers and some tins of Kit-E-Kat. On reaching home, she would feed Tibby and Tibby's Daughter, then take a bottle of Booth's gin from the bottom of her wardrobe and get straight into bed. Sipping gin and tonic or Guinness and crunching salted crackers, she would read a historical romance (*The Remarkable Young Man* by Cecil Roberts or *Mary of Carisbrooke* by Margaret Irwin) until it was time for sleep.

Other than Miss Ball, she had little contact with her neighbours in Castle Street, even though there were several with whom we had much in common. In that particular quarter, near the Union Street junction, seaside trade seemed to have all but died out; as well as several other disused pubs, there were two or three disused shop premises with still-occupied dwelling quarters behind them. Concealed one ghostly shop window lived a family named Archer – a huge, gap-toothed man, his prematurely aged young wife and a brood of noisy children to whom Grandma Norman regularly doled out sweets, though she disliked their father, complaining that 'he smells of bed'. Next door to the Archers was a long-shut-down tobacconist's inhabited by an elderly woman who, despite her years, still had a reputation for 'entertaining sailors'. Each night, dressed in a tailored grey suit, she would set off a little unsteadily to ply her trade in the Redan pub, just across Union Street. She, too, had a couple of cats, which spent all day asleep curled among the petrified dummy cigarette-packets in her front window. Late at night, you would sometimes hear her calling them in with the eerie cry of some threatened marsh bird.

*

To ME, ALL THIS seemed like purest Heaven. At the end of the 1956 spring term, shortly before my thirteenth birthday, I had left Ryde School's boarding-house, as my father had promised, to revert to being a day boy and live with Grandma Norman in Castle Street. I remember the calendar I made of the weeks, days, even hours remaining until my release. It was illustrated by a drawing of the Kiosk with her in the window, handing a stick of rock to a customer with one hand and waving welcome to me with the other.

Since her bed was now only a single one, we could no longer sleep together the way we'd always done. But I still shared her room, occupying an even narrower bed along the

inner wall. It was miraculous to be warm at night, no longer
hungry or hounded over face-flannels and counterpanes or
threatened with the slipper or jabbed in the small of the back
by Matron for not sitting up straight. As I lay in the electric
firelight, watching Grandma Norman move from wash-stand
to commode chair, I thought of my late dormitory-mates
under their chill white coverlets, the Turkish and Iranian boys
huddled beneath dressing-gowns and overcoats for extra
warmth. My supper would be sandwiches of cheese, tomato
and Ryvita, made by her at the Kiosk and brought round in
the wheeled basket along with the Guinness and the Kit-E-
Kat. I'd munch them in the firelit dark, pretending I was
Captain Hornblower eating ship's biscuit in his cabin in
HMS *Sutherland*.

Also resident in the house during its inaugural weeks was
Mrs Dunwoody, Grandma Norman's Geordie friend, who
still came down each season to help her in the Kiosk (wearing
a thornproof 'costume' under her nylon overall to underline
her seniority to mere paid employees). Mrs Dunwoody occupied the top front bedroom with her Pekinese, Sue-Sue. Early
each morning, she would come into our room, sit down
with a plonk on my bed and spend half an hour or so discussing old ladies' ailments. I'd be lulled back to sleep by the
familiar litany of rheumatism, arthritis and what sounded like
'flea-bitis' – a by no means implausible hazard of lodging at
5 Castle Street.

It was a small price to pay for the joy of here and now,
late at night with Grandma Norman: the electric firelight
playing on Regency-striped wallpaper, the shadows of her tall
chest-of-drawers and sentinel-like commode chair. The last
thing she did each night was set her old Ingersoll wristwatch
deliberately half an hour fast, so that when she awoke in
the morning she'd think she was late, then remember she had

another half-hour. On top of the chest I could just distinguish the familiar photographs of my father and Uncle Phil in their respective wartime uniforms, and another of my cousins and me with our mothers on the sea wall in our earliest Ryde days, all throwing back our heads and laughing as if none of us had a care in the world. 'Ugh! *Eugh!*' would come from the bed by the window, her familiar settling-down sounds, followed – perhaps – by a 'rude below-noise', then a heartfelt sigh of 'Peace came to Peckham,' the words that had always signified that her long, energetic day really was over at last.

The electric firelit room seemed equally a sanctuary to her, as if we had each made our separate journeys, like Mole and Ratty, through the cold and frightening Wild Wood to the warm refuge of Mr Badger's house. In these bedtime moments, she ceased to be the only tycoon and dynamo in our family, instead adopting the idiom of some simple cottage-dweller in the long-ago West Country of her girlhood. 'We may not be very grand to look at, but we'll always have a bit o' comfort . . . a nice bit o' crusty bread and butter and cheese and a pickled onion . . .' I remembered the poem we'd read with Charlie when I was a famished boarder, which could have been Grandma Norman talking there in the classroom:

> There's plenty cheese and plenty bread
> And russet ale, and apples red . . .

What others might have considered drawbacks to 5 Castle Street were to her causes for pride. She often spoke glowingly of having access to 'a nice commode' rather than straight-forward chamberpots whose contents were not tactfully concealed by a padded tip-up seat. Nor did she wish it to be thought for a moment that the flat's lack of hot water and a bathroom encouraged standards of cleanliness lower than in any modern establishment. 'There's a nice wash-stand . . . a bowl and jug, I can always have a good Wash-Down.' She could indeed, although I never saw her do so in all the nights we slept in that room together.

Often, as we settled down, she'd say, 'You know, Phil, I always think that, no matter what happens to me in the daytime, I'll be coming back here to spend the night in my own bed.' I couldn't imagine what could 'happen' to her during the day, other than serving sweets and cigarettes and talking to customers and confectionary travellers and having an afternoon rest in a deckchair among piled-up rock-cartons. Still, it was a nice thought to snuggle to sleep with – the cold seashore outside; the distant yowling of tomcats in the cellar; the two of us together again, like the old days. 'Thank goodness we've got this little place,' she would sigh almost like a prayer. 'It's a safe haven.'

*

BUT NOT ONE I was destined to have to myself for very long. Soon after my arrival, I learned that Grandma Norman had also offered sanctuary to my cousin Roger, who had fled the Island with his mother and sister while I was shut away in boarding-school. His period of exile among Auntie Lorna's relatives in London had evidently proved no happier for Roger than life in the eventful orbit of Uncle Phil. He had elected to come back to Ryde and, from the shelter of 5 Castle Street, resume a cautious relationship with his father.

The news did not fill me with unadulterated joy. Roger and I had never got on particularly well, he regarding me as a namby-pamby and I considering him a slightly dangerous yob. Moreover, as a rival victim of divorce, he would have his own powerful claim on Grandma Norman's attention. I resolved to make the best of it, however, after another heartening heart-to-heart with my father. 'Make a pal of old

Rog', won't you,' he urged me in his most winning manner. 'The poor old chap's had a bit of a rough time of it, one way and the other.' Certainly, when Roger arrived, he bore little resemblance to the swaggering character I remembered, who used to talk like Marlon Brando while chewing imaginary gum. He looked pale, haggard and utterly crushed. 'Hel-*lo*, Rog',' I said, trying to swell my voice with a bonhomie that had never existed between us. ''Lo,' he answered, barely audibly.

It may have been a sheer coincidence but with Roger's reappearance the long rift between my father and Uncle Phil ended as suddenly and unexplicably as it had begun. Late one evening, after a visit to the Commodore cinema, I found myself being wordlessly ushered with Mrs Salsbury into the side door of the adjacent Star Hotel, where Uncle Phil now dwelt alone. We joined him in an after-hours gathering in the old-fashioned bar-parlour, which to me still evoked radio stars like Richard Murdoch and Semprini. True to his reputation for esoteric knowledge and unusual tastes, he cut slices from a strange black vegetable called a kohlrabi and handed them round as a relish with the drinks. I saw again that look of superior knowledge on his face as he cut slivers of kohlrabi and, in his portentous, heavy-breathing way, described how it repeated even worse than onions or radishes. 'Lit-tle, ti-ny burps,' he mused, lapsing into a comically singsong tone, 'that go on for ever and ever . . .'

He did not rejoin the business: my father continued 'helping' him single-handedly, as before. But he was back within the family circle once again, as was his gloomy pub. In the absence of a bathroom at 5 Castle Street, I was told – as Roger was – that when we wanted a bath, we had only to walk to the top of town and we could have one at the Star.

For all the weight of Uncle Phil's intellect, he was still as disinclined as ever to spend money on educating his children. Roger had always had a hankering to join the merchant navy, fired, like so many Island boys, by the nearness of Portsmouth and Southampton and the constant passage of big ships up and down the Solent. With his undoubted academic brightness, Uncle Phil might have been expected to enter him for the officers' navigational college at Warsash. Instead, it was decided he would train to become a ship's steward. Meantime, he and I were put together in 5 Castle Street's top back bedroom, from which you could see the pier extending slantwise beyond the Esplanade house-tops. Miss Ball supplied the furnishings, including a second commode chair, a metal sun lamp that had last worked some time around 1930, and a bedside table mounted on antelope-horns.

At night, as we lay in our adjacent beds, I tried to please my father by making 'a pal' of Roger, on the basis that we now had broken homes, at least, in common. But he seemed sunken in a trauma and misery almost too deep for words. He said nothing about the circumstances of his departure from Ryde, the day his sister Dina hit Uncle Phil with the cookie-jar. And being the sort of boy I was, I made no attempt to draw him out. Despite the reconciliation with his father, he seemed still to expect violence of some sort from Uncle Phil, and even to be training himself for it. 'I know I'd only have time to get in one punch,' he told me one night, 'because when Dad gets me with that right of his, I'm a goner.'

Even in stabler family times, Grandma Norman had always referred to him as 'poor old Rog', cherishing the prickly and aggrieved side of him and the nerviness that was the legacy of his scalded arm. Now she took him under her wing in a way which – she communicated convincingly – even I did not need. One of her first acts was to buy him a whole new outfit from Fred Brooker, the Ryde outfitter where the newfangled Teddy boys got their clothes. Roger's gloom lifted a little as he unpacked it in the Kiosk's back room to show her – a yellowish tweed jacket, midnight-blue rayon trousers, black shoes with mudguards. Until his sea-training began, he spent most of his time in the visitors' gallery at Ryde Magistrates Court.

Roger had been in residence at Castle Street only three or four weeks when I learned, with feelings even more mixed, that yet another tenant was soon to join us. After less than a year of running the Cross Keys, my mother was leaving the hotel – was, indeed, leaving the hotel trade altogether for work even more fortuitously glamorous and prestigious. She had always had an artistic knack with make-up and now, despite her age, had a chance to train as a beautician with the Elizabeth Arden company. I was jubilant at the news, for the soft, fragrant world of hairdresser's shops and department store cosmetic counters had always seemed to me the place she rightfully belonged. But if she accepted the traineeship – which, if completed successfully, would involve constant travel between Arden salons all over Britain – she could no longer maintain custody of my little sister Tracey. So Tracey, too, was to come back to Ryde and be cared for jointly by my father and Grandma Norman.

I accompanied him when he went up to London for the handing-over ceremony, which took place in a big, almost-empty tea lounge on Waterloo station. It was the first time I'd been with both my parents since their divorce – and one of the few occasions in my life I remembered us out anywhere together. They spoke to each other with impersonal politeness, focusing most of their remarks on Tracey (and, now I come to think of it, none on me). I had not seen my sister since she was only a few months old. Now just over two, she turned out to be a smiling little thing in a harness, still with her spectacular mop of bright golden curls. That day, she wore shoes called Jumping Jacks ('They give more support at the heel,' my mother said) which, on the journey back to Portsmouth, she made us repeatedly take off and then put back on her again. My father was at his most genial and gentle as we both struggled to please her.

When we returned to Ryde I had to suffer all over again the mortification of seeing Grandma Norman deluge Tracey with huge hugs, smacking kisses and the multiple endearments ('My little love, my little pet, my little bit o' fluff, my little bit o' fat, my little bit o' all right . . .') which had once been my exclusive tribute. I was totally unused to having a little sister and – to my shame now – totally uninterested in the experience. I viewed Tracey as no more than a tiresome interloper, disrupting our safe haven in Castle Street.

On the other hand, my father's boundless gentleness, patience and good humour with her were comforting; further evidence of the wonderful change that seemed to have come over him. I remember him putting his arm around my shoulders and drawing me close as Tracey tottered ahead of us on her Jumping Jacks, her reins dangling down behind her. 'Best thing that ever happened to you and me,' he murmured into my ear.

The arrangements for looking after Tracey were complex, made more so by the fact that my father's address in Ryde remained still ostensibly a secret. Why he should have been so determined to keep it so still mystifies me to this day. The whole world knew by now that he had run off with Miss Salsbury and was living with her in what that era still termed 'sin'. No doubt he felt some residual shame and embarrassment in facing the scrutiny of former friends of my mother's, like the Dorley Browns and Mr and Mrs Bailey of the Royal Esplanade Hotel. My explanation to myself at the time was that, just possibly, he was keeping his options open in case the arrangement with Miss Salsbury should fall apart and he decided to return to my mother. There was that crumb of comfort in being kept so slightingly in the dark.

In fact, his secret hideaway was in Spencer Road, just a few minutes' walk from Castle Street, and was a secret only from his official family. During the past couple of years – when I so fondly hoped I had ceased to know them – Miss Salsbury's parents had prospered in the private hotel trade, and now owned one of Ryde's grandest old seafront mansions, Westfield Park, latterly transformed under their aegis into Westfield Park Hotel. The entrance to its spacious grounds was a stone archway surmounted by a stag's head. As a grace and favour concession from Mr and Mrs Salsbury (how gladly granted, I'm not sure) my father and Miss Salsbury were living in the adjoining gatekeeper's lodge.

Tracey saw him only in daylight hours, just as I did, and mainly down at the Pier Pavilion, now awaiting its second summer season in its new character as the Seagull. The arrival on the scene of a small child by my father's divorced wife cannot have delighted Miss Salsbury, especially in this early stage of their relationship. She could easily have seen Tracey as a rival for his affections, and maintained a hostile or frigid distance from her. But, I must admit, she accepted her immediately, supplementing my father's ministrations with the skill and finesse of an obviously experienced mother, although seldom relaxing her grimly sceptical look. Tracey, too, was supposed to address her as 'Miss Salsbury', which in her case came out as 'Miss Alsbury', but with increasing frequency she would forget and say 'Mummy'. At such moments, I always seemed to catch Miss Salsbury's eye, then we'd both look away in the same silent seizure of embarrassment.

Another old acquaintance was unexpectedly renewed when my father mentioned that 'young Robert Kennie' would be joining his employees that season. Struck as I was by a sudden memory of the bewitching Kenney at school, it took a moment to realize he meant Mrs Kennie's youngest son, whom I hadn't seen since we were enforced companions at Dunraven. Though now almost sixteen, Robert was still the puny, pale-skinned boy I remembered, with black hair thickly slabbed across his forehead and a back as straight as a Brigade of Guards Sergeant-Major. As a further concession from Miss Salsbury's parents, he was now living with his mother in Westfield Park's former coach house (which he spelt 'caoch house'). He rode to the pier-head each day on a low-slung black bicycle equipped with every conceivable gadget including an old-fashioned car indicator, fixed on the back wheel, which raised an orange tongue-like object to warn of a turning right or left.

Robert's role was a simple one – to help with whatever my father might be doing every day of the week, including Sundays and bank holidays. In this pre-season period, his duties also frequently included looking after Tracey, which he did with loving conscientiousness and would have done even more often (my father explained to me quietly) if his whole skin had not appeared to be covered with a thick film of engine oil. So I would be deputed to 'watch the baby' with him. When time came for her to have a nap, we'd wheel out one of the deep basketwork skips that were used for empty bottles in the bars. Its metal slop-tray would be taken out, its floor padded with blankets and pillows, and Tracey would be put down in it.

Each evening she was brought back to 5 Castle Street by Mrs Kennie, who would bath her in a bowl on the kitchen table, put her into Grandma Norman's bed, and babysit until

Grandma Norman's return from the Kiosk at around 9.15. Grandma Norman would then get into bed beside her, with the gin bottle and the historical romance, invariably waking her up and then plying her with sweets, chocolate, crisps and fizzy lemonade. 'I want crisps,' the sleepy little voice soon learned to say in the half-light, or, 'I want pop.'

Grandma Norman spoiled her in the way I remembered so well, lauding her to the skies at every second ('She's her Nan's bit of all right! There's not a flaw in her!'), never reprimanding her or restraining her. When Tracey filled a teacup with water and poured it into the pink powder that fed the Kiosk's candy-floss machine, turning it into useless paste, Grandma Norman just laughed. When she went to the open till and began handing out money to customers at the windows, Grandma Norman sternly forbade any of the staff to stop her. 'Never thwart the instincts of generosity in a child,' she told them with the air of one profoundly versed in infant psychology.

She referred to Tracey as 'Baby' in the Victorian manner ('Don't wake up Baby') that suggested some lace-bonneted infant in an iron perambulator, and taught her rhymes and songs similarly reminiscent of nurseries in the 1890s:

> Nelly Bly, caught a fly,
> Tied it to a string,
> Put it in a pitty-hole,
> O, poor little thing.

*

MY FATHER AND I continued to get on wondrously well. Despite his adoration of Tracey and his obligations to Miss Salsbury, her parents and Lynette, he continued to imply a special understanding between the two of us that excluded

everyone else. One afternoon as we sat together in the twilight
Amplifier Room, he told me that whatever bad thing I ever
did in my life, I could aways go to him and he would help me.
'Doesn't matter what it is . . . If you get a girl into trouble . . .
anything . . . just come to me and we'll see what we can do.'
He took his pipe out of his mouth and smiled. 'Excepting if
you did a murder,' he added. 'Then it'd be out of my hands.'

I had no idea what he meant by 'get a girl into trouble'
other than telling tales behind her back, whoever she might
be. With all my heart, I prayed I would never do a murder and
so put myself in that terrible position of being beyond his
help. Sometimes he would even pay me the compliment of
seeking literary advice on the advertising campaign he was
preparing for the Seagull's second season. One day, he read me
a poem he had written for an advance display ad in the *Isle
of Wight County Press*:

> When at Ryde you're arriving
> Or up the pier you've been driving,
> There's a bar at the end
> Which is in the modern trend,
> And on draught we have a brew
> Which you'll find is good for you . . .

I felt confident enough even to offer criticism; we'd just
started doing scansion with Charlie at school. 'It'd be better
as "When at Ryde you *are* arriving," ' I said. ' "Or up the pier
you *have* been driving." '

' "When at Ryde you *are* arriving," ' he repeated thoughtfully, writing it down with his Yard-O-Led propelling-pencil.
' "Or up the pier you *have* been driving . . ." '

Before I returned to school for the summer term, he
bought me a bicycle, the first I'd ever owned. It was a dark
green Raleigh 'All-steel', a clanking heavyweight, impossible

to pedal up Ryde's precipitous hills. Riding it along the pier against the wind was like pushing against a breath-snatching wet wall. With the wind behind me, I often did not have to pedal at all, only keep my front wheel clear of the long, sea-green plants. As I coasted along, with the sea almost all around me, I'd pretend I was Captain Hornblower and my bicycle was a three-decked ship of the line. I had an imaginary first lieutenant named Mr Cargill, to whom I used to murmur terse navigational commands.

In those early days of freedom – as it seemed to me then – the pier-head was hardly less a safe haven than Grandma Norman's Regency-striped bedroom. Often, on a lengthening spring evening, I'd walk across the car-park to the western-most side of the concrete peninsula, where a white wooden tower with a flagstaff marked its occasional use for starting yacht races out in the Solent. Around the pier-head rim at regular intervals were thick wooden posts, about eight feet high, banded with rusty iron. Standing in the lee of a post, looking out at the urgent grey waves, I'd recreate my old mind-game of being in a fort, awaiting attack from somewhere out there between Fishbourne and Southampton Water. In my pocket would be the reassuring bulge of a water pistol (the see-through plastic space-gun type) filled and ready. And in my heart, the glow of certainties as strong as any ramparts: no more boarding-school, Grandma Norman in Ryde all the time, my father being so wonderful to me.

I was always going back to Castle Street at night with news of something else he'd given me – two more half-crowns, a matching green saddlebag for my bicycle, a Babycham jotter or propelling pencil or key-ring. 'Yes, he's a good dad,' Grandma Norman would agree, looking almost sternly over her glasses at me as she sat in bed with her gin and tonic and bag of salted crackers. I remember one day pleasurably trying to calculate exactly how many months had now passed with him liking me and me pleasing him and not even the faintest shadow of a row.

The very next afternoon, I was guilty of a minor procedural error. What precisely I can't remember, only that it was terribly minor – I'd been at the Kiosk when I was expected at the Pavilion, or at 5 Castle Street when I was expected at the Kiosk. It was a mistake to which my father in his new persona might have been expected to respond with an understanding smile, or perhaps the very mildest word of deprecation. Secure in that belief, I did not apologize very humbly.

I suddenly realized he was looking at me, not in his new way but in his old one. The dark V of hair on his forehead seemed to twitch as it had at so many unpleasant moments far behind us. As he stared at me, the hazel brown pupils of his eyes seemed to brighten to angry yellow.

'Well, it's not *good* enough, Philip . . .' he began.

Seventeen

I HAVE IN FRONT OF ME the quarter-page display-ad for the new Seagull Ballroom and Bars which appeared in the *Isle of Wight County Press* at the start of the 1956 summer season. On the upper right-hand side is a line drawing of a seagull, with its black-tipped wings fully extended and its beak pointed downward, as if to pluck a tasty morsel of garbage from the sea's surface. Its one visible eye is blank, giving it a dazed, even nauseous look. Beside and below it, lines of faintly 1930s-looking black sans-serif type set out the whole range of exciting innovations now to be found at Ryde's revamped Pier Pavilion. The wording has the slightly archaic formality of all my father's promotional announcements; as I read, he could be speaking into my ear.

THE SEAGULL
RYDE PIER HEAD

where you first place foot on the Garden Isle

*

DANCING
every afternoon and evening throughout the season to
the perfect tempo of NICK OLSON *of B.B.C. Fame*
on the Compton Melotone Electric Organ

ADMISSION FREE
Fully Licensed Bars   Free House

✳ GALA EVENING EVERY THURSDAY ✳

Morning Coffee ✳ Luncheons ✳ Teas
at popular prices

Parties of up to 100 persons catered for in the spacious
licensed restaurant with sea outlook and dancing if desired.

By 1956, the public tea dance had become almost as out-
dated a form of seaside holiday entertainment as the beach
Pierrot show or 'concert party'. Yet every afternoon, from
2.30 to 5.30, such an amenity was offered at the Seagull –
dancing, a pot of tea and a plate of fancy cakes for three and
sixpence (17.5p) per head. And every afternoon, a maximum
of half a dozen or so middle-aged couples, the men usually in
brass-buttoned blazers, would make the half-mile seaward
journey by tram or foot to shuffle and glide around the spaces
of the old skating-rink while Nick Olson at the Compton
Melotone organ pumped his way through 'Mack the Knife',
'Tulips from Amsterdam', 'Poppa Piccolino' and 'The Poor
People of Paris'.

The appointment of Nick Olson as the ballroom's resident
organist was something of a coup on my father's part. Electronic organists in these days were superstars of the music
world, many having their own hugely popular peak-time
radio shows. While not quite in the lofty firmament of
Reginald (Blackpool Tower) Dixon or Sandy (Chapel in the
Valley) McPherson, Mr Olson's was a name to conjure with;
he had played in top London ballrooms like the Hammer-
smith Palais and the Streatham Locarno, and broadcast on the
Home Service (hence 'of BBC Fame'.) For many years, he
had been principal organist on the Granada cinema circuit,

performing in the intermissions that used to be necessary when cinema programmes comprised two full-length films. As the house lights came on, Mr Olson would rise from the pit at the terraced keyboards of a Mighty Wurlitzer, playing tunes whose lyrics were simultaneously projected on to the screen, with a bouncing white dot to indicate tempo.

He was not the husky Swede his surname suggested, but a slight, balding man with gilt-rimmed glasses and a quiet Tyneside accent. It took some years to dawn on me that 'Nick Olson' must have been a pseudonym, derived from Nicholson or perhaps Nicolson. Goodness knows what tempted him from his broadcasting and luxury cinemas to play at an untried dance hall on the end of Ryde Pier. But he came, bringing with him a Compton Melotone organ that was not only brand-new but also, fortuitously, salmon-pink and so perfectly in tune with the Pavilion's new décor. It was transported over to the Island by car-ferry and assembled on the stage in its two bulky components, the keyboard section and free-standing amplifier. Mr Olson then spent hours lovingly crawling around it with pots of touch-up paint.

Despite his pen-pusher's appearance, he could play up an absolute storm, peering through his gold glasses with what seemed only mild interest at the ever-changing sheet-music before him while his left leg schizophrenically jumped back and forth over the maplewood rhythm-bars. By pulling out a stop or flicking a switch in the green baize console above his double keyboard, he was able to mimic the sound of almost any instrument – trumpet, trombone, piccolo, tuba. When he played '12th Street Rag', one waited with delicious anticipation for the moment when he flicked two switches in unison and played a whole twelve bars of rousing, hilarious 'doo-wacka-doo-wacka-doo-wacka-doo'.

Apart from the colour scheme, and aspirations, of its

dominant building, the summertime pier-head looked the same as when I'd last inhabited it two years earlier. Packed ferries from Portsmouth still arrived every few minutes, heeling over almost to the waterline. As the crowds struggled down the wooden gangways, Taffy's amplified voice still greeted them from the railway station with a bardic rolling of the r's: 'Good afternoon, ladies and gentlemen, good afternoon. This is R-r-ryde Pier, R-r-ryde Pier-head ...' As they streamed towards the ticket-barrier, Alfie Vernon's voice struck up from the rock shop in the same old pleasant, persuasive light tenor: 'Hello, ladies and gentlemen ... now, just across here at the shop ... we'll serve you straight away ...' As they filtered through the barrier, my father's boom joined in, with a few slight changes to the formula I used to know by heart, but still as solemn and pessimistic as ever: 'Hot or cold meals, tea, coffee and light refreshments can be obtained in the restaurant on the ground floor or on the sun-roof upstairs. The entrance is on the tramway station. Make certain of your meal in comfort before you leave the pier.'

The other great development during my absence was that the war with Mr Vernon had ended. No longer did my father speak of his broadcasting rival belittlingly as 'Alfie', misappropriate his Wall's ice-cream tins or attempt to wrench his shirt off his back. At about the same time that my sister Tracey was born, Mr Vernon's auburn-haired wife had, perhaps equally unexpectedly, presented him with a baby son. But at barely a year old, the little boy had died in a tragic accident, drowning in a few inches of water in Ryde's Canoe Lake. My father's belligerence had instantly melted into heartfelt sympathy, no doubt heightened by the fact of having a vulnerable tot of his own newly in his life. As a result, the former deadly rivals had become friends; my father now called Mr Vernon 'Alf' on a note of fraternal respect and was often to be seen drinking with him in the new Seagull Bar or at pubs or clubs on shore.

Around the Pavilion were many new faces for me to get to know as well as old faces with whom to become re-acquainted. The improvements to its fabric had included few for the saving of labour, and for its rebirth season my father had hired a larger-than-ever contingent of waitresses, bar staff and kitchen workers from the itinerant pool that came down each summer from London and the southern mainland. Side by side with the unfamiliar Southamptonians, Brightonians and Bournemouthians were the nucleus of local people who'd worked for us as long as I could remember – Mrs Cook, whom we called Cookie, Mrs Bishop whom we called Bish, Mrs Trueman, Mrs Field, Mrs Dibben and Mrs Gallop. Cookie and Bish, in particular, counted almost as family friends and had often been unwilling ringside spectators of upheavals within the family. Both of them greeted me with a surprised 'El-*lo*, Phil-op' as if, in the totally changed land-scape, I was the last thing they had expected to see.

Whatever idea my father may have had of keeping Miss Salsbury on a pedestal soon vanished under the pressure of summer business. By day she worked in the kitchen, pre-paring food for the sun-roof and downstairs restaurant, clad in a white overall with – very obviously – only an underslip beneath. It was exactly my mother's former role and her co-workers included many who had liked and respected my mother. Unswervingly loyal to my father, they accepted Miss Salsbury's authority without comment. But I caught more than one eloquent exchange of glances behind her back as she washed lettuce leaves under the ancient brass tap or sliced a hard-boiled egg into eight wafer-thin slivers. 'I always liked yer Mum,' Bish would say to me in a mutinous murmur. 'Yer mum was a *lady*.'

On the pier-head's westerly promontory stood a circular stone building, one storey high with a railed observation roof, which had been erected by occupying military forces during the war. Known as the Round House, it had previously been used by the pier authorities as a ticket-office for the Red Funnel steamer line and a deckchair store. This summer, it – or the major part of it – had been absorbed into our domain. The largest of its rooms had been turned by my father into a café of the basic tea-and-buns variety; the adjacent narrow kitchen had become a repair shop for the few slot-machines we still had in service outside.

This workshop was the preserve of Robert Kennie, the young assistant to whom my father was teaching all the multitudinous technical skills I had never shown any interest in acquiring. Robert had already learned everything there was to know about repairing slot-machines, and was now being taken through plumbing and gas fitting and also being given driving lessons. In return, he worked seven days a week, from nine in the morning to past midnight, never seeking, or being granted, a holiday or even a day off. Whatever one of a hundred possible daily jobs my father might be engaged on, Robert would always be in close attendance with his black busby hair, ramrod-straight back and a white coat grubby above the waist and filthy below it. Like some sacred regalia, my father had passed on to him the tarnished chain of slot-machine keys and identity-discs; to find him anywhere on the pier-head, you simply followed the jingle.

He was only three years my senior and, despite an innate solemnity, quite willing to join me in covert games of 'He' or water-pistol duels. These would usually be broken off by a spasm of guilty alarm on Robert's face and a mutter of ''Ere's yer dad.' Even his lair at the Round House did not afford much refuge from the demands endlessly made on him. On the wall above his workbench was a loudspeaker connected to my father's Amplifier Room over in the main Pavilion. Like Big Brother in George Orwell's *Nineteen Eighty-Four*, this could not be turned off at the receiving end. Periodically, it would crackle into life and my father's voice deliver a terse command in RAF code: 'Scramble, Robert, scramble . . . Ten-forty, Robert, ten-forty . . .'

I remember standing and watching the first ferries come in at Easter, wondering with pleasant anticipation what their cargoes would make of all my father's new improvements. Surely they could not fail to be impressed by the oceans of grey and red paint that had been poured out for their benefit? How could they fail to marvel at the breathtaking modernity of the Seagull Bar, with its sky-blue Formica and red plastic? How could they not savour the bookish humour of the frescoed Porpoise Bar, the whiting winking over its shoulder at the heavy-treading porpoise, the Walrus and the Carpenter seated on a rock before a trusting audience of little-legged oysters?

But whatever surprise and delight these innovations inspired remained hidden – from me at any rate. The crowds that poured from the ferries seemed to spare the transformed Pavilion as few glances as ever in their headlong rush to their trains and trams. Such customers as found their way to the ground-floor restaurant ate in the usual preoccupied haste, seemingly unaware that the walls around them were decorated with faces in the style of Picasso and recipes for cocktails like Crème-de-menthe frappé. As in the shabby old Victorian First and Last, the clientele of the brand-new, ultramodern Seagull Bar just stood there, singing 'Let's All Go Down the Strand', 'Knees Up, Mother Brown' or 'Bye-Bye Blackbird', and getting drunk.

*

THE EVENING DANCES, especially the Thursday Gala Nights, were a different matter. For the first time since we'd opened our skating-rink, an idea of my father's seemed to hit the jackpot.

I cannot think of them without also picturing the loud-speaker van he also brought into service that summer to tour Ryde's seafront, extolling the pleasures of the evening ahead. It was a 1948 'Series E' Morris of the most basic utility design, drab green in colour, with a vestigial black dashboard and an empty metal shell behind. My father had bought it sixth or seventh hand from a local tradesman, then taken his customary satisfaction in bringing its engine to a peak of efficiency it could hardly have known even when brand new. On its roof he mounted a back-to-back pair of trumpet-shaped grey loudspeakers. On each of its sides he fixed a red and grey signboard: 'DANCING, THE SEAGULL, RYDE PIER HEAD, ADMISSION FREE, LICENSED BARS, CHILDREN'S ROOM AVAILABLE'.

I would often ask to go with him on these afternoon broadcasting tours, not because I could be any practical help but just to be a part of something I found exciting and inspiring. Also it reminded me how he was always at his best behind the wheel of a vehicle, any vehicle, be it vintage Wolseley limousine or decorated carnival float: unflappably calm and deliberate, never speeding or hesitating or taking the smallest risk. Even my mother, at her bitterest moments, always acknowledged what an expert driver he was, adding wryly that it was about the only time you could completely trust him.

So we would make our way down the pier at its regulation 5 mph, then along the Esplanade and back again, my father holding the wheel with his left hand and speaking into a small microphone cupped in his right one. 'Tonight is Carnival

Night at the Seagull on Ryde Pier,' the twin loudspeaker would boom as mournfully as if giving notice of a mass funeral, 'with balloons, competitions and prizes...' Sometimes Mr Olson came with us, crouching in the van's seat-less rear, holding the microphone and reading out the announcement from a piece of paper in fractionally more festive tones, with an ever-so-slight emphasis as he reached the bit that mentioned himself ('... with dancing to the music of Nick Olson ...') My dearest hope, which of course I never mentioned, was that one day I would be granted the privilege of doing it.

Whether the lure was the newspaper advertisement, the loudspeaker-van tour or the fame of Nick Olson, I don't know. But by 7.30, the grey metal tables and chairs around the dance-floor would be filled by a seething, expectant throng. Children were not allowed into the dance area because of licensing restrictions but could watch from the encircling balcony, to which we charged admission of nine old pennies (4p) per head. This was the 'children's room' mentioned on the side of our loudspeaker-van – a linguistic inexactitude that always made me worry vaguely to myself. Clearly, the balcony fulfilled the legal requirement of keeping the impressionable young apart from adult drinking and carousing. But 'children's room' seemed to be stretching it a bit, especially since the balcony was bare of any amenity, child-oriented or otherwise, except for an old wooden table and a few chairs borrowed from the upstairs restaurant.

By eight, Mr Olson, wearing a double-breasted grey suit with silver lapels, a white shirt and a grey bow tie, would be in full swing on his salmon-pink Compton Melotone. The Pavilion floor would be packed with couples, young, middle-aged, old and sometimes very old, men and women or women partnering each other, mostly shuffling around at an unadventurous walking pace, but with the odd pair of 'real' ballroom dancers, lunging and twirling on unpredictable courses as disruptively as jet-skiers among rowing-boats.

The dances were the traditional ones – quickstep, waltz, slow foxtrot, with occasional digressions into the more exacting disciplines of the tango, the rumba and its almost indistinguishable relation, the samba. There would be an 'Old Tyme' interlude in which the more seriously grey-haired elements would resurrect stately Victorian formation dances like the veleta and the military two-step. Nor was an evening complete without the Gay Gordons, which may prompt sniggers today but back then was straight-facedly known as a mass Highland reel (combining 'Scotland the Brave' and 'Bladon Races' in Mr Olson's version), when the dancers mouthed unintelligible words and uttered the manic whoops with which English people show empathy with Bonnie Scotland.

The renovations had provided the main Pavilion with a brand-new bar also, stretching along the curve of the windowless wall where the arcade's rifle-range used to be. Compared with the splendiferous Seagull Bar, it was a makeshift construction of plain wood rather than luxurious Formica – a kind of eleventh-hour manifestation of economy and common sense. Customers could come to the bar to fetch their own drinks or be served at their tables by a contingent of white-jacketed waiters.

Throughout the evening, unless called away by the demands of management or showmanship, my father stationed himself at the counter-flap end of this bar, just to the right of the main entrance, where the waiters came to place their table-orders. As one of the genteel breed of publican, he himself did not serve behind the counter, but stood on the same side as the customers, standing drinks to friends and favoured members of the night's crowd in rounds that never ceased, and telling stories of the wondrous RAF-blue past. Though I shall never run a pub – or, at least, pray I won't – my boyhood taught me the essential difference between a successful and an unsuccessful landlord. Those who make money stay always behind the bar-counter, watching their staff's every move. The 'too-good-for-all-this' kind socialize with their customers while their employees rob them blind.

Here also, all evening, every evening, sat Miss Salsbury, perched on a high stool and sipping her favoured tipple, gin mixed with dry ginger-ale rather than the usual tonic water, orange or lime. Her stool was always pushed right into the corner and my father stood close at her side, as if to protect her from the hostility of a still-censuring world. Her lean-featured face was, as always, unsmiling; despite the summer heat, she usually clutched the cardigan of a twinset around her slightly hunched shoulders. There was something faintly waif-like about her, as if she'd lately been rescued from some ordeal and been told to sit and wait until someone brought her a cup of cocoa.

This air of tight-lipped reticence was confounded, however, as one looked lower. For the legginess of the roller-skating Joan I remembered was nothing compared with the legginess of Miss Salsbury as revealed by the Seagull's inaugural seasons. Previously, her legginess had to some degree been imposed by the demands of skating. But now she had become leggy of her own inscrutable free will. In an era when the great preponderance of ordinary women's clothes were still calf-length and bell-shaped, Miss Salsbury's were short and figure-huggingly tight. Her skirts and dresses broke just on the knee and exposed the calves in their entirety, a sight more riveting to male eyes in 1956 than a full nude body would be today. The display was most astounding when she sat cross-legged on a bar-stool – the way she usually sat – her skirt-hem slipping up her thighs and exposing the forbidden cleft behind the knees. Yet it was noticeable that she seemed no more at ease with her own blatant legginess as Miss Salsbury than she had as Joan. As she perched there in the lee of my father, her narrow eyes flickered around continually to see who might be looking; every minute or so, she would lift her tautly encased rear from the stool in order to tug her skirt-hem down another irrelevant couple of centimetres.

For all his keyboard pyrotechnics, Mr Olson in performance had a certain aloofness, as if he realized only too well this was not the BBC or the Granada cinema, Tooting. He did not speak to his audience, smile at them or even look at them other than to acknowledge their applause with a brief, rhythmic turn of his bald head and glint of gold spectacles as he segued into the next number. The only lapse into informality came during intermissions, when he slid off his salmon-pink bench and discreetly vanished through the door that led to the backstage lavatory. Before retiring, he placed a little red-and-grey notice on a miniature easel at the stage-front. PLEASE EXCUSE ME, it said, WHILE I GO AND HAVE A DRINK.

In the face of Mr Olson's steadfast non-verbalism, there was no alternative but that the job of compère, continuity announcer – and, on Gala Night, master of the evening's revels – should fall to my father. He made no concessions to the role, taking the stage in his usual soft green shirt, lovat trousers and RAF squadron tie, often with Dunhill pipe still in his hand. But at least the deathbed solemnity of his usual microphone work was temporarily put into abeyance. He spoke in his most charming ex-Wing-Commander manner, with lots of dimply smiles and an edge of old-world courtliness: 'Now, ladies and gentlemen, will you take your partners, please, for a quickstep . . .' Although nothing like his customers expected, he must have seemed an attractive figure, to the women particularly, and they accepted him and followed his direction without protest, even if it did sometimes include words and expressions not often heard at seaside pier-head dances. There was, for instance, his explanation of the 'supper-hour' extension, whereby customers could enjoy an extra hour's drinking after 10.30 closing time if they bought a supper from the cold buffet in the Porpoise Bar. 'But remember, please, ladies and gentlemen,' his address concluded, 'to enjoy this facility, it *is* necessary to purchase a modicum of food.'

Most alluring of our Thursday Gala Nights were those whose prizes were donated by the Babycham company – furnished in such generous profusion, as I have said, that the occasion was dubbed 'Babycham Night'. In the three years since Grandma Norman's cider-making cousins, the Showerings, had launched their 'Genuine Champagne Perry' on the world, it had became one of Britain's best-known brands. When commercial television began in 1955, Babycham was one of the first products to feature in its advertisements, along with Cadbury's Dairy Milk chocolate, Stork margarine, SR toothpaste and Murraymints. Everyone now knew its bow-tied little ersatz Bambi, leaping on spindly legs down trails of tinkly stardust. Working-class girls throughout Britain had learned to refuse port and lemon or gin and lime but, instead, to wrinkle their noses, giggle like debutantes and exclaim, 'I'd *love* a Babycham!'

I liked to think it was the family connection that made Babycham sponsor our Gala Night so generously, but, with their brilliant PR, they probably did it for all kinds of functions, seaside and otherwise. By happy coincidence, they had just introduced the first six-pack cartons, implanting the extraordinary notion of buying more than one bottle at a time and – more revolutionary still – buying it to drink at home rather than at the pub. The sky-blue cardboard six-packs made ideal prizes, as did gold-rimmed Babycham champagne glasses, scribbling blocks, pencils, key-rings, tea towels and plastic models of the bountiful little chamois.

The Pavilion all set for Babycham Night was a stirring spectacle. On every grey metal table beside the dance-floor would be a scatter of Babycham drip-mats and a fold-out cardboard model of the chamois. Along the balcony's fancy wrought-iron railings and on the stage above the Compton Melotone hung white banners imprinted with tilted champagne glasses, smiling chamois heads, blue ribbons and the legend I'D LOVE A BABYCHAM. Below the stage stood a table covered with sky-blue six-packs, plus a squad of individual brown and blue bottles for consolation prizes. High in the dome, two horizontal joined Union Jack flags concealed their waiting cargo of balloons, all but for the occasional one that would come prematurely floating down. As a final touch, my father would walk backwards around the dance-floor, sprinkling thick skeins of a white powder called Slipperene that made dancers' feet slide along more easily.

In Robert Kennie's workshop over at the Round House, the wall-mounted loudspeaker would then crackle warningly. 'Neons, Robert,' my father's voice would say, as if calling on Spitfire pilots to 'scramble'. 'Neons, Robert... *Neons*, Robert...' Robert would cross to the Pavilion, open a coffin-sized wooden fusebox above the main staircase and throw an outsize black switch. On the wall above the Seagull Bar, our giant Babycham neon sign would flicker and buzz into yellow and white and blue-tubed, fitful life. And so the evening's revels would begin.

The first hour or so consisted of general dancing, punctuated by what we called 'spot prizes'. A roving spotlight, operated from the balcony by Robert, would play over the circling multitude, settling on couples at random. My father would call them to the stage (but never up on to it), bend down with his hand-microphone to enquire their names and place of origin, and ceremonially present them with a Babycham six-pack, a Babycham ball-pen, scribbling block, key-ring or tea-towel. However blatant a piece of free advertising the prize, it was always greeted with delight. Then, having run through the entire dance-inventory from slow foxtrot to veleta, Mr Olson would abruptly cease playing, shut down a few stops on his keyboard and swivel around on his bench, cradling one knee in his hands. And my father would descend to the floor with his hand-microphone to do the competitions.

These were all the old seaside favourites – knobbly knee contests, glamorous granny contests, races to knock back a pint of beer or eat a saucer of cockles with a wooden cocktail-stick. Whenever some judging decision proved difficult, my father would call Miss Salsbury from her place at the bar to render an impartial verdict. If bystanders were puzzled by her exact role, they at least recognized in her the kind of woman naturally cut out to be a magician's assistant or, smiling submissively, to spin a giant wheel of fortune on a television quiz show. Clutching her cardigan around her shoulders, her exposed calves followed by every pair of male eyes present, she would clack across the floor on black suède high heels to confirm that this contestant's bared knee truly was the most grotesquely knobbled, or that that one truly had speared and eaten his cockles to the last vinegary gulp.

From time to time, as if in an effort to raise the tone, my father would include a game of his own invention. They were always elaborate affairs involving recognition of tune-titles played by Mr Olson and a mass distribution of pencils and paper – things that many Babycham Nighters must have come away to the seaside to forget. Holidaymakers are usually game for anything, and they did their best to understand the rules that my father would sometimes patiently run through three or four times over. 'Nick is going to play a medley of eight tunes [or, he pronounced it, "*choons*"] . . . In the title of each tune is the name of a month in the year . . . You write down the initial letter of each month . . .' Despite the customers' steadfast goodwill, these tended to be moments of mass exodus to the lavatories.

At other times, he seemed content for the tone to sink as low as it pleased. As additional prizes, he kept a store of novelties that went far beyond normal mild seaside risquéness. The most popular was a giant red rubber phallus with an elastic loop that allowed it to be worn (by women usually) as a false nose. Also much sought-after was the 'Mucky Pup', a plaster dog's mess with a horribly realistic upward twirl, and a little Scotsman made of hollow rubber. When you squeezed him, his sporran flew up, revealing outsize genitalia of the pale pink of uncooked sausages. The supplier was a company in Southsea called U-Need-Us Ltd. I used to picture its production-line of giant phalluses and dogs' messes, the quality-control inspectors squeezing each rubber Scotsman in turn to ensure that its genitals flopped out satisfactorily.

Babycham were not the only generous sponsors of our Gala Nights. The prizes might equally well have been presented by Double Diamond, the bottled beer whose slogan was 'A Double Diamond Works Wonders' and whose mascot was a beaming little City gent with rolled umbrella and briefcase. Double Diamond were just as generous with their crested jotters, pencils and drip-mats and, in addition, offered a novelty that even Babycham did not. This was a solid yellow globe filled with soapy liquid that one could see through a thick glass peephole. You shook the globe, then asked it a question such as 'Will I get married in the next five years?' Into the peephole would float a black ticket with the answer printed on it in silver letters: 'Probably' or 'I doubt it' or 'My sources say No.'

Double Diamond had an even more effective secret weapon against Babycham. Their area sales rep, a Mr Stark, bore an uncanny physical resemblance to the little City gent who was their trademark. To be sure, he cultivated it, growing the same kind of blobby black moustache and always wearing a black coat, pinstripe trousers and an expression of dizzy conviviality. On very special Double Diamond Nights, Mr Stark would attend in person and my father would invite him up on to the stage, so that the audience could derive fullest enjoyment from comparing him to the figure depicted on posters, placards and beermats all around them. One memorable night, he was even persuaded to take the hand-microphone from my father and sing the Double Diamond song, also newly launched via commercial television. To the tune of 'There's a Hole in My Bucket', this ran:

> A Double Diamond works wonders
> Works wonders, works wonders.
> A Double Diamond works wonders,
> So drink one today.

The extraordinary thing about those beery, crowded mid-fifties nights, I now see, was their total lack of violence. Hundreds of people would be inside the Pavilion, drinking and enjoying themselves to the limit, yet we had no need to employ a single bouncer or security man. Having managed a pub in London's West End during the war, my father was well used to dealing with unruly or discontented customers. To Miss Salsbury and his circle of rapt auditors, he often described how he had fought off groups of drink-maddened Canadian servicemen with the help only of a 'salmon priest' – a bludgeon for killing salmon which sentimental fishermen equate with the last rites. He also owned a little cosh made of dark brown leather and weighted with lead, which he claimed to have taken from one of those rampaging Canadians. He once told me that if you bent back the cosh's flexible handle and merely flicked at it someone, its lead-weighted ball would break any bone it struck. But neither cosh nor salmon priest was ever needed on Double Diamond or Babycham Night.

My father's final appearance onstage would be at about ten minutes to midnight. 'And now, ladies and gentlemen, will you take your partners, please, for the Balloon Waltz...' Mr Olson would begin 'I'll See You Again', seguing into 'Charmaine', 'Goodnight Irene' and the theme from *Around the World in 80 Days*. On the balcony stood Robert Kennie, in the same white coat he'd worn since nine o'clock this morning, and holding a string that stretched vertically upward. The other end of the string held together the two horizontal Union Jacks with their waiting cargo of balloons, thirty-odd feet up inside the dome. Half-way through 'Around the World In 80 Days', at a thumbs-up signal from my father – *Wilco! Roger! Chocks away!* – Robert would pull on the string, separating the flags and bringing the balloons down in a slow-motion shower on the heads of the dancers beneath.

After midnight, our customers got their tram journey back to shore free of charge. I was especially proud of that. It seemed to prove how my father had thought of absolutely everything.

Eighteen

FOR THE FIRST FEW WEEKS of that season, I imagined that after the dancing was over, my father locked up the Pavilion and went with Miss Salsbury in the loudspeaker van back to their hideaway in the lodge at Westfield Park. Not until about mid-June did I learn that the hideaway had moved half a mile out to sea and that they now lived in the little stage-side dressing-room where we used to watch *I Married Joan* on winter Sunday afternoons.

Why my father chose to make the two of them the only end-of-pier residents (to my knowledge) in the entire British Isles was puzzling at the time and is even more so in retrospect. This was, after all, still an early stage in his relationship with Miss Salsbury, when he might have been expected to want to impress, not to say spoil her. Economy can hardly have been the motive since acceptable accommodation on land was easily available for only a few pounds a week – and he seemed to have ample funds for other purposes, like custom-made aquamarine wallpaper and murals of the Walrus and the Carpenter. Spending all day and evening at the Pavilion as they both did, it was certainly more convenient to sleep there. That was about all you could say for it.

The dressing-room-turned-bedroom was a narrow, high-ceilinged space, roughly triangular in shape, with a floor of torn green linoleum. All along its outer wall ran a window, hung with net curtains to blot out the looming wooden screen of the pier-head railway station. After a bed had been installed – a low-slung double divan with a green mattress – there was space for no other furniture but a couple of wooden restaurant chairs deputizing as bedside tables. A walk-in cupboard, where prewar Pierrots had hung their bobbles and flounces, provided the only storage space. An inner door led to the backstage passageway which connected with the Amplifier Room. At the other end of this passage, screened off by a hardboard partition, were a hand-basin and ancient wooden-seated WC.

As a love-nest, it could hardly have been less secluded. Outside, at the foot of the short staircase, hundreds of chattering holidaymakers consumed café meals by day and danced to electric organ music by night. Nor were the backstage washing facilities the love-nesters' exclusive preserve; in dancing hours, the WC and basin were also used by Mr Olson. Looking back, I can only marvel that Miss Salsbury let herself be persuaded to live in such conditions, dotingly unassertive though she clearly was. It can only have been intended as a temporary measure, though they were to end up staying there almost five years.

The Pavilion's lease did not permit use as a private residence, so their occupancy had to be kept secret from my father's landlords, British Railways, whose officials thronged the adjacent pier-head station. None of his employees was supposed to know – or, at least, let on they knew – that he and Miss Salsbury did not leave the Pavilion each night and go to a normal home like everyone else. Nor was I supposed to know, nor indicate that I knew after I'd found out. He always referred to their new quarters as 'the Rest Room', implying that its divan was used merely for relaxation during off-peak daytime hours. Its door into the main Pavilion was kept firmly closed and was never used by either him or Miss Salsbury. They came and went via the Amplifier Room on the opposite side of the stage, and along the connecting passage.

The militarily exact procedures which my father evolved to preserve his secret unfortunately served only to draw more attention to it. At nine o'clock each morning, when the Pavilion restaurant opened, his faithful servitor Mrs Kennie had the job of heating shaving-water for him in the coffee-urn. Bearing the hot water in a jug balanced on a saucer, she would then go, not to the nearby Rest Room but all the way across the dance-floor to the Amplifier Room. There, she would mount the steps and tap on the door. My father would make his way backstage from the Rest Room; the Amplifier Room door would open just a crack, a hand would take in the jug, and the door quickly close again.

In fact, long before I myself finally tumbled to it, the 'secret' had become common knowledge, not only to his own staff but everyone else who worked on the pier. One day, as I was travelling up by tram, the conductor stopped beside me on his swaying walk through the carriage. ''Ere,' he said with his Island twang, 'does your Dad *live* at the Pavilion?'

'Yes, I think so,' I said.

'With that there Miss Salsbury?'

'I think so.'

'Whoar!' The conductor grinned. '*He's* all roight for the noight, then.'

I mulled over the exact meaning of this for days afterwards. For the amazing truth is that at thirteen, despite having lately seen my home destroyed by it, I still did not really understand about sex. Boys in those days matured far more slowly than today, of course; I had had pubic hair for barely a year, and several more months were to pass before my first wet dream. I was, besides, more dreamily naif even than your usual fifties adolescent. Although I had seen the reproductive act crudely depicted on innumerable walls – including those of the pier-head public toilets we controlled – and heard it described in innumerable smutty jokes, I couldn't quite believe that was *really* what happened: it seemed altogether too crude and farcical and obvious.

My father had brought up the subject only once, and with extreme obliqueness. 'If there's anything you ever want to ask me, Philip,' he said, giving me a searching look, 'you know you can always ask me, don't you?'

Here, I saw, was a matchless opportunity to learn from someone who must be as well-informed on the subject as anyone in the world. But I never did take him up on it. The mystery was too many-faceted to be framed by a single question.

All my vague fantasies now centred on 'the Rest Room', after the Compton Melotone had shut down, the last tramload of Babycham Nighters had departed and he was 'all right for the night'. I had the impression of something that was both companionable and vaguely intimidating, like sleeping with all the bedclothes pulled out and a draught whistling around one's untucked feet. I imagined, as clearly as if I could see it, the shadowy space with its black sea view through dingy net curtains . . . the low green divan . . . my father's pale forehead with its deep V-shaped hairline . . . Miss Salsbury's face with the familiar look that was both grim and compliant . . . wind thudding against the Victorian timbers . . . the waves threshing around iron legs, far beneath. The vision made me feel as guilty as if I'd actually spied on them, the way I had on the auburn-haired woman and him up above the sun-roof so many years before.

Even when Miss Salsbury wasn't in her skimpy kitchen overall or seated on her bar-stool, sipping 'gin and dry' and wrestling with her errant skirt-hem, I found it increasingly difficult not to look at her. Her dresses and jumpers almost all had a deep V at the front, revealing a prominent breastbone although little in the way of actual bosom. This jutting bone created a slight shadow where her cleavage began which, to my furtive and oblique gaze, resembled dark hair. I knew she was aware of my constant scrutiny, for she would often look up suddenly or wheel around as though to catch me at it. She would meet my eye with the same knowingness, then look away again with the same shyness, as at our first encounter, long ago on the skating-rink when she was Joan.

My father, too, must have sensed my interest, for in these summer months, when her overspilling physique was most on public display, he became even more insistent on the strict protocol governing my relationship with her. At meals he always kept stern watch lest I should sit in the chair she always occupied or unthinkingly help myself to something he had specially reserved for her. He had a way of referring to her, in her presence, in a kind of regal third person that also seemed to be a kind of lingering denial that she was there at all. 'You may not want another cup of tea, Philip,' he would say, 'but *Other People* might . . .' Any lapse in respect was treated with extreme severity. Late one afternoon, as I leaned over the ballroom's balcony rail, Miss Salsbury emerged from their secret backstage area, groomed and made up for the evening and wearing a new, shorter-than-ever dress in vertical black and gold stripes. As she clacked across the dance floor beneath me on her black suède high heels, I let out a facetious wolf whistle. There was a brief pause; then my father came into view, walking backwards and scanning the balcony with a thunderous look on his face.

'Did you whistle at Miss Salsbury then?' he called up to me.

'Yes, Dad,' I answered.

'That's not what boys who go to Ryde School do, Philip,' he said in an icy voice, audible to everyone below. 'That's only what nasty little guttersnipes do.'

*

MY LIFE, meanwhile, had been arranged into its own military routine. I got up in the morning at 5 Castle Street, had a cold wash – sometimes no wash at all, because it was so difficult – and pushed my cumbersome Raleigh 'All-steel' bicycle up the connecting steep hills to school. At ten to one, I swooped down the hills in a whirring, clanking couple of minutes, then tacked my imaginary wooded-walled battleship HMS *Sutherland* out along the pier-planks for my lunch in the Seagull's restaurant, barking navigational instructions to Mr Cargill, my imaginary first lieutenant. When school ended at five past four, I returned to the Seagull to have tea and do my homework up on the balcony, which didn't open until evening. (That's what I'd been doing when I let out the unfortunate wolf whistle.) At seven or seven-thirty, just as Nick Olson was getting going on 'Mack the Knife', I cycled back up the pier, bound for Castle Street and bed.

In the Seagull restaurant we had our own grey metal table, with a permanent 'Reserved' sign, near the servery entrance, where the beginners' bars of the old skating-rink used to be. Mr Olson, whose salary included meals, generally sat with us, his few cross-combed hairs often damp from recent swimming. Both he and my father did the *Daily Telegraph* crossword every day, and would confer about its clues – ' "Could be used for arranging the rice in Bengal." Nine letters. I think it's an anagram . . .' My father kept his paper open at the crossword page and folded into a neat strip. When he went off to do some job, he left stern instructions that it wasn't to be removed, turned to another page or interfered with in the slightest way. Those strips of grey newsprint and black-and-white squares, to me, were like sticks of gelignite that I could not touch or even approach too closely without causing disastrous damage. For years, I hardly realized the *Daily Telegraph* contained anything but a crossword or came in any shape other than that folded, sacred oblong.

I visited the now forbidden backstage area only to use the lavatory that adjoined my father's Amplifier Room. Standing or sitting there, I would do my best to ignore the cluster of female toilet preparations above the adjacent washbasin, and other telltale signs of illicit domestic occupancy. Sometimes, if no one was about, I would creep further down the passage, through a raw hardboard door that still bore the chalked name of a wartime Royal Naval signaller: 'Sergeant Swindells'. In the yellow twilight ahead, I could see my father's dry-fly rods in their green canvas jackets stacked against the wall, and a small bookcase, one of his few souvenirs from Dunraven, with the familiar spines of Izaak Walton's *Compleat Angler* and *Round-the-Year Stories*. The door to the Rest Room often stood wide open, but I never approached it nearer than about ten feet. I would glimpse an edge of the low divan, and a strappy evening shoe lying on torn green lino, then hastily retreat back into bounds again.

My father's most conspicuous keepsake from our old life was his grey bronze head of Pharaoh Rameses II. So attached was he to the head that he did not keep it in his private quarters, along with other precious mementos like his rods and RAF shield, but displayed it in the most public of places – the counter of the Pavilion bar. The soulful grey face that had been my companion through so many solitary nights at

Dunraven now stood next to the bar-flap and the orange-squash dispenser, where Miss Salsbury perched on her stool each evening. Sometimes in his cups, to his circle of listeners, my father would hint that it possessed the same occult powers as had cursed the invaders of Tutankhamun's tomb. 'I've often thought of throwing it in the sea,' he would say, 'but, quite honestly, I'd be scared to.' When drinking, he tended to repeat himself with greater and greater emphasis. 'Quite honestly . . . quite *honestly* . . . I'd be *scared* to.'

My pier-head diet was an unchanging one of beans on toast, 'luncheon meat' salads, silver-wrapped triangles of Dairylea cheese spread and Jacob's cream crackers. Only a single triangle per meal, and no more than three cream crackers to accompany it. One day, after I had asked the waitress for four, my father took me aside and told me with an air of weary patience that there was a halfpenny profit on each cracker, and it was no good his working the hours he did if I just 'woofed up' the profits. The bond between us that I'd so wantonly broken by being at Castle Street instead of the Kiosk – or whatever it was – had never quite been re-established. Now I was seldom able to count more than a couple of days between occasions when I disappointed, angered or exasperated him.

He remained determined that I should not grow up into 'one of those boys who spend their time hanging around street-corners', even though all the boys my age that I knew were of that breed and, between attendances at the pier-head, I had few places but street-corners to go. While taking no interest in my school work or activities, he often made that objective reference to me as 'a boy from Ryde School', both to dissuade me from low company and remind me of the still sizeable fees he was obliged to pay for me. 'Eighteen guineas a term!' he would sometimes exclaim, to leave me in no doubt of his sacrifice and of the expectations that devolved on me.

Though we might live under different roofs – a dome in his case – he regulated my existence in a way that sometimes put me in mind of Westmont, Matron and Blase. Despite the chaos elsewhere in Grandma Norman's establishment, I was under strict instructions to make my bed every day, and liable to spot-checks whenever his loudspeaker van happened to be in the vicinity. He was also deeply exercised by my table manners, even though himself preferring to sit sideways at the table, taking outsize gulps and poring over his paper or crossword puzzle. 'Old son . . . don't make that clashing and clattering noise with your knife and fork when you eat . . . Eat *carefully*!' I would usually receive such reproaches in front of Mr Olson, the organist, and almost always in the presence of Miss Salsbury.

Though she never volunteered any comment about me, the look on her face needed no articulation. ('Well, you made a nice mess of that, didn't you?') My misdemeanours seldom amounted to much, Heaven knows – a fact I have regretted ever since. My bed might have been left unmade; I might have been caught messing around with Robert Kennie, so distracting him from his thousand-and-one daily duties; spots of rust might already be disfiguring the new chromium of my Raleigh 'All-steel' bicycle. Usually, when being told off, I hung my head in silence even though this was to risk being charged with 'dumb insolence'; but now and again I would be goaded into blurting out a riposte that made my father's face quiver momentarily as if it had sustained some small impact. 'Now don't be saucy, Philip,' he would say; the hardly-serious word made me almost smile until I saw the look in his staring, yellow-flecked eyes.

He never showed me any of the physical violence he had

used on my mother. What I dreaded even more was being cast out of the magic sphere of his good opinion, his soft-rough tweed, his pipe smoke, his manly gentleness. For days at a time, he would ignore my existence completely, taking care to be even more attentive and loving to Tracey in front of me. Often, while so exiled, I would have a half-erotic vision of him lying in Miss Salsbury's arms late at night in their wind-blown dressing-room, and telling her what a disappointment I was to him. Grandma Norman would listen to my side of the story with apparent total sympathy, but make me feel even worse by reminding me how good and kind he was, how hard and unselfishly he worked, what a sweet, selfless little boy he had once been and how adorably he had mispronounced words like his brother's name Phil ('Til') and 'lovely' ('ludley').

Then, suddenly, my crime would be forgotten; his dimples would be all smiling at me again, and his arm go back around my shoulders. 'I know I get a bit irritable sometimes,' he'd say in the familiar words of all emotional tyrants. 'But you know it doesn't really *mean* anything . . .'

*

DESPITE THE MANIFOLD demands of his new bars and entertainments, not to mention his new relationship, there was never any doubt as to whom he owed his primary devotion. Side by side with running the Seagull, and often to its detriment, he ran Grandma Norman at the Kiosk. Every day, the restaurant provided a salad lunch, not only for her but for her entire staff. Robert Kennie would be released from his other numerous duties to travel down on the tram with the hefty pile of plates and grey metal rings. It was seldom that my father's afternoon tour with the loudspeaker van did not include a stop-off at 5 Castle Street to pick up fresh supplies of cigarettes, sweets and rock (and check that I'd made my bed that morning). 'This is my son, y'know,' Grandma Norman never failed to inform customers proudly as he knelt beside her, packing away jars and cartons and tins of candy-floss powder.

The two of them continued to look after Tracey, as a co-operative effort, transferring her continually between the separate hemispheres of their daily lives. Grandma Norman had never visited the Pavilion in its new incarnation and still seemed not to know – or want to know – of Miss Salsbury's existence. Her only contact with my father's pier-head life were the salads he sent her each day. As she so often repeated, symbolically closing her eyes, she made a point of never asking Any Questions.

At the beginning of the season, they had between them hired a woman named Mrs Spreckley to become Tracey's full-time nursemaid. A stout, handsome widow, with brown skin and luxuriant white hair, she lived on the mainland and had to be coaxed over to the Island by a range of generous fringe-benefits including free lodgings and all her meals. She had the faintly genteel, too-good-for-all-this air that always impressed Grandma Norman, and so enjoyed a meteoric, if brief career in our employ.

After a few weeks of caring for Tracey, it became clear that what Mrs Spreckley really wanted was to work at the Kiosk, where the hours were shorter, the company was livelier and employees were allowed to help themselves to single sweets as they pleased. With minimal delay, she was given a white coat and took her place at the panoramic serving windows with Mrs Dunwoody, Phyllis, Dorothy and Maria. She would stand resting her broad brown arms with seeming non-chalance on the boiled-sweet jars that formed a rampart between server and customers. One hand, meanwhile, would be covertly unscrewing a jar-lid and the other hand lowering itself inside to extract a toffee or fruit drop or Nuttall's Minto.

She was a Roman Catholic of extreme devoutness who attended mass every day as well as on Sundays and prayed extensively and loudly, so we heard, at her lodgings in Monkton Street. Two of her Kiosk co-workers, Maria and Phyllis, were also Catholic and, when counter trade was quiet, Mrs Spreckley would berate them for their 'immorality' in wearing make-up and lipstick. Her employment came to a sudden end after she was found to have stolen hundreds of pounds' worth of cigarettes, which she kept stacked under her bed, ready to be shifted off the Island at season's end.

The problem of finding a replacement was finally solved by Grandma Norman's friend and seasonal helper Mrs Dunwoody, who had lately sold her house in Clapham and moved back to her native South Shields. Up in 'Shields', it transpired, Mrs Dunwoody had a friend named Nellie Marshal, not long since widowed, who needed a job and did not mind how far afield it took her. She was a little, bird-like woman in her late sixties who, even on high-summer days, still clung to her thick tweed skirt and jacket. Despite her years, she looked after Tracey – whom she called 'Trixie' – capably enough and was unfazed by any of the bizarre domestic arrangements with which she was confronted. I remember her crawling on her hands and knees into the bare back of the loudspeaker van, showing a flash of old-fashioned pink satin bloomers. Under Nellie's influence, a Geordie note soon crept into my little sister's voice. One wet morning, she came into my room and told me, 'You canna go to schoo-ul to-dea. It's teemin' o' rain outside.'

In provisioning the flat, as opposed to the Kiosk's back room, Grandma Norman was oddly parsimonious. Consignments of groceries would periodically arrive from Johnson's

Stores on the Esplanade, but they always came in tiny amounts – single cut loaves, quarter pounds of ham, never more than four apples at a time. At night, when I returned home with a thirteen-year-old's desperate appetite, Nellie would stand in front of the meat-safe as if protecting some sacred shrine. 'There's oanly one egg,' she would inform me, 'and that's for the babby's breakfast.'

Catering arrangements took an occasional turn for the better when Mrs Dunwoody forsook her post at the Kiosk's windows and cooked a ceremonial meal at 5 Castle Street. She was an immensely gluttonous woman whose meals even in the Kiosk's tiny back room tended to run to almost as many courses as a Lord Mayor's banquet. Periodically, she would bully Grandma Norman into giving her leave (and money) to do an expensive shop up in the town and roast a large chicken or piece of beef in the flat's otherwise unused gas-stove. The usual reason would be a visit to Ryde by her daughter, Connie, a younger replica of herself, also jowly and mole-studded and equally 'fond', as they put it, of her food. Connie was wealthy, having married a Pole named Igor (pronounced 'Eega' by Mrs Dunwoody) who'd invented a unique type of water-softening plant for use on ships. He and Connie had a house in the Surrey stockbroker belt and a sixteen-year-old daughter named Virginia, recently chosen to be photographed for *Woman* magazine's series 'Undiscovered British Beauties'.

For all her wealth, Connie was a good sport, never batting an eyelid at the decor of 5 Castle Street, cheerfully rolling up her sleeves to help her mother scrape mounds of new potatoes at the cold-water sink, then serving them up in Miss Ball's least repulsively-chipped china tureen, draped in thick rags of sodden mint and shiny with melted butter.

The ranks of Geordie widow women staying at or passing through 5 Castle Street were further swollen by a mutual

friend of Mrs Dunwoody and Nellie Marshall, Gertie Lindbergh by name (but no relation to the famous aviator), whom
they persuaded to come down on holiday from South Shields,
where she ran a sailors' boarding-house. She was a little, pear-
shaped woman with a Latin-looking face and legs so fat that
they overhung the tops of her shoes. Like the others, she was
cheery, convivial and kind to me, though it was clear that with
the 'Eee's' and 'Wha-heys' and the tree-trunk legs went a
yearning, passionate nature. I once heard her singing half to
herself, 'Some day he'll come along . . . the man I love . . . and
he'll be big and strong . . .'

If there was company at the flat, Grandma Norman would
vary her usual after-work routine of retiring straight to bed
with the Booth's gin-bottle and a historical romance. Instead,
she would entertain the guests to bottled stout – for medicinal
purposes only, of course – seated in the dreadful kitchen on
a bentwood rocking chair (also supplied by Miss Ball) with
Tibby or Tibby's Daughter, or sometimes even both, curled
on her lap. 'Pass your glass,' she would say in her familiar
incantation. 'Or should I say "Pass your glass you silly arse"?'

After one such late-night session, Gertie Lindbergh had to
be helped down the narrow stairs by Nellie Marshall and Mrs
Dunwoody, very carefully lest she should topple into the
piled-up cartons of Senior Service and Gold Flake cigarettes.
Slipping out of their steadying grasp, she cocked one little tree
trunk over the banister rail and made as if to slide down it.

I was no longer sharing the top back bedroom with my
cousin, Roger. Having completed a short course at Gravesend
Nautical Training School (catering section), he was now a
laundry boy on the P & O liner *Alcantara*, bound for South
Africa. I had the gloomy chest-of-drawers, the second
commode chair of the house, and the antelope-horn bedside
table all to myself.

When darkness finally came, I would lie awake listening to the Esplanade's summer sounds through my wide-open window – the whirr of ice-cream-making machinery from Dinelli's Café next door; the piano-playing and singing from a glass-roofed back bar of the Wellington Inn. The singing went on every night and always included 'Down at the Ferryboat Inn', with 'Ferryboat' loyally changed to 'Wellington':

> Come on and join us and let's be gay,
> Sing your blues away, ta-ra-ra-boom-de-ay.
> Give all your troubles a holiday
> Down at the Wellington I-i-inn!

*

I MISSED my mother all the time, in a low-burning, hopeless way, as usual mentioning the fact to no one. But my longing for her was mitigated by my excitement at her new job as an Elizabeth Arden beautician. She had by now completed her training and was working in Arden salons as far afield as Bradford and Inverness: she stayed in hotels, wore nice clothes, ate in restaurants, had an expense account, in every way lived the life I'd so much wanted for her. As well as providing her proper environment of soft lights, thick carpet and sophistication, her new employers were kindly and beneficent; there was still a real Elizabeth Arden who knew all her 'treatment girls' by name, took an interest in their families and sent their children presents at Christmas (something Tracey qualified for, but not me). I listened avidly to my mother's stories of department stores and buyers and, especially, the wonderful annual staff cocktail party given by 'Miss Arden', where a fountain in the middle of the room spouted Blue Grass perfume. I thought of her, painfully but proudly, every time I passed Pack's drapery store in Union

Street and glimpsed the cosmetic counters inside. As other boys supported football teams, I rooted for the turquoise-script Elizabeth Arden logo, silently booing its rivals, Yardley, Coty and Helena Rubinstein.

My father's attitude to her varied, according to the amount of Tavern ale he had consumed at any given moment. When he spoke about her to me, he always called her 'Your Mummy' in a tone of reverent respect she had never received as his wife. Sometimes, deep in his cups – and when Miss Salsbury was not in earshot – he would intimate that he still loved her, regretted losing her, knew she would never return but still could not stop himself from indulging in hopeless romantic gestures. 'On her birthday *every* year,' I remember him slurring late one night, 'two dozen red roses are delivered to her door . . .' He also often spoke fondly about her parents, Grandma and Grandad Bassill, of Grandma's fortitude in caring for Grandad, and the cockney Sunday high teas ('Haddock with poached egg, and pints of prawns!') he had once enjoyed with them. Every Christmas, in another of his romantic gestures, he sent them a hamper of groceries. Of course, I had never told him that they'd blotted out his face in the photograph on their mantelpiece.

At other times my mother caused him severe exasperation, particularly when she telephoned him and – as she always did – reversed the charges. I suppose these calls must have concerned the £5 per week he was still supposed to be paying her, though my father always suggested she was demanding money for fripperies. 'Now she's telling me she wants to buy a car,' he would report to me with a more-in-sorrow-than anger grimace. 'But if I give it to her, I *know* the next time I see her, she'll be wearing a nice new outfit from Harvey Nichols . . .' Once, as I approached the Amplifier Room, I heard his side of an all-out row, apparently connected with her temerity in going out and getting a job. 'You've had a whale of a time this past year, Irene . . . No, I know it wasn't through me, but you've had a *whale* of a time . . .'

Every couple of months, she would get leave from the salon in Bradford or Inverness and travel down to Ryde to check on the standard of child-care Tracey was receiving. I remember arriving at the pier-head from school one afternoon and finding her out on the sun-roof, talking to Miss Salsbury – and, now I come to think about it, drinking Babycham. Her past hatred and contempt for her successor had now given way to an elaborate politeness. She cannot have been displeased by the encounter, since Miss Salsbury was fresh out of the food-preparation area, in white overall and headscarf, while my mother was in a smart navy-blue and white business suit (with matching two-tone shoes) and talking in the posh voice she now used all the time about West End shows and restaurants.

She was appalled by the conditions in which Tracey was kept, though the satisfaction in creating difficulties for my father and Grandma Norman must also have been considerable. She would criticize the clothes and shoes that had been bought for Tracey ('*Much* too small for fat little feet!'), the frequency with which her hair was washed and her lately-acquired Tyneside accent. But the main target of my mother's wrath and contempt was Grandma Norman's 'flat'. Rolling up the sleeves of her business suit, she would turn out every pot and pan from Miss Ball's rickety kitchen-cabinet and scrub each one ostentatiously, murmuring sentiments such as 'filthy old witch' under her breath. Sitting in the Kiosk's back room or sharing a late-night gin and tonic at Castle Street, she would harangue Grandma Norman about Tracey's diet and wardrobe, and the amounts of grease or mould she had scoured from every utensil. 'Oh, you and your microbes,' Grandma Norman would growl back.

She would not stay at Castle Street – how could she? – but at the nearby Royal Esplanade Hotel, which was still run by her old friends, Mrs and Mrs Bailey. Sitting in the dining-room there with her and Mrs Bailey, I would catch many a murmured reference to the ménage at the pier-head. 'My *dear*, they've got no proper washing facilities, nothing... God alone knows why *she* puts up with it... anyway, he apparently knocks her about worse than he ever did me...' I realized the effect of Castle Street on me, too, when I saw a famously bitchy female friend of the Baileys staring intently at me. 'Phil,' she said with affected kindliness, 'I know you're very excited when Mum comes down to see you – but don't you think you could have given your neck a bit better wash than that?' I then had to crane my neck forward while the whole company inspected its grimy tidemark.

I was always heartbroken when my mother returned to her Elizabeth Arden world, though I showed it to no one, least of all her. One morning, I remember, she left on an early ferry, and I went to the pier-head to see her off before school. It was long before the Pavilion opened and the whole place was still locked, with no sign of my father. We needed to ask him something – I forget exactly what, but it was vital at that particular moment – and so had to tap and hammer on the Pavilion's tramway station door until he heard us, far away in his dressing-room retreat. After a long time, he came into view, striding across the dance-floor, still tucking in his shirt and zipping up his trousers. As he drew back the long bolts, his expression was volcanic; I knew I would catch it later in some way for having thus overtly acknowledged he was there. I still shiver inside, remembering his first coldly furious words. 'And you can take *that* expression off your face, Irene, for a start!'

*

I SPENT the summer holidays of 1956 selling refreshments – tea, minerals, packets of crisps – from a red metal and glass trolley to the ferry queues on the pier-head. The tea came from a grey urn that was changed only once each day, leaving it darkened and stewed to the consistency of sump-oil by the afternoon's end. My father invented hyper-inflation twenty years early: a paper cup of disgusting tea was sevenpence, a packet of biscuits was elevenpence rather than the usual threepence, a warm cherryade or cream soda was one shilling and threepence rather than the usual eightpence or ninepence. 'I'm sorry, I don't make the prices,' I replied to outraged customers dozens of times each day.

Often when I was working, a rival trolley would issue from Alfie Vernon's shop, piled high with rock and sweets and pushed by an elderly but spry man in a grey jacket and highly polished shoes. I regarded him as Hornblower would a battleship from Villeneuve's fleet but, with my father and 'Alf' now such friends, hostilities were impossible. Instead, our two vessels would pass each other in silence, observing minimal maritime courtesies.

My father, I knew, watched every circuit I made from his eyrie in the Amplifier Room. One long sunny evening, to my surprise, he came out and helped me push the trolley a couple of turns, complaining vociferously about his British Railways landlords, their greed and short-sightedess. Despite the Pavilion's new grey and red livery, he said, BR had insisted that the sun-roof railings – which lay directly above their tram station – should still be painted institutional green. He explained how infinitely better things had been before the post-war Labour government had nationalized the railways, making me feel, as usual, nostalgic for golden times I had missed. 'Competition, that's the key,' he said. '*Competition!*' He put his arm around my shoulders as he said this, and I tried to signify agreement from the depths of my loyal little Tory soul.

He spurred me to greater efforts on the refreshment trolley by telling me about a wonderful young employee named Peter who'd operated it during the previous summer when I was still locked away in boarding-school. Peter, he said, had been wonderfully bright and hard-working in all sorts of jobs around the Pavilion, but nowhere had his abilities been better demonstrated than in plying the trolley up and down beside the home-bound queues. Where I was bringing in only six or seven pounds from a day's work, Peter used regularly to bring in twelve or fifteen. Of course, this really had nothing to do with the fabled Peter's abilities, being solely dictated by the size of the queues, which had been unusually long the previous summer. But each day, I wheeled the trolley forth, determined to surpass Peter in my father's good opinion; each evening I wheeled it in again, dismally conscious that I had failed.

Then came a Sunday evening when some hitch occurred in the usually efficient ferry-timetable, and an immense queue of home-goers snaked around the pier-head and nearly half-way down the plank walkway. I could not sell my stewed tea, warm minerals and overpriced biscuits fast enough; the grand total, when the last voyagers cleared at around 7.30, was almost eighteen pounds. In a fever of triumph I rushed to the Amplifier Room with the leather money satchel to show my father.

'Peter took twenty-five one Sunday,' he told me.

*

THAT SEASON'S closing weeks brought the Suez Crisis, an episode that would allow future historians to pinpoint the exact moment in the twentieth century when Britain ceased moving hopefully forward and began chaotically falling back. It may have ended as a fizzling damp squib of humiliation for British arms and diplomacy, but it began with a horrible, fatalistic thrill. Here, at long last, seemingly, was the Third World War everyone had been expecting since 1945. The Egyptian leader Colonel Nasser, who had dared to nationalize the waterway that ran through his country, was portrayed as Hitler reborn. And, as Grandma Norman remarked ominously to many a confectionary traveller in her back room, 'We shan't have Churchill to look out for us this time.'

There were newsreel pictures of British Tommies embarking at Portsmouth, as no one yet doubted, to go and teach this audacious upstart a lesson. With their packs and rifles, grinning and giving thumbs-up signs, they looked little different from the expeditionary forces of 1939 – or of 1914. I remember cycling up the pier on my Raleigh 'All-steel' against a stiff headwind and seeing the grey troopships in a far-apart convoy five or six miles to the east, making their way towards Spithead and the open sea beyond. I assumed that global war was about to break out, and wondered vaguely whether I would survive.

However, there were far more pressing concerns on my mind. Tonight was Babycham Night. And, for the very first time, I would be helping behind the bar.

Acknowledgements

Thanks are due to the copyright holders for permission to quote from the following songs:

'Little Things Mean A Lot'. Words and music by Edith Lindeman and Carl Stutz. © 1954 EMI Catalogue Partnership, EMI Feist Catalog Inc and EMI United Partnership Ltd, USA. Worldwide print rights controlled by Warner Bros. Publications Inc/IMP Ltd. Reproduced by permission of International Music Publications Ltd. All Rights Reserved.

'We'll Gather Lilacs'. Words and music by Ivor Novello. © 1941 Chappell Music Ltd, London W6 8BS. Reproduced by permission of International Music Publications Ltd. All Rights Reserved.

'The Man I Love'. Music and lyrics by George Gershwin and Ira Gershwin. © 1924 (renewed) Chappell & Co Inc, USA. Warner/Chappell Music Ltd, London W6 8BS. Reproduced by permission of International Music Publications Ltd. All Rights Reserved.

'The Queen of Tonga'. Words and music by Jack Fisherman. © copyright Campbell and Connelly Limited. 8/9 Frith Street, London, W1D 3JB. Used by permission of Music Sales Limited. All Rights Reserved. International Copyright Secured.

ACKNOWLEDGEMENTS

Thanks are due to the copyright holders for permission to quote from the following:

'Little Fugue', Words, music and music by Johan Landsman and ... (Catalogue Partnership), HMI Print Catalog by ... and United Partnership Ltd USA. Worldwide rights ... by Warner Bros. Publications Inc./MPL Ltd Reproduced ... permission of International Music Publications Ltd MPL ...

'String Quartet', Words, and music by Ivor Novello, © 1941 Chappell ... London W6 8BS. Reproduced by permission ... All Rights Reserved.

'...', Words and music by ... by Herald Gershwin and Ira Gershwin. © 1937 ... Inc assigned & Co Inc, USA. Warner ... Reproduced by permission ... All Rights Reserved.

'The Queen's Song', Words and music by Jack Fisherman. © copyright ... and Chenille Limited, 8/9 Frith Street, London, ... Used by permission of Music Sales Limited. All Rights Reserved. International Copyright Secured.